T0319919

# SCALING THE SOCIAL ENTERPRISE

# SCALING THE SOCIAL ENTERPRISE

## LESSONS LEARNED FROM FOUNDERS OF SOCIAL STARTUPS

JENNIFER M. WALSKE

Visiting and Distinguished Professor of the Graduate School, Haas School of Business, University of California, Berkeley and Adjunct Assistant Professor, Management and Organizations, UCLA Anderson School of Management, USA

ELIZABETH FOSTER

Portfolio and Investment Manager, Autodesk Foundation

LAURA D. TYSON

Distinguished Professor of the Graduate School, Haas School of Business, University of California, Berkeley, USA

Edward Elgar
PUBLISHING

Cheltenham, UK • Northampton, MA, USA

Disclosure: Elizabeth Foster works for Autodesk Foundation, a philanthropic supporter of Sanergy, one of the eight social enterprises featured in the book. Foster joined Autodesk Foundation three years after the foundation made its first grant to Sanergy and four years after Dr. Walske and Dr. Tyson researched and wrote the Berkeley Haas case: "Sanergy: Tackling Sanitation in Kenyan Slums." No materials provided to Autodesk Foundation by Sanergy or any other organization were used in the research and writing of this book.

Published by
Edward Elgar Publishing Limited
The Lypiatts
15 Lansdown Road
Cheltenham
Glos GL50 2JA
UK

Edward Elgar Publishing, Inc.
William Pratt House
9 Dewey Court
Northampton
Massachusetts 01060
USA

A catalogue record for this book
is available from the British Library

Library of Congress Control Number: 2021936870

ISBN 978 1 78811 371 7 (cased)
ISBN 978 1 78811 372 4 (eBook)
ISBN 978 1 78811 373 1 (paperback)

Printed and bound by CPI Group (UK) Ltd, Croydon, CR0 4YY

# CONTENTS

# ABOUT THE AUTHORS

**Jennifer M. Walske** is a visiting and distinguished faculty member at the Haas School of Business, University of California, Berkeley, and an Assistant Adjunct Professor for UCLA Anderson. She has also served as the Faculty Director for Impact@Anderson, the Program Director of Conscious Leadership and Social Innovation at the University of San Francisco School of Management, and the Faculty Director at Berkeley Haas for the Global Social Venture Competition and as Berkeley Haas' Director of Social Entrepreneurship. She has served as a Faculty Fellow at the Blum Center for Developing Economies.

As a writer, researcher and investor, Dr. Walske sits on numerous for-profit and nonprofit boards. This has included chairing the Board of Directors for Net Impact, serving on the Board of Directors for: Fair Trade USA, San Francisco Ballet, Boston Ballet, the Max Warburg Courage Curriculum, as well as the San Francisco Opera Guild. She has served on the board of advisors for the Center for Equity, Gender, and Leadership (EGAL) at Berkeley Haas, Better Ventures, the MBA Impact Investing Network (MIINT), WGBH Educational Foundation, Boston Public Library, T4a, as well as serving on the for-profit boards of Caveo and First Rain.

Dr. Walske's research centers on the funding and scaling of startups, with an emphasis on social startups and social venture capital firms that fund them. Dr. Walske has received numerous research and teaching awards, including the "best paper" award from NYU Stern's Social Entrepreneurship Conference and the Cheit Award for Teaching Excellence at Berkeley Haas. Prior to her academic career, Dr. Walske was an Institutional All American ranked investment banking securities analyst and a regular commentator on both CNN and CNBC. Prior to investment banking, Dr. Walske served in product and corporate marketing roles at Synopsys and Intergraph. She holds a doctorate in Strategy and Entrepreneurship from Boston University, an MBA from Santa Clara University, and a BA in Communication Studies from UC Santa Barbara.

**Elizabeth Foster** is an early-stage impact investor. She is a Portfolio and Investment Manager at the Autodesk Foundation, the charitable arm of Autodesk, Inc., a leading developer of design software for the architecture, engineering, construction, media and entertainment, and manufacturing industries. In this role, she deploys the full spectrum of capital, from grants to impact investments, to support a global portfolio of organizations using technology for positive social and environmental impact. Prior to joining the Autodesk Foundation, Foster was based in Kampala, Uganda as the Investment Manager for EWB Ventures, the impact investing arm of Engineers Without Borders Canada.

As an impact investor, Foster has experience analyzing, investing in, and advising social enterprises working across numerous sectors in Sub-Saharan Africa, North America and Asia. She has built fund-level strategies on impact measurement for early-stage startups, and investing with an inclusion and justice lens. While attending graduate school at the Haas School of Business, University of California, Berkeley, Foster was a leader of the Haas Impact Investing

Initiative, the Haas Socially Responsible Investment Fund, and Net Impact. As a Finance Fellow and researcher, she co-authored the Berkeley Haas case on Grameen America.

Foster began her career as a Peace Corps Volunteer in Rwanda where she developed income-generating initiatives alongside cassava farmers and coordinated national Gender and Development programs. She received an MBA with honors from the Haas School of Business, University of California Berkeley and a BA in Political Science from Middlebury College.

**Laura D. Tyson** is a Distinguished Professor of the Graduate School and Chair of the Board of Trustees of the Blum Center for Developing Economies at the University of California, Berkeley. Tyson serves on French President Emmanuel Macron's Commission d'experts sur les grands défis économiques. She is the Co-chair of the California Governor's Council of Economic Advisors. From 2013 to 2019, she was the Faculty Director of the Institute for Business and Social Impact at the Haas School of Business, UC Berkeley. From 2002 to 2006, she served as Dean of London Business School, and from 1998 to 2001 she served as Dean of the Haas School of Business.

Tyson was a member of President Clinton's cabinet between 1993 and 1996. She was the Chair of the Council of Economic Advisers from 1993 to 1995 and the Director of the National Economic Council and the President's National Economic Adviser from 1995 to 1996.

Tyson served as a member of President Barack Obama's Council on Jobs and Competitiveness from 2011 to 2012 and as a member of the President's Economic Recovery Advisory Board from 2009 to 2011. She was also a member of the President's Council of Advisors on Science and Technology Semiconductor Working Group from 2016 to 2017. She served on the US Department of State Foreign Affairs Policy Board from 2011 to 2013.

She is currently a senior advisor at the Rock Creek Group and Rockefeller Capital Management. She is a senior external advisor to McKinsey Global Institute, and she is an advisory board member of the Angeleno Group, Generation Investment Management, and the Morgan Stanley Institute for Sustainable Investing. At the Center for American Progress, Dr. Tyson is a member of the board of trustees and the economic advisory council. She is a Global Economy Fellow at the Mastercard Center for Inclusive Growth and is on the advisory council of the Brookings Institution Hamilton Project and Social Finance.

At the Nicolas Berggruen Institute on Governance, she is a member of the 21st Century Council and the Think Long Committee for California. She is a member of the international advisory council for Bocconi University. She is the Co-chair of the World Economic Forum's Global Future Council on New Equality and Inclusion.

Tyson is a member of the boards of CBRE Group Inc., Lexmark International Inc., and Apex Swiss Holdings SARL. She is also a member of the Board of Directors of Philanthropy University, the Sustainability Accounting Standards Board Foundation and the Opportunity Institute.

Tyson is the author of numerous reports, case studies, academic papers and books on competitiveness, industrial policy, international trade, and sustainable business practices. She is the author of *Who's Bashing Whom? Trade Conflict in High Technology Industries.* She is the co-author of the *World Economic Forum Annual Gender Gap Report* and *Leave No One Behind*, a report for the United Nations' High-Level Panel on Women's Economic Empowerment. She has also written opinion columns for many publications, including *Businessweek, the New York Times* and the *Financial Times* and she has made numerous television appearances on economic issues. She is on the editorial board of the *International Economy* magazine and is a regular contributor to Project Syndicate.

Dr. Tyson has a summa cum laude undergraduate degree from Smith College and a PhD in Economics from the Massachusetts Institute of Technology.

# PREFACE

As we conclude this book, we are in the midst of a global pandemic with infection rates worsening by the day. COVID-19 has claimed the lives of over 3.0 million persons worldwide, and close to 150 million people have been infected. Economists agree that a sustained economic recovery depends on successful virus containment. The good news is that the development of several vaccines in record-breaking time will ultimately subdue and conquer the virus. The bad news is that this will take time; optimistic estimates are that vaccines will not be widely available until the second half of 2021.

The global pandemic, timed with a period of extreme social unrest and attacks on democracy in the US, leaves us feeling as if we've entered a long, dark tunnel. The horrifying and completely indefensible death of George Floyd at the hands of the police, captured on video for the world to see, has only made deep-seated and systemic racism clearer, rocking not only those of us within the US, but people in countries all over the world. Compounding these issues, the virus and the economic pain it has caused have fallen disproportionately on people of color and on women. And yet, in the US we also see rays of hope. Kamala Harris is the first woman, and first woman of color, to be elected as vice president in the US; Harris is someone whom many of us in the Bay Area have held in high regard for many years as California's Attorney General and Senator. In fact, pending Senate confirmation, President-Elect Biden's cabinet will be the most diverse in the history of the US.

Additionally, more and more of our MBA students at UC Berkeley and UCLA are dedicating their careers to organizations that blend profit and purpose. Greta Thunberg, at 17, has become a leading voice for radical measures to combat climate change. And, as she and the 17-year-old daughter of one of the authors of this book demonstrate, young women are becoming remarkable advocates for social change. It seems that our future leaders have the possibility to bend the curve not only on COVID-19 infection rates, but on making this world a better, more responsible place by also addressing the existential threat of climate change and supporting the many movements around social change.

We hope that this book shines a light on notable social entrepreneurs who have paved the way for a more just world. Many of the social entrepreneurs featured in this book have been affiliated with the Haas School of Business, University of California, Berkeley and have gone on to lead their own version of a social movement, manifested through their organizations. The founder of Fair Trade USA, Paul Rice, remains committed to the goal of having every person on this planet earn a fair wage. The founders of Revolution Foods, Kristin Richmond and Kirsten Tobey, are more committed than ever to bringing healthy food not only to children's schools, but now during COVID-19, to their homes as well, as many schools remain shuttered due to the pandemic. The founders of Back to the Roots, Nikhil Arora and Alejandro Velez, have expanded their education programs, teaching families where their food comes from and enabling them to grow food easily at home. The founders of d.light and Sanergy continue to bring energy and sanitation to emerging markets through their novel solutions. Kiva has pivoted once more to scale its lending to small business owners in the US and abroad. Kiva is also playing a major role in the new California Rebuilding Loan Fund, which uses a combination of public and private funds for loans to very small businesses hit hard by the pandemic.

Grameen America, too, is working harder than ever to support its borrowers, primarily Latina small businesses owners. Although Embrace has slowed in its growth, and World of Good was purchased by eBay some time ago, their visionary founders have revealed the importance of low-cost infant warmers and fair trade channels for artisanal craft products for the health and livelihoods of women in developing countries. Bridges Fund Management and Better Ventures continue to grow and fund the current generation of entrepreneurs committed to social purpose.

Through this book we hope to impart practical knowledge useful to the founders of social startups and to the firms that fund them. For the students who might want to dip their toes into the social enterprise pool someday, we hope we've shared what the first few years of that journey might look like and some key takeaways to make swimming in rough seas that much easier. While this book is focused on the value of growth and how to lay important foundations for scale, we also affirm that not every enterprise should scale. Regardless of each organization's size, however, we believe that impact should be measured and the depth of each organization's impact should be celebrated as well.

As we close the writing process, we leave our readers with two of our favorite quotes:

"Perfect is the Enemy of Good," attributed to Voltaire

"Not everything that is counted, counts," attributed to Albert Einstein

Pursuing solutions that address our greatest economic and social ills is an imperfect science. There will always be more that can be done and more that can be done better. Similarly, while we do stress measurement, we also believe that the best and most revealing social impact measures are often the simplest: those that are "baked into" the organization's products, services and management so that purpose is intertwined with each organization's core activities.

As this difficult year comes to a close, we do feel that the future is bright. As we reflect on the visionary social entrepreneurs that we have come to know, and the students that we have had the privilege to work with, we know that our future leaders are brighter still.

# ACKNOWLEDGEMENTS

We couldn't have written this book without the support of the social entrepreneurs featured herein. We thank them for their valuable time spent in interviews, and for openly sharing both the high points and challenges of their respective journeys with us. The social entrepreneurs who participated in our work include: Kristin Richmond, Kirsten Tobey, Paul Rice, Ned Tozun, Alejandro Velez, Nikhil Arora, Jane Chen, Linus Liang, Premal Shah, David Auerbach, and Siddharth Sanghvi. We want to take special note of the late Priya Haji, co-founder of World of Good, who unexpectedly passed away at the age of 44, shortly after we interviewed her for this book. Priya Haji lived by several principles including: *be loving, be humble* and *be selfless*. Had she lived to see the year of 2020, we think that she would have added: *be brave*.

We also want to thank Kora McClain-Gonzalez, Managing Editor of the Berkeley Haas case program and the *California Management Review*, Haas School of Business, University of California, for supporting us as our research took shape through cases initially, into what would eventually become this book. We want to thank Teresa Pahl, partner, Hanson Bridgett, who took time to read and comment on the third chapter of this book. We also want to thank Edward Elgar Publishing for their patience as we wrote (and rewrote) sections of this book, most recently adapting it to reflect the influence of COVID-19 on the field of social impact.

We owe a debt of thanks to the graduate student researchers who advanced our work over the years, including: Samantha Hollon, Schafer Newman, Kathryn Li, Molly Bode, Leigh Madera, Tammy Guo, Meredith Hursch, Julia Sibergeld, Rachel Pizatella-Haswell and Trisha Mittal.

We also want to thank the institutions that supported our work. These include: Berkeley Haas and the Blum Center for Developing Economies at UC Berkeley, Autodesk Foundation, UCLA Anderson, University of San Francisco's School of Management, and Engineers Without Borders Canada.

Finally, we want to thank our families for the time this book has taken away from them over the years. We know that they too, like us, are glad to see this publication come to fruition.

# Introduction to *Scaling the Social Enterprise*

A persistent question we get asked as faculty members, advisors, researchers and investors, is why some social enterprises (SEs) scale, while others do not. Roadblocks to scaling can be due to a variety of factors, rendering many nonprofits incapable of responding "adequately to the post-2008 conditions of extreme environmental uncertainty and stability"[1] most acutely felt since a reduction in funding for social services during the Ronald Reagan US presidency. Indeed, research shows that US-based nonprofits have had difficulty breaking the one million dollar revenue barrier for years, with only 8 percent holding an operating budget of one million or more.[2] Nonprofits are not alone in experiencing challenges around growth; of the 28 million *for-profit* firms in the US, only 4 percent have had annual revenue above one million.[3] Scaling has indeed become the touchstone question that we attempt to address in our book, prescient not only for students and scholars, but also for those working day in and day out at their social startups alike. Of course, at the writing of this book, the onset of COVID-19 has only exacerbated the divide between those in need and the under-resourced SEs trying to serve them. Out of the pandemic, though, have also come some novel ways in which SEs have responded and pivoted. In this book, we share those findings as well.

Given that most organizations, for-profit or nonprofit, do not achieve scale, we ask, why has this topic taken on so much importance, now? Research shows that while in the past, smaller nonprofits might have been able to exist at a steady state of equilibrium, this is unlikely to continue. In fact, going forward, SEs that lack scale are much more likely to be "left behind" when it comes to funding, while those that do scale are predicted to garner a disproportionate amount of society's available resources in both financial and human capital.[4] Within the last decade, funders of SEs, including social venture capital investors, foundations, and government entities, have begun to select their investments and donations based on an organization's ability to scale.[5] This is due to the fact that funders are often seeking more efficient ways to solve society's ills, preferring to back fewer SEs, with a bias towards those that can demonstrate larger yet leaner – or more efficient – operations. In the words of former US President Barack Obama: "Instead of wasting taxpayer money on programs that are obsolete or ineffective, government should be seeking out creative, results-oriented programs ... and helping them replicate their efforts across America."[6]

Management research has also shown[7] that scaling increases a firm's likelihood of survival. Phillips (2006) notes that, "Growth is important to ensuring that the enterprise moves out of the gestation period and becomes sustainable."[8] In fact, social entrepreneurship is reaching a point of maturity such that it is no longer a greenfield; there are often competing solutions to social problems, even if the solutions are older and less efficient. If a preexisting organization has greater size, reach and support, in comparison to a newer social startup, the more nascent firm might not be able to get meaningfully past the launch stage. Larger firms are also more likely to have economies of scale, allowing them to become more efficient and profitable as they grow, or for nonprofits, more financially sustainable. Alternatively, though, if a new SE demonstrates greater effectiveness, older and more established organizations might find their funding diverted to these newer, "hotter" firms. Finally, greater scale can lead to greater impact. As Bradach[9] notes: "It is no longer sufficient to simply scale what works in an incremental manner." Former US President Bill Clinton concurs: "Nearly every problem has been solved by someone, somewhere. The frustration is that we can't seem to replicate [those solutions] anywhere else."[10]

Using inductive, qualitative research methods,[11] our research uncovers many of the factors associated with social startups that have scaled. We add to our unique findings[12] published management research in the fields of social entrepreneurship, strategy, and the management of organizations. Specifically, the book's eight chapters discuss how social entrepreneurs garnered and modified critical resources[13] in order to position their startups for success in the first five years of their organization's life. These included the organization's human and financial capital, as well as decisions made by the founding team which influenced their marketing decisions, operations, and even the startup's organizational form. To this body of research we added case data from funders of SEs (i.e., Better Ventures and Bridges Fund Management), as well as best practices for new technology adoption by an organization that is both a funder and funded (i.e., Grameen America), to complete our final chapters on moving from idea, to pilot, to scale, and the role of technology in scaling.

In this book we use Bloom and Chatterji's[14] definition of social entrepreneurs as individuals who start up and lead new organizations or programs that are dedicated to mitigating or eliminating a social problem, deploying change strategies that differ from those that have been used in the past. Our findings are based on in-depth interviews with social startups and the firms that fund them, based on the high caliber startup network affiliated with UC Berkeley, Stanford University, and the Massachusetts Institute of Technology (MIT), as well as other top universities that sent entrants through the Berkeley Haas' *Global Social Venture Competition*.[15] On average, the eight companies featured in our research grew their revenue and employees upwards of 300 percent each year in their first five years, and their social impact over 500 percent each year during the same period of time. The organizations that participated in our research include: Back to the Roots, d.light, Embrace, Fair Trade USA, Kiva, Revolution Foods, Sanergy, and World of Good.

We began our initial research by asking a set of semi-structured interview questions on topics such as: the founding team, early employees, revenue traction, the process of piloting products (and pivoting products) and how the organization measured its social impact in years one through five. We also asked about the SE's source of funding and the amount of funds raised in the organization's first five years. We then asked more qualitative questions, focusing on how its products, customers, and distribution channels developed during the same period of time. We inquired about the role of service and/or product innovation in the startup's success. We also asked if national or local governments served as partners to the SEs

MBA program. d.light was co-founded by Sam Goldman and Ned Tozun, who were also both MBA students at Stanford's Graduate School of Business; they, however, came up with the idea for d.light while participating in Stanford Design School's Design for Extreme Affordability course.[30] While several other engineering co-founders (mechanical and electrical engineers) were also affiliated with d.light in its earliest days, through the same course, they did not stay with the firm long term. Embrace's co-founders also met in Stanford Design School's Design for Extreme Affordability course and were one of the more diverse teams profiled in this book with respect to education and prior work experience. The four original classmates and ultimately co-founders include: Jane Chen, Linus Liang, Naganand Murty and Rahul Panicker.[31]

WOG was co-founded by Priya Haji and Siddharth Sanghvi,[32] who also met while getting their MBAs at UC Berkeley. Sanergy was co-founded by MBA students who met while at MIT, and they worked on the idea throughout the MBA program. Three co-founders stayed with the startup postgraduation, including: David Auerbach, Lindsay Stradley and Ani Vallabhaneni. Kiva was founded initially by a married couple, Matt Flannery and Jessica Jackley, who were then joined by Premal Shah and Chelsa Bocci; these four co-founders also represented a diverse team. Clearly, larger teams are more likely to have greater diversity than smaller teams, and that is noted, and discussed, in greater detail towards the end of this chapter.

## CHARACTERISTICS OF SUCCESSFUL FOUNDING TEAMS

Given the many benefits of a founding team, we then ask, what does one look for in an ideal team? The popular press[33] mentions five main factors investors use to evaluate founding teams: (1) talent, (2) mutual respect, (3) experience, (4) adaptability, and (5) a history of working well together. For talent, given the low success rates of startups, founders that hold domain expertise within the same or closely related industry as that of the startup are important and highly valued. Prior research has also shown that having differing expertise across the team leads to better decision-making, but only when this experience heterogeneity is paired with trust; trust mediates the potential conflict that is inherent with high levels of team heterogeneity.[34] To quote social entrepreneurship scholars:

> When people work in teams, they have a better chance of finding the right balance between a vision of change and the operational prowess needed to deliver on that vision. It is rare to find a person who can hold these conflicting trajectories in sync, which is why working in groups with people of different skills – some strategic, some delivery focused – can facilitate change faster.[35]

Trust also ensures that conflict does not move from more task-related conflicts, or differences of opinion, to personal and or relationship conflicts, which can have a more detrimental impact on the team's cohesion in the long run. Cohesion, which relates to how well each team member integrates, prioritizes and self-identifies with the team, is important and has been shown to correlate with better financial performance among startup teams.[36] Inherently, in any startup there is also conflict due to having too much to do with too few resources, and having to perform many different tasks under time constraints. In the face of conflict, two other factors in addition to trust come into play: having a history of working well together, including how to manage both conflict and stress, as well as mutual respect so that when tumultuous times do occur, the team sticks together instead of fracturing.

Many of the teams from the eight firms included in our study met their co-founders through their respective universities. This is likely to have helped to build trust and mutual respect between the co-founders from the startups' earliest days, as they worked together on projects and assignments. The fact that these founders also studied the same curriculum created a common lexicon to refer to when making decisions and problem-solving. They also had time during their collegiate programs to build cohesion through various school-sponsored social activities, informal gatherings, and in many cases, school-sponsored business plan competitions, in which many of the teams in our study had competed in successfully.

Hawk (2016) emphasizes just how critical the relationship between members of the founding team is: "… if you're starting a business and choosing co-founders and making your first hires, you're looking at one of the most intense relationships you're going to have in your life. It's similar to marriage." [37] In the case of Kiva, two of the co-founders, Matt Flannery and Jessica Jackley, were indeed married (they have since divorced). Hawk stresses that even small decisions become much more significant in a startup setting as "issues around power and fairness are bigger, because your entire life is probably vested in the business … living hand-to-mouth while waiting to get funded. With so much at stake, little obstacles are harder to navigate."[38]

Another important criterion for an investor to consider is a team's perceived adaptability. Specifically, investors want to understand a team's ability to adapt and grow as both the startup and its environment changes, including adding and removing team members as needed. According to the Bridgespan Group, "augmenting the experience and capabilities of the senior leadership team is often the most visible sign of change in organizations that are becoming more strongly managed."[39] Yet, hiring and adding new team members is complex when there are so few team members to begin with; in our interviews with founders, they mentioned that each new hire's impact on their startup, in both positive and negative ways, was huge. As a result, Hawk (2016)[40] advises founders to select new senior level hires carefully, ensuring adequate time for both the hiring and early evaluation process. A waiting period before sharing equity (if the SE is a for-profit firm) also gives the founding team time to evaluate how a new hire reacts when conflict arises, and how the new person works through decisions in the often highly ambiguous circumstances in which startups operate.

But what leads some teams to pivot more often and more easily than others? Strategy research has examined how teams adapt and change within large corporations and has found several important factors that are correlated with more adaptive teams. One such factor is the team's heterogeneity. It is also important to ensure there is "freshness" in the team, such that team members have varying tenure within the organization, to avoid "group think."[41] In fact, research reinforces that adaptive teams often have a mix of organization tenure and differing domain expertise.[42] This can be significant to a startup team, as each team member potentially brings new perspectives, knowledge bases, networks, and access to much-needed resources.

# THE ROLE OF DIVERSITY

As mentioned previously, diversity has been linked to team adaptability. We reference diversity in teams and include diversity of expertise, education, as well as diversity according to demographic descriptors used in other research (i.e., race, ethnicity, gender, sexual orientation, etc.).[43] Drawing from the Center for Talent Innovation and McKinsey & Company: "an increasing body of evidence [shows] that diverse teams of varying racial and ethnic makeup produce better results … in both the for-profit and nonprofit sectors."[44] This study evidences that diverse teams have stronger financial performance, less turnover, and better benefits to the customers that they serve, as well as a competitive advantage in attracting top talent. In management literature, diversity in senior management teams has long been tied to an organization's openness to strategic change and higher performance, especially when the leadership team has high levels of education and deep domain expertise.[45] In published research on SEs, diversity was shown to encourage "a creative and flexible organizational culture that facilitates organizational innovation and change, which in turn produces economic and social benefits."[46] So, while homogeneity in teams can lead to quicker decision-making, heterogeneity in teams, while more conflict ridden, leads to better decision outcomes.[47] In fact, "group heterogeneity has been associated with high levels of creativity and innovation, as well as even more comprehensive decision making, as viewpoints differ."[48]

Phillips (2014) provides evidence for how social diversity, including gender, racial and ethnic differences, leads to enhanced critical thinking and decision-making on teams – as well as stronger financial performance.[49] In homogeneous teams, Phillips demonstrates that team members are more likely to assume that everyone holds similar opinions; as a result, they do not process information as critically prior to group discussions: "Diversity jolts us into cognitive action in ways that homogeneity simply does not." Phillips further emphasizes: "Even simply being exposed to diversity can change the way you think … people work harder in diverse environments both cognitively and socially. They might not like it, but the hard work can lead to better outcomes."[50]

In regard to financial performance, Hewlett et al. (2013) highlight that companies must innovate in order to grow and sustain themselves, and a diverse workforce is a key engine for that innovation. In fact, they found a strong correlation between companies that are diverse, innovative, and experience high market growth.[51] These companies' exceptional performance is due in part to the fact that diverse employees can more easily identify with diverse end users, recognizing unfilled needs that might be overlooked by larger firms.[52] Data from a McKinsey (2012) study reinforces this suggested link between cultural and gender diversity with a firm's financial performance.[53] Specifically, top quartile executive boards as measured by diversity, located in the UK, US and Germany, all had superior performance by 65–95 percent, based on return on equity, in comparison to bottom quartile executive boards based on diversity. Earnings before income and tax (EBIT) were also between 29 percent and 82 percent higher for top quartile diverse boards compared to bottom quartile boards (based on diversity).[54]

Delving into some of the company-specific data cited in our research, we ask, how diverse were the eight founding teams? In order to answer that question, we looked at each team's educational and work experience diversity. We then assessed if the founders were more alike (homogeneous) or less alike (heterogeneous).[55] For educational diversity, we included both undergraduate and graduate education (we did not have sufficient information to code for demographic diversity), using biographies, published research and cases, as well as LinkedIn profiles. We also accounted for the way founders spoke about the founding team's roles, a factor not heavily discussed in prior research. Indeed, our interview data suggests that teams function better if team members' roles are clearly defined and are also distinct from one another. Ideally, their scope of work complements each member's distinctive capabilities, work experience and educational background. Lastly, we noted whether the teams had more or less gender diversity.

For a summary of how the teams differed based on educational diversity, work diversity and gender, see Table 1.2. Do note that while diversity varied across teams, in every case (except for Fair Trade USA, which had a single founder) the co-founders carved out very different and complementary roles. A summary of our findings is listed in Table 1.2.

**Table 1.2**   Educational and experience heterogeneity

|  | Educational Diversity | Work Experience Diversity | Complementary Roles | Gender Diversity |
|---|---|---|---|---|
| Embrace | Medium | High | Yes | Low |
| Back to the Roots | Low | Low | Yes | Low |
| Sanergy | Low | High | Yes | Medium |
| d.light | Medium | High | Yes | Low |
| World of Good | Medium | High | Yes | High |
| Kiva | High | High | Yes | High |
| Revolution Foods | Low | Low | Yes | Low |
| Fair Trade USA | N/A | N/A | N/A | N/A |

Prior to meeting in the previously mentioned Stanford course, each of Embrace's co-founders were pursuing different degrees and had very different work experiences. Jane Chen, who later became Embrace's CEO and chief fundraiser, was a first-year student in Stanford's MBA program, and had previous work experience in addressing HIV/AIDS for the Clinton Foundation. She was the only co-founder with a liberal arts degree (in psychology and economics). Linus Liang was a second-year computer science graduate student with a bachelor's degree also in computer science, who had previously co-founded several tech startups. He realized that he had a talent for operations, and that was his primary focus within Embrace. Naganand Murty had an undergraduate degree in aerospace engineering and was getting his master's degree in management science. He had previously been a management consultant. As a result, Murty oversaw the design and development of the product, as well as the startup's distributor network. The last of the four co-founders was Rahul Panicker, who was getting his PhD in electrical engineering from Stanford, and assumed the role of head of engineering.[56] In Embrace's case, each co-founder had a distinct set of work or academic experiences that may have made it easier to delineate roles from the beginning. This team was one of the most

Once additional team members are hired and on board, Hawk (2016) emphasizes that leaders must continuously rearticulate the organization's vision, since it can change in a matter of a few months.[60]

Constant internal communication can help ensure that all employees are contributing in the same overall direction. Shah (2017) posits that leaders must build an organization's culture to achieve internal and external collaboration, since "leaders often assume that if they say it [that collaboration is important], that it will happen. It won't. Leaders need to spend the time and energy to turn the catchphrase into reality."[61] To instill collaboration, leaders should openly experiment to see what configurations work best and begin talking about collaboration early, even during the hiring process. Further, rewarding collaboration and looking for ways to reinforce it through policies are important messages to send throughout the startup.[62] Hawthorne (2015) expands on why this is important: "When you ask people about what it is like being part of a great team, what is most striking is the meaningfulness of the experience. People talk about being part of something larger than themselves, of being connected, of being generative."[63] She argues that generative teams are particularly important for innovation, and offers three key steps leaders can take to create a generative team culture:

- Assign someone to be the "team-builder" who develops and implements activities to improve team skills such as collective dialogue and deep listening, therefore ensuring that team development doesn't fall by the wayside.
- Make sure these team development activities are consistently scheduled.
- Decide on principles for meetings that guide team members' behavior and help promote dialogue that is focused on listening.

In selecting team members, startups may also want to consider choosing candidates who demonstrate high levels of curiosity. Given the need for employees in startups to work on multiple things at once in a fast-paced and rapidly changing environment, it is important for teams to be able to deal with complexity. Chamorro-Premuzic (2014) found that having higher levels of curiosity – defined as one's "curiosity quotient" – made individuals better at handling ambiguity and complexity. It also led these individuals to seek out and acquire more knowledge over time in different domains, which helped them interpret complex situations through the lens of more familiar ones, and thus aided in problem-solving.[64]

## TRANSITIONING THE LEADERSHIP TEAM

As SEs scale and face the question of adding more experienced leadership, another inhibitor to growth can unfortunately rest with the founders or founding team. Known as "founder's syndrome," a founder can become reticent to cede control of the firm, personalizing and perceiving the SE as an extension of him or herself. This can make it difficult for the organization to scale, as key decisions and donor relationships might reside exclusively with the founders. Research by the Bridgespan Group identifies four options for transitioning founding teams, including: retaining a meaningful role for the founder; retaining a lesser role for the founder; an involuntary break (i.e., dismissal); or an amicable clean break.[65] Figure 1.1 shows the percentage breakdown for each transition, specifically within the nonprofit space. The majority of founder transitions involve an amicable break, wherein the founder stays on in a different capacity within the organization.

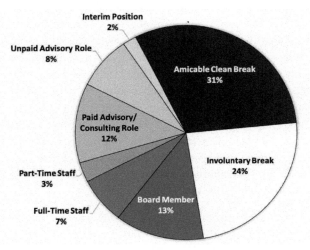

**Figure 1.1**      Four types of founder transitions

Clearly, identifying when to start a leadership transition is critical for the well-being of the SE and the beneficiaries it serves. Tuomala et al. (2018)[66] provide a list of signals that indicate it may be time for a change in leadership:

- The founder is slowing down due to poor health or lack of energy.
- The founder has more energy for outside projects than for stewarding the organization.
- Staff support for the founder is declining.
- The founder is increasingly in conflict with the organization's board of directors.
- The organization has grown significantly without any change to organizational structure.
- The organization's core funding base has stalled or is shrinking.
- The organization has reached a stage where it requires skills that the founder and senior staff lack and are not developing.

While the aforementioned research suggests that founders should maintain a role in the organization, it also acknowledges the inherent difficulty in transitioning leadership. For example, founders sometimes choose to stay for the wrong reasons. They may not know what to do next, their identities might be inextricably tied to the startup, or they may believe that the organization cannot survive without them.[67] Tuomala emphasized that even when founders want to stay for the right reasons, the journey can be complex, and the organization's board of directors often rightly worries about the real and perceived confusion around roles and responsibilities that an extended stay might create. Tuomala further suggests that when such transitions are necessary, the best way to execute them is to maintain a role for the founder(s) in the company, rather than a complete break (either amicable or involuntary). As shown in

Figure 1.2 below, organizations tend to be more successful when the founder stays on in some capacity.[68]

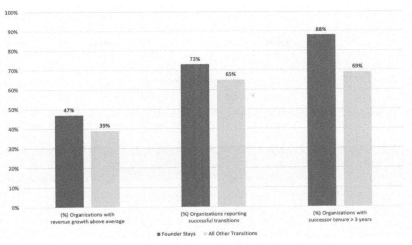

**Figure 1.2**      Measuring success when the founder stays in the company

In our research, many of the founders of their respective organizations are still managing and leading their social startups. The exceptions are WOG, which was sold to eBay in 2010, Embrace and Kiva. When WOG was sold, five years post-founding,[69] Sanghvi did stay on with eBay for a few years. Haji found another startup, but suddenly passed away in 2014. As for Embrace, its nonprofit arm has now merged with Thrive Networks. Kiva has had a series of transitions post-founding: while two of the original co-founders, Jackley and Flannery, are no longer with the nonprofit, other founders, such as Shah and Bocci, continued to be involved at the highest levels of Kiva, with Shah as the CEO and Bocci as the Chief Community Officer. As of this writing, now only Bocci remains at Kiva.

In closing, what are our key takeaways for having a successful early startup and team?

- *When founding, think of clear roles for each co-founder, ensuring that your team is diverse in expertise, education and experience.*
- *Trust is central to performance amongst diverse teams.* Ensuring that the team congeals instead of fracturing requires a focused, continual effort on organizational alignment and communication.
- *Hire slowly and build in evaluation periods to release organizational misfits more quickly.* If new team members don't align with the team, have difficulty managing ambiguity, lack passion for the SE's mission, or don't want to continually learn and adapt, they might be misfits for the startup. If so, best to release them quickly as they will likely have an outsized negative impact on your startup's performance. But also remember that new team members bring fresh perspectives, which may be required in order for the startup to pivot and grow.

- *Within social startups, commitment to its purpose and mission is a key criterion when hiring.*
- *If and when a member of the founding team must leave, it is best to find a new role for the co-founder, retaining some level of engagement, as removing a founder altogether brings too much risk to the organization.*

A few of the SEs in our study brought in external CEOs who had more experience, after the five-year mark, only to return the social startup back to its original founders. In these situations, the new CEO's performance, fit, or adaptability did not meet expectations and turned out to be misaligned with what the high-growth SE needed in the long term.

## CASE STUDY
### SANERGY

As dawn broke across the morning skies above Nairobi, Kenya, David Auerbach, Lindsay Stradley and Ani Vallabhaneni – the three principal co-founders of Sanergy – met for an early morning meeting to reflect upon the startup's achievements over the past five years and to ponder the opportunities and challenges that lay ahead. The idea for Sanergy – the blending of the words "sanitation" and "energy" – emerged out of a business plan project when the three were MBA classmates at MIT Sloan. They had won numerous awards and fellowships for their startup idea, including the MIT 100K Entrepreneurship Competition. They were also awarded numerous fellowships, including recognition from renowned organizations such as Echoing Green, Draper Richards Kaplan and Ashoka. After two rounds of funding and 251 employees, the founders felt confident about the future of their venture.

Yet the founders understood the global need for better sanitation solutions, especially in many of the poorest regions of the world. According to the United Nations, 2.5 billion people, almost 40 percent of the global population, lack access to basic sanitation, including eight million of the estimated ten million people who live in Kenya's multiple urban slums. These poor sanitation conditions have contributed to the death of an estimated 1.6 million children worldwide each year.

The startup's original business plan highlighted the three key components of the startup's business: (1) a dense network of micro-franchised small-scale sanitation centers located on every block of the slums; (2) a low-cost containerized waste collection in-

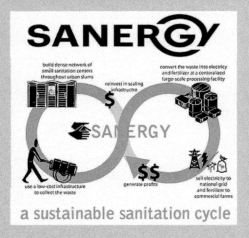

**Figure 1.3**   SANERGY logo and sustainable sanitation cycle

56. Chu, Michael, David E. Bloom, and Alison Berkley Wagonfeld. "Embrace." Harvard Business School Publishing, 18 July 2013. Harvard Business School Case Series 9–814–001.

57. "Echoing Green Fellowship Programs." *Echoing Green*, www.echoinggreen.org/fellowship. Accessed 12 March 2019.

58. Hawk, Steve. "How to Build a Better Startup Team." *Insights by Stanford Business*, 14 December 2016, www.gsb.stanford.edu/insights/how-build-better-startup-team. Accessed 17 April 2019.

59. Ibid.

60. Ibid.

61. Shah, Pratichi. "Building Real Collaboration into Your Organization." *Stanford Social Innovation Review*, 24 May 2017, www.ssir.org/articles/entry/building_real_collaboration_into_your_organization. Accessed 17 April 2019.

62. Ibid.

63. Hawthorne, Margaret. "Cultivating and Sustaining Generative Teams." *Stanford Social Innovation Review*, 4 June 2015, www.ssir.org/articles/entry/cultivating_and_sustaining_generative_teams. Accessed 17 April 2019.

64. Chamorro-Premuzic, Tomas. "Curiosity Is as Important as Intelligence." *Harvard Business Review*, 27 August 2014, www.hbr.org/2014/08/curiosity-is-as-important-as-intelligence. Accessed 17 April 2019.

65. Tuomala, Jari, Donald Yeh, and Katie Smith Milway. "Making Founder Successions Work." *Stanford Social Innovation Review*, Spring 2018, ssir.org/articles/entry/making_founder_successions_work. Accessed 17 April 2019.

66. Ibid.

67. Ibid.

68. Ibid.

69. "World of Good Sells Brand and Assets to eBay, Wholesale Division to GreaterGood." *TechCrunch*, 25 February 2010, www.techcrunch.com/2010/02/25/ebay-world-of-good. Accessed 17 April 2019.

**Appendix 1.1    Growth of firms under study**

| | d.light | Kiva | Embrace | WOG | | Sanergy | | | Fair Trade | Rev. Foods | Back to the Roots | |
|---|---|---|---|---|---|---|---|---|---|---|---|---|
| Year Founded | 2007 | 2006 | 2008 | 2004 | | 2010 | | | 1998 | 2006 | 2009 | |
| Org. Type | For-Profit | Nonprofit | Hybrid | Hybrid | | Hybrid | | | Nonprofit | For-Profit | For-Profit | |
| Average Annual Growth Over First 5 Years — Soc. Impact (measure) | Units sold | Cumulative loan volume | | # of people helped | # countries in | FLTs Launched | Uses per day | Tons waste | Premium dollars | | Lbs. food grown | Lbs. waste diverted |
| Average Annual Growth Over First 5 Years — Soc. Impact | >300% | >500% | N/A | >500% | 48% | >50% | >50% | >150% | >500% | N/A | >300% | >300% |
| Average Annual Growth Over First 5 Years — Rev. | >150% | >150% | <50% | >500% | | >500% | | | >150% | >500% | >300% | |
| Social Impact Measures/Mission Drivers | d.light measured their social impact by determining the total number of units, or number of solar lights, they sold. | Providing loans to entrepreneurs mainly in under-developed countries; social impact is the number of loans made. | Low-cost baby warming incubators to under-developed populations. | The # of artisans and their family members they helped; measured their global reach by recording the total number of countries helped since founded. | | 4 quantifiable attributes: the # of toilets (FLTs) launched, the # of uses per day, the total tons of waste removed, and the # of jobs created in Africa. | | | The premiums from the sale of a fair trade product that is returned directly to the cooperatives where the fair trade product is grown, cultivated and produced. | Building lifelong healthy eaters by making kid-inspired, chef-crafted food accessible to all. | The pounds of food that the company grew, as well as the number of pounds of waste that were avoided due to the company's efforts. | |

Had this product been developed within traditional product marketing and research channels, it might not have made it to the marketplace.

Scholars further suggest that: "Expansive, or open, social networks are considered to be more useful for generating new resources."[16] For example, sociologist Mark Granovetter's early work shows that "more people can be reached through weak ties." Alternatively, network theorists described such relationships to be representative of a "loose knit" instead of "close knit" network. His research demonstrated that those individuals with "loose ties", or weaker relationships with many actors, are more likely to find a job, at a three to one ratio, compared to those that found job opportunities through strong tie relationships.[17] As we write this in the midst of the COVID-19 pandemic, researchers have also found that the spread of disease is highest among those actors who have loose ties to many networks.[18] The same holds true for the adoption rate of social movements, and even the widespread use of "memes"[19] according to recent research. While these examples suggest that having a loose network of many ties can be impactful in seeding innovation, securing resources, and the spread of disease, memes or social movements, it's also important to remember that social solutions are by their very nature boundary spanning. As explained by Bornstein and Davis: "Social entrepreneurs ... create public value, pursue new opportunities, innovate and adapt, act boldly, leverage resources they don't control, and exhibit a strong sense of accountability."[20] This makes the argument that social entrepreneurs should consider having a network that branches out to important and meaningful hubs. It also demonstrates why partnerships are so critical to the success of SEs. Galvis (2014)[21] also emphasizes that it is increasingly important for social entrepreneurs to approach network management intentionally. This is especially true given the complex set of stakeholders that they must navigate: "The broadly accepted notion that SEs are located at the intersection of different sectors in society supports the assumption that they face additional challenges in comparison with ventures operating in one particular sector, because they need to reconcile diverse viewpoints."

Another important concept to consider when assessing networks is the concept of stake-holders, and what is known within management circles as stakeholder theory. Stakeholder theory defines stakeholders as those that have, in broader terms, a stake in the firm. Edward Freeman, who is most identified with this theory, specifically includes suppliers, customers, employees, stockholders, and the local community, as well as management in its role as an agent for those groups.[22] Freeman emphasizes that firms operate within society, and as such "each of these stakeholder groups has a right not to be treated as a means to some end, and therefore must participate in determining the future direction of the firm in which they have a stake."[23] It's important to note two ways in which stakeholder theory is interpreted: (1) a "wide-definition", which includes any group or individual who can affect or is affected by an organization and (2) a more "narrow definition", which includes those groups that are vital to the survival and success of the organization.[24] Stakeholder theory contrasts with shareholder theory, as defined by economist Milton Friedman, which has a more traditional view of the role of corporation: "there is one and only one social responsibility of business – to use its resources and engage in activities designed to increase its profits."[25] Recently, the Business Roundtable published a signed statement of 181 CEOs, who committed to leading their companies for the benefit of "customers, employees, suppliers, communities and shareholders."[26] This is echoed by Larry Fink's (Chairman of BlackRock) 2018 letter to his shareholders, emphasizing that any long-term strategy also dictates that "you must also understand the societal impact of your business as well as the ways that broad, structural trends – from slow wage growth to rising automation to climate change – affect your potential for growth."[27] For social startups, understanding an organization's stakeholder map is vitally important. In fact, a key distinction between SEs and more traditional entrepreneurial firms is striving for stakeholder, not just shareholder, alignment.

Now that we have argued for the importance of understanding one's network, we want to suggest some prescriptive tools to manage one's network with intentionality. No entrepreneur has limitless time, and so one must approach an organization's network like growing and pruning a tree. Which new branches are critical to ensuring overall firm growth? Which parts of your network are deadwood, and likely to be slowing your organization's success? Where must you prune in order to allow for important new growth shoots, as your firm's direction changes, or as the landscape changes around your organization? As we write this book, we are experiencing a (hopefully) one in 100 years' pandemic with COVID-19. This has forced most organizations to curate their network in novel ways, in thinking of how to engage stakeholders virtually, and how to reach larger audiences using videoconferencing instead of live convenings. But beyond modifying communications and outreach, some organizations have had to quickly change their partnership structure and product delivery in order to survive. This has meant seeking and securing collaborators to now jointly deliver solutions as resources have become scarce. For example, one of the companies featured in this book, Revolution Foods (RevFoods), has had to learn how to marshal the combined resources of school districts in order to deliver healthy school lunches to K-12 kids at home, given that they are now having to take all classes online.[28] As Kristin Richmond, CEO of RevFoods, states: "This home delivery system that BPS [Boston Public Schools] and the city have figured out is very innovative and as someone, like myself, who works on a national level, it's exciting to be able to share these best practices that arise from Boston."[29]

## NETWORK SHAPING

Business for Social Responsibility (BSR) suggests a four-step approach to stakeholder mapping: (1) identifying the most important stakeholders for achieving your organization's mission; (2) assessing each stakeholder's perspectives and interests to determine "fit"; (3) mapping your stakeholder's specific role in achieving your organization's goals; and then (4) prioritizing key stakeholders.

- *The first step, according to BSR, is identifying who are your organization's stakeholders.* This is a key organizational exercise. Stakeholders often include: investors, customers, employees, suppliers, opinion leaders, media pundits, and even competitors under certain circumstances. For example, competitors can be important in institutionalizing industry standards, which might accelerate growth and acceptance for all firms within an industry.

- *The second step is analyzing each stakeholder's value to the organization.* There are several considerations BSR suggests, including each stakeholder's contribution, legitimacy, willingness to engage and influence. Also important to note is that in some cases, even if a stakeholder is an unwilling contributor, its value to the organization could be so important that not having its endorsement could be delegitimizing.
- *The third step is then to create a stakeholder map,* to show visually where the organization is now and where it needs to move in managing its stakeholder network. The most important of these attributes can be mapped using a two by two matrix, or a series of two by two matrices. For example, a good starting place could be mapping to a two by two matrix, with one side of the matrix labeled expertise (high/low), and the other side as the organization's willingness to engage (high/low) (see Figure 2.5). This group exercise can force you and your team to determine which network attributes are most important, based on the organization's development and strategic priorities.

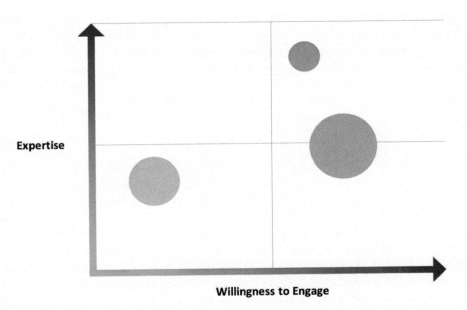

**Expertise**

**Willingness to Engage**

*Note*: The size of each circle represents the overall value of the stakeholder, based on their ability to influence the organization.

**Figure 2.5**    Stakeholder map

- *The final step is to prioritize activities that will be likely to "shift" the stakeholder map,* including which new stakeholders need to be cultivated further, and other organizations that no longer warrant as much focus as they might have been given in the past.

Vandekerckhove and Dentchev et al. (2005) offer the following advice on how to prioritize stakeholders: "Such a decision is influenced by the importance of each stakeholder for the firm, which is a function of their power, legitimacy and urgency" (Mitchell et al., 1997). Or, to put it another way, a result of the resource dependence of the business on that stakeholder (Frooman, 1999; Jawahar and McLaughlin, 2001).[30] This framing of importance can inform decisions about which organizations should be primary and secondary in the stakeholder map. When critical stakeholders have been identified, that's the time to look through your organization's own network map: Who has the best connections to key stakeholders to make introductions? What events do they attend? What are likely incentives to get them to align with your social startup? These are important and strategic assessments to be made and remade as shaped by additional insights and information from the organization's leadership team.

# IDENTIFYING STAKEHOLDERS

According to Burga and Rezania (2016), one of Freeman's core arguments is "the principle of who or what really counts," indicating that it is critical for SE founders to identify their stakeholders and assess their significance relative to the success of the SE.[31] As such, in this section, we spend time delving into the possible type of stakeholders that might reside within your organization's stakeholder map, to better delineate the "who and what." We start with one of the most important stakeholders for your organization: your paid staff, and in many cases unpaid volunteers, creating a larger set of internal stakeholders.

## Staff

Chapter 1 was dedicated to an organization's founding team. In this chapter we expand that view to include the entire organization. This is likely to be the first place to really dive deep into one's network map. Galvis (2014) notes that 90 percent of changes to products within SEs were driven by staff, as they are often closer to the day-to-day operations of the business than founders are.[32] For example, while Sanergy had a large founding team composed of classmates from MIT, as the company relocated to Kenya and began scaling, the composition of its employees changed. Within a few years, 93 percent of Sanergy's 251 employees across its eight key departments – sales, marketing, operations, toilet manufacturing, waste management, processing, technical, and administration – were Kenyans, with 40 percent of them under the age of 25. According to David Auerbach, Sanergy's co-founder and CEO, having such a strong Kenyan team was key to the company's success: "We've worked hard to establish a Kenyan leadership team to be the ones running country operations on a daily basis. Our managers have a strong intuitive understanding of the cultural context, which is critical for solving problems and which our expat teammates will never have at the same level."[33] Similarly, for RevFoods, a key and unexpected area of impact was providing local employment as the organization expanded its lunch program nationally. In fact, the founders discovered that they were serendipitously hiring family members of their prime beneficiaries (i.e., K-12 students), including students' parents, grandparents, aunts or uncles. These family members became key advocates for RevFoods' products, helping to seed their early success and acceptance by the local community.

## Partners

Partners is another important stakeholder group, and includes co-solution providers, suppliers, distributors, and all those who enable a social startup to provide end-to-end solutions more easily to its beneficiaries. Partners can aid an SE in understanding the nature and scope of its chosen social problem and provide insight into the feasibility of certain solutions within the local context.[34] This is especially important when working with communities that the founders are not already a part of: "Local partners in developing economies can often serve as interpreters, cultural guides, and importantly, sources of credibility within otherwise distrusting communities."[35] Building relationships with nongovernment organizations (NGOs) in related issue-areas can improve the SE's credibility through third-party validation, as the NGO can verify that the SE is actually accomplishing its mission.[36] Partnerships can also make collective action more impactful: "Because no one is responsible for the entire community, no one is tallying up impacts across service providers in order to ascertain a total impact … most programs serve a very small clientele and as a result, their impact is rather limited."[37]

An example of an early and important partner for three companies in our research is Whole Foods. Several executives from Whole Foods supported RevFoods in its earlier days due to their belief in its mission and helped RevFoods build its supply chain. "Initially, we could order from their bake house, produce distribution center, and other suppliers, and the Whole Foods truck would come and deliver things to us," said RevFoods' co-founder, Kirsten Tobey. Whole Foods executives further advised RevFoods on what equipment to put in their kitchens. Whole Foods was also important to Fair Trade (FT) USA, and continues to be important as FTUSA introduces new product categories, under their joint collaboration titled WholeTrade.[38] According to Paul Rice, FTUSA's founder and CEO:

> What we're doing with migrant farm workers in Northern Mexico who grow fruits and vegetables for Whole Foods, Costco, and Sam's Club, has been hugely successful. We've launched 20 new estate-grown fruit and vegetable products in the last two years like tomatoes, bell peppers, asparagus, and watermelons, all helping to improve wages and working conditions for farm workers.

Whole Foods also served as the first distributor for Back to the Roots (BTTR)'s first mushroom in a box product. Co-founder of BTTR, Nikhil Arora, recalls: "The regional buyer told us if we could figure out a way to get him enough product, he could 'blow this business up'."[39] Subsequently, within three months BTTR went from one Whole Foods store to 89 stores across 11 states.[40] With BTTR, Whole Foods was a supplier, distributor, investor and advisor.

## Customers and Beneficiaries Are Clearly Important Stakeholders

Customers and beneficiaries are often used interchangeably within the SE context. However, referring to users of a product or service as a customer often implies ability to pay, whereas the term "beneficiary" implies those consuming the product or service, who might not be paying at all. With RevFoods' subsidized lunch program, the students are the beneficiaries, and the meals are served at no charge due to government reimbursements. In the impact canvas developed by Jorge Calderon (2015),[41] he distinguishes between customers "who provide economics for the value you deliver" and beneficiaries who are "the target of your theory of change." Regardless, understanding the ultimate user and underwriter of the product is critical to assess how an SE's solution is being valued, and to inform future iterations of the product or service. As Galvis (2014) notes: "This group in particular is considered by both participants as the most important stakeholder because it is both fundamental to an SE's economic sustainability, as well as the main beneficiary of the social impact that the company aims to generate."[42] Employing a design thinking observation technique to discover customer needs and pain points that otherwise wouldn't surface from other research methods, such as surveys, can also be critical to an SE's early success (Walske et al. 2017):[43] "Observation reveals the subtleties of society that a polite home-dweller might not tell you about in your lean startup-inspired sit-down interview, much less so in an online survey platform." This also prevents the "Hawthorne Effect,"[44] also known as the observer effect, by which a customer may be using a product only because a representative of the providing organization is present.

Kennedy (2016) also discusses that as SEs expand, there is potential for competing claims to develop—particularly between socially and economically interested parties (Smith, Gonin, & Besharov, 2013). Firms faced with claims from a multitude of stakeholders need to determine ways of identifying which claims are most credible and pressing, including determining how to allocate resources based on the salience of each stakeholder (Mitchell, Agle, & Wood, 1997) and issue (Bundy, Shropshire, & Buckholtz, 2013)."[45] Kennedy (2016) sees founders' early decisions around the SE's business model as the biggest determinant of its relationship with beneficiaries. For example, the business model will determine whether the enterprise interacts with beneficiaries by donating proceeds to them (i.e., utilizing a one-for-one model, as TOMS shoes uses, such that when a customer buys a pair of shoes, a pair of shoes is similarly donated to a beneficiary in a target country). Kennedy emphasizes, "Once the intervention is determined, there is some potential for the interaction to evolve, but the core enterprise-beneficiary relationship is likely set during the ideation phase of the organization."[46]

Alternatively, the customer and beneficiary could also be one and the same, which is the case with BTTR's mushrooms in a box products: "We're on a mission to reconnect every family and kid back to where food comes from by helping them experience the magic of growing it themselves – no green thumb or backyard needed."[47] BTTR also has a "grow one give one" model with their products; if the paying customer posts a picture with one of BTTR's products, BTTR will then in turn donate the same kit to an elementary school classroom of the customer's choice. For FTUSA, the customer is the large corporation that has adopted and pays for fair trade certification practices, while the beneficiaries are the workers who receive fair wages and a portion of the certification fees for worker identified programming through farmer cooperatives (i.e., healthcare, childcare, education, safe drinking water, etc.).

RevFoods' founders discovered that their chosen population of beneficiaries, K-12 students mostly in charter schools, were not always quick fans of the healthy food choices offered in RevFoods' school lunches. The founders learned that presentation and taste were two important factors in having kids eat their meals (learned painfully after some early meals ended up in trash cans instead of empty stomachs); if kids didn't like what they saw, they wouldn't eat it. For

**Table 2.1**   Fellowship programs for social entrepreneurs

| Fellowships | Benefits | Recipient Companies | Website |
|---|---|---|---|
| Echoing Green | Funding, healthcare benefits, access to a peer group and mentor network | Sanergy, Embrace, Teach for America, College Summit, One Acre Fund | https://www.echoinggreen.org |
| Schwab Foundation for Social Entrepreneurs | High-level connections; association with World Economic Forum | FT USA, Revolution Foods, d.light, Embrace, Kipp Foundation, La Fageda, Barefoot College | https://www.schwabfound.org/ |
| Skoll Fellows | Over $1m in funding; high-level visibility at the Skoll World conference | FTUSA, Kiva, Revolution Foods, Code For America | https://skoll.org/community/awardees |
| Draper Richard Kaplan | Unrestricted, multi-year funding. Board engagement and ongoing coaching | Kiva, Room to Read, Sanergy | https://www.drkfoundation.org |
| Mentor Capital Network | Feedback on one's business plan; peer and investor connections | Back to the Roots | http://mentorcapitalnet.org |
| Thiel Fellowship | $100k in funding and mentor support for founders less than 23 years old | Workflow, Ethereum, The Ocean Cleanup | https://thielfoundation.submittable.com/submit/45338/apply-for-the-thiel-fellowship |

focused on hardware, education, healthcare, and other domain specializations. For example, LearnLaunch[66] is an accelerator focused on EdTech startups. Lemnos[67] is a funder and accelerator that takes equity in exchange for hands-on coaching, development, and capital for hardware startups. Startup Health[68] is exclusively focused on healthcare-related startups. (See Table 2.2.)

Accelerators and incubators are also important in gaining funding, having access to co-working space, and in finding both mentors and advisors. The main difference between incubators and accelerators is that incubators can house entrepreneurs for a longer period of time, whereas accelerators typically have entrepreneurs as participants for a shorter duration.[69] Hub Ventures has now been folded into Better Ventures,[70] but in its early years, it did run an accelerator program out of the San Francisco-based Impact Hub,[71] ultimately hosting three cohorts before changing its business model to become a venture capital firm. Impact Hub[72] is an important co-working space in its own right, for social entrepreneurs, long before the rise of WeWork space.[73] Co-working spaces provide "the opportunity to interact with peers and advisors."[74] Impact Hubs are a vital part of the social entrepreneurship community, with over 92 locations worldwide, including in Europe, Africa, US, Central America, Latin America, Mexico, the Middle East and Asia. Impact Hub also has over 15,000 members.

The value of incubators is much more than space. Village Capital is a fund and organization that supports early-stage social entrepreneurs, with its VilCap Communities: "The goal of VilCap Communities is to unlock capital for communities outside the major venture capital centers. Entrepreneurs in these communities are solving real-world problems – like health,

**Table 2.2** Incubators and accelerators for social entrepreneurs

| Incubators and Accelerators | Benefits | Recipient Companies | Website |
|---|---|---|---|
| Unreasonable | Unreasonable has a collection of accelerators and incubators depending on the focus of the startup | Eneza, Pivot, BioSense, Rising Tide Car Wash | https://unreasonablegroup .com/initiatives/ |
| Mass Challenge | Up to $3m in funding without loss of equity, co-working space and mentorship/coaching | Ksplice, RelayRides, Thinx, Drync | https://masschallenge.org/ |
| NewMe | Pay to participate in a weeklong accelerator | Hard Fork! | https://www.newme.in/ |
| Civic Accelerator | 10-week bootcamp for-profit or nonprofit early-stage ventures focused on solving social problems | Impact Lab, La Cocina, The Dress Project | https://cvcx.org/ |
| Techstars | Three-month incubation; demo day in front of potential funders. Includes but does not focus on social startups | Digital Ocean, PillPack, ClassPass | https://www.techstars .com |
| Fast Forward | Tech nonprofit accelerator; provides funding, coaching and connections | MedicMobile, Quill, UpSolve, Dost | https://www.ffwd.org/ |
| Y Combinator | Founded in 2005, the largest tech-focused accelerator. Main focus is tech instead of social mission-oriented startups | Dropbox, Airbnb, Stripe, Reddit, PagerDuty, Instacart | https://www.ycombinator .com/apply/ |

education, water sustainability and advances in agriculture."[75] Some co-working spaces offer centralized business services (i.e., business planning, accounting, and office support). Another US-based co-working space is Propeller in New Orleans, which has a $1.4 million annual budget (at the time of this writing) and had 100 startups that have gone through it. Other incubators include the LIFT Economy, Koga Impact Lab (Paraguay), Impaqto (Ecuador), Advance Humanity (Vermont), China Australia Millennial Project (Sydney), and Singularity University (California).[76] There are also many accelerators listed in India, like the Deshpande Foundation, which has been around since 1996,[77] and Fledge runs programs in Seattle, Lima and Barcelona.[78]

Universities have also joined the ranks of accelerators, with too many to mention in this chapter. Table 2.3 shows a sampling of accelerators affiliated with the UCLA, University of California Berkeley, and University of Chicago. If you live near a university, are an alumnus/alumna of a university, or have team members still affiliated with a university, it's important to see what the university might offer in terms of space, monies and mentorship. Often, accelerators are not restricted to students or alumni, so it's important to check with nearby colleges to see what they might offer. SkyDeck, out of UC Berkeley, for example, was formed as a collaboration between the Haas School of Business and Berkeley Engineering, as well as the Vice Chancellor of Research at UC Berkeley.

**Table 2.3**   University incubators and accelerators

| University incubators and accelerators | Benefits | Recipient Companies | Website |
|---|---|---|---|
| The Global Social Benefit Institute, Santa Clara University | Since 2003, 1000 social entrepreneurs have raised over $1 billion in funding. | Juhudi Kilimo, Jacaranda Health, Global Alliance for Clean Cookstoves | https://www.scu-social-entrepreneurship.org/gsbi |
| Anderson Venture Accelerator, UCLA | At least one team member at UCLA Anderson | KPOP Foods, Hansel, Split Decision, Predictev | https://www.anderson.ucla.edu/centers/price-center-for-entrepreneurship-and-innovation/anderson-venture-accelerator |
| Berkeley Skydeck | For founders and UC affiliated founders | Eko Devices, Ensighta Security, Sutro | https://skydeck.berkeley.edu/ |
| NewVenture Challenge, University of Chicago | At least one team member at Chicago Booth | GrubHub, BloomNation, Braintree | https://polsky.uchicago.edu/programs-events/new-venture-challenge/ |
| Launch, UC Berkeley | At least one team member at UC Berkeley | TubeMogul, Medinas, Revolution Foods | https://www.uclaunch.com/ |
| Edward L. Kaplan Business Model Competition, University of Chicago | Social New Venture Challenge is a track that accepts mission-oriented social ventures. Yearlong launch process | GrubHub, Braintree, Bump Technologies | https://polsky.uchicago.edu/programs-events/new-venture-challenge/ |

Competitions also serve as another source of funding, recognition and peer engagement employing a "cohort" cycle during the competition process. A large social entrepreneurship competition, which was in existence for 20 years and seeded much of the field before shuttering, was the Global Social Venture Competition (GSVC),[79] which originated out of UC Berkeley. Prior competitors in the GSVC included: BTTR, Kiva, RevFoods (which won first place), Sanergy (which won GSVC's impact award), d.light, and the World of Good. Sanergy was also the winner of MIT's $100k competition.[80] Sanergy's win in the $100k challenge is an example of an SE performing well in a competition open to all types of entrepreneurs (not just social entrepreneurs). Not only was the prize money significant to Sanergy, but the distinction of winning further propelled Sanergy to national recognition on National Public Radio (NPR), which ultimately led to important funding from USAID. There are many entrepreneurship competitions that aren't specifically for SEs, but which might have a benefit to social startup founders nonetheless. BTTR did well in Berkeley's business plan competition, as did World of Good. The Hult Prize is an issues-based competition, that also has an accelerator for the finalists, followed by a final competition whereby teams can win up to one million dollars in funding. Winning such a prize could provide important seed funding without loss of equity, and may also provide global recognition. Many universities are also starting to embrace alumni as well. For example, Harvard Business School's New Venture Competition has a track specifically targeted towards their alumni.[81]

Criticism of incubators, accelerators and competitions is that they are often focused on "idea development," which means that entrepreneurs have to create their own network for scale. As such, "far too much attention and resources are devoted to studying the problems and talking about ideas, rather than implementing them."[82] Outside the university system, there are many important organizations that can help social entrepreneurs build their network and continue finding a sense of community. These include membership organizations such as Social Venture Circle,[83] which has been around for 30 years and has notable alumni such as: Ben Cohen and Jerry Greenfield, founders of Ben and Jerry's; Chip Conley, founder of Joie de Vivre Hospitality; Neil Grimmer, President and co-founder of Plum Organics; Kara Goldin, founder of Hint Water, and Chid Liberty, co-founder of Liberty and Justice. Net Impact professional chapters, and a variety of local convenings sponsored by Sustainable Brands,[84] can also be important places to find one's tribe.

## BUILDING A BOARD

Within the stakeholder map, one should think carefully about building a formal set or informal set of advisors. For the more formal route, the benefit of an advisory board is that it *isn't fiduciary*, so more formal meeting minutes and governing processes are not required. Also, an advisory board can be, and often should be, decoupled from investors. Advisors can simply be that – there to advise the social startup – and there can be more than one set of advisory boards. For example, a company like RevFoods could have both a culinary advisory board, and an advisory board composed of educators. They could further have a parent advisory board. Ultimately, a strong board of advisors can create trust and transparency – as well as providing "strategic advice" to the new entrepreneurs, often in a targeted way based on their industry experience.[85] If one had an EdTech startup, for example, an important advisory board could be made up of educators. This could include teachers, school district administrators, and luminaries in the field like Wendy Kopp,[86] founder of Teach for America, or Arne Duncan,[87] former Secretary of Education. Another potential advisory board in the same EdTech example could be a parental advisory board, likened to a virtual parent teacher association (PTA), to give insight into what is important in having their children adopt the innovative EdTech product.

Even though these are nonfiduciary boards, it's important to employ some tips to building an effective advisory board. First and foremost, prior to ever forming an advisory board, think about how your organization will incorporate the advice given. Is your personal style and that of your organization more informal, such that feedback and advice is ongoing and formal meetings are infrequent and short? Or, will scheduled, in-person meetings be catalytic to you and your team in having deeper discussions around topics that are central to your organization's growth? The larger the organization, the less ad hoc feedback is likely to become, and the more formal the feedback from an advisory board needs to be managed and heard. Regardless of size, the social startup should formally convene a board of advisors anywhere from two to four times a year to evidence that being a member of this board is worth the advisors' time (note: in the early days, these can be shorter meetings, held by video conference call; the coaching and relationship between formal meetings is most important to the social entrepreneur).

Second, ask yourself if the goal of an advisory board is to have advisors that can give you the advice, provide the social startup greater credibility, and/or build the organization's network. Sometimes founders will debate: Is it worth getting a literal "rock star" on their advisory board to build the organization's visibility – even if that person has little to no time for the organization? For sure, there are times when it is advantageous to have a key influencer as an advisory board member, but it is also important to balance that star power with having someone also engaged in your business. Having a disengaged influencer as part of your advisory board can actually hurt your startup; ask yourself: How would he or she respond when asked about the organization's mission, performance, or even you as a part of the leadership team? If you don't know – there is a high risk in having this person closely wedded to your new enterprise. From the perspective of a future advisory board member, an advisor might want an affiliation with your startup, but not want the fiduciary responsibility, nor the time commitment often associated with serving on a more formal board of directors. So, serving as an advisory board member is then the right level of commitment and not in any way a step down from having a full board position. Finally, think about term limits for your advisory board, which allows you the opportunity to change your advisors as the organization changes, in a less confrontational way than asking someone to leave your advisory board.

Eventually, you will also want to grow your board of directors outside of the founding team; having a board of directors is a legal requirement for those launching an SE in the US, irrespective of whether the organization is a for-profit or nonprofit entity. A board of directors has fiduciary responsibility for the SE, which means watching over the finances of the organization, approving annual budgets, and also weighing in on difficult financial situations, such as cash flow shortages which might impact payroll. They also typically manage the chief executive officer (CEO), including ongoing performance reviews, and other key hires. As the SE grows and matures, the board might include only one or at most two of the organization's original founders, but in the early years, the board might be composed of only the founders and perhaps one outside advisor or financial supporter. As an SE grows, only one founder might retain a board of directors seat, and that is usually the founder with the CEO title. For example, when RevFoods had its first formal venture round, the lead investor asked Tobey (the organization's original Chief Operating Officer) to step off of the board, favoring instead Richmond, RevFoods' CEO, as the sole board member representing senior management.[88] While both Tobey and Richmond balked at the idea, and were able to retain two board seats, this is not an unusual request, most particularly from investors who demand a board seat as part of their investing criteria.

This leads to the next question: Are investors automatically board members, or can boards be composed of non-investors also? This depends on a few factors. First, what is your organization's form: For-profit, nonprofit or hybrid? We'll go into more detail in the next chapter on the differences, but it's important to remember that your organization's form of incorporation will dictate the composition of your board of directors, as board seats can differ greatly between for-profit and nonprofit boards. Significant investors in for-profit entities will often require board representation as part to their investment criteria (if there are multiple investors participating in a round, usually only one or two formally join the board). However, just because an investor wants to be on your SE's board, it doesn't mean they *have to* be on your board. Sometimes offering board observer rights is enough; being a board observer allows investors to attend board meetings but does not give them voting power. For for-profit boards, adding new members to the board of directors should be carefully considered, as a board member cannot easily be removed, most particularly if he/she is an investor, as that is a requirement of the investment.

Nonprofit board members are important, as nonprofits have a public service obligation, and an outside board of directors ensures that the nonprofit's public benefit is being met. In this case, it is unusual to have the management team as part of the voting body within a nonprofit board. However, in some instances the CEO or Executive Director (ED) has negotiated a board seat with voting rights. Nonprofit board members also have fiduciary responsibility, in vouch-safing the organization's finances, and supervising the nonprofit's ED or CEO, depending on which title the primary leader of the nonprofit holds. In both cases, board members of SEs are held to a higher standard of representing stakeholders (for a for-profit board, not just share-holders), in keeping with our discussion on stakeholder engagement, earlier in this chapter.

In both nonprofit and for-profit boards, board members are sometimes kept in service well past their value to the organization. So, consider in advance having terms for service, so that board membership can be re-evaluated in a pre-defined time period.[89] Do you require a certain level of board attendance? For nonprofits are you expecting a certain level of financial support? For for-profit board members, is this board seat at risk if the investor chooses not to participate in future fundraising rounds? With respect to your organization's network, mapping out the network of one's board, and where one lacks network "coverage," can by helpful.[90] Specifically, "start thinking in terms of a network versus 'Who do we know who has this skill?', create a social network map of your board members' and staff's networks. It can help you see where the 'holes' and the 'silos' are in your network, and help you reveal new networks and people to connect with to reach your goals."[91] Board members are often attractive because of their pow-erful networks, but if their network largely overlaps your senior management team's network, or that of other board members, it is likely to stifle innovation, and create groupthink, leaving the organization blind to potential threats, weaknesses and opportunities.

## KEY TAKEAWAYS

In closing, there are a few important takeaways from this chapter. First and foremost, if nothing else, we've advised you to build and manage your network thoughtfully and judi-ciously. It takes time, but it is an important strategic advantage, and helps build the credibility of your startup. Second, given that time is a founder's scarcest resource, prune your network to focus on engaging those most aligned with your organization's stakeholder map. This doesn't mean ignoring authentic friendships and advisors who might not serve your startup's needs today. Nor does it mean ignoring your role in "educating the field" or helping out those who are new to the field. It just means being mindful of those who take time away from your startup without providing any benefit. Third, you and your management team will have to proactively seek those stakeholders that are necessary to your startup's success. This IS a group exercise and one that should be thoughtfully and authentically executed within your management team, as well as communicated. So, engage in a stakeholder map exercise, and make that, at a minimum, part of your annual strategic planning process.

## CASE STUDY
## FAIR TRADE USA

As 2014 drew to a close, Paul Rice, founder, President, and CEO of Oakland, California-based nonprofit Fair Trade (FT) USA, was deep in thought about how to scale FTUSA in the coming years. Since its launch in 1998, FTUSA had become the dominant certification organization for fair trade amongst US-based companies, growing from certifying one million pounds of coffee in its first year to certifying over one billion pounds of coffee since 1998.

Over its 16-year history, FTUSA had also forged notable partnerships with leading US brands and retailers including: Starbucks, Keurig Green Mountain Coffee, Ben & Jerry's, PepsiCo, Hershey's, Sam's Club, Costco, Dunkin' Donuts, and Whole Foods. By 2014, FTUSA had also garnered approximately 55 percent brand recognition amongst US-based consumers; yet, the organization was still certifying less than 6 percent of all United States-consumed coffee. This led Rice and his team to question how the $10 million-dollar nonprofit should best focus over the next decade, and how FTUSA should catalyze deep and effective social impact, with real market penetration that better matched its widespread consumer brand recognition.

Prior to founding FTUSA, Rice had spent 11 years working with farmers in Nicaragua, where he saw that international aid programs failed to create lasting change and sustainable development in rural villages. Accordingly, he and his wife decided to return to the United States so that Rice could pursue an MBA at the Haas School of Business at the University of California at Berkeley. It was a competition at Haas that prompted Rice to write the business plan for the organization that would eventually become FTUSA.

Early on, Rice received recognition for his groundbreaking work in fair trade. He was awarded an Ashoka Fellowship for social entrepreneurship in 2000, which was catalytic; it came with a $50,000 per year stipend for three years, allowing Rice to pay himself and bring on other early employees. Rice then went on to win many additional awards, including being named a four-time winner of *Fast Company*'s Social Capitalist of the Year, the Skoll Award for Social Entrepreneurship, and the Schwab Foundation/World Economic Forum Award for Social Entrepreneurship.

**Figure 2.6** Fair Trade USA logo

As a social enterprise, FTUSA had sought to reduce dependency on grants and donations by building a strong earned revenue stream, which came from its certification services and by licensing the Fair Trade Certified label to brand partners' product packaging. By 2013, FTUSA had not only grown to $10.4 million in total revenue, it had also become a bellwether within the social enterprise community for how to create an internal "economic engine," earning 80 percent of its revenue from audit and certification services, and thus requiring that only 20 percent of its revenue come from donations.

However, despite consumer, commercial and financial success, by the close of 2014, Fair Trade Certified products were less than one percent of the overall US-based consumer market. As Rice reflected on his organization's past accomplishments, he could not help but feel discouraged that FTUSA had not made more of a dent in consumer goods more broadly, and that two billion people around the world still continued to live in extreme poverty:

> All of our accomplishments sound like scale, but it's not. At the grocery store, consumers still don't see our label in every aisle. We've proven our concept, but now we need to innovate our model in order to truly scale our impact to hundreds of millions of farmers and workers around the world.

As part of this ambition to scale, Rice and his team had recently initiated a five-year strategic business plan focused on answering the question of how to grow FTUSA's reach and impact. This effort included reaching out to external constituents, such as companies that might increase the scope of their certification, as well as NGOs focused on related issues. As part of this plan, Rice and his team launched a $25 million capital campaign to fund five key projects, one of which was to launch new product categories for which FTUSA could apply its business model.

As Rice grappled with options around product diversification, it forced him and his team to think about their own definition of scale.

> Should our goal be to get from six percent to 20% in coffee because that will be a tipping point of credibility and prove that fair trade can go beyond a market niche? Or should we focus on creating a fair trade option in thousands of different product categories and take a longer-term view of market share?

Another part of FTUSA's five-year plan was to build shared value between two key stakeholders: farmers/workers and companies seeking to improve their supply chains. After enacting the business plan, the organization rewrote its vision to reflect this intention:

> We seek to innovate and evolve the fair trade model, taking impact to scale. We aim to elevate the social side of sustainability and emerge as the preferred model for ethical sourcing, sustainable development, and supply chain security. Our shared value and positive impact will reach millions of farmers and consumers around the world.

Against a backdrop of concern over the future of FTUSA, Rice couldn't help but to reflect on his past. But, drawing his attention back to the issues at hand, Rice knew that he needed a deliberate approach to sustain his organization into the future.

organizations such as United Way of America, The Salvation Army, and the American Red Cross,[2] all of which are well known for their charitable activities.[3] Rarely though do we consider that the nonprofit corporate structure is also predominantly used by hospitals, academic institutions, sports leagues (including the National Hockey League) and National Rifle Association. In fact, several identity groups, including the KKK, also hold a nonprofit corporate form. Simply being a nonprofit also doesn't preclude an organization from charging high prices for products and services; both hospitals and academic institutions often pay high salaries and charge high rates for their services as nonprofits. Nonprofit arts organizations like ballet and opera companies, theaters, as well as sports leagues, including the NHL and the National Football League[4] (which recently converted from a nonprofit to for-profit in 2015) also pay high salaries and charge steep ticket prices for events. Are these organizations understood to be committed exclusively to the generation of social value? And what about nonprofits that are focused on preserving gun rights or that promote views around white supremacy? These examples might not be what most consider fitting the image of a nonprofit, and challenge the blanket "halo" effect that is frequently entrusted to this organizational model.

Therefore, simply adopting a nonprofit corporate form does not excuse SEs from an obligation to contribute to society, have well-run organizations, and to be financially sound, as mismanaged nonprofits are a disservice to their beneficiaries and their mission. Promisingly, a current trend among nonprofits is a reexamination of management practices with an eye towards efficiency in mission delivery, and an increased focus on creating opportunities for earned revenue to supplement contributed revenue, lessening a nonprofit's dependence on grants, philanthropists and foundations. Indeed, a nonprofit organization cannot provide social impact, nor can it scale, if its funding streams are not secure and its financial stability is of ongoing concern. Even with sources of earned revenue, nonprofit organizations are still foreseen as less conflicted than for-profit firms, as any profit (or "surplus," as is more commonly used in nonprofit accounting), is automatically reinvested into the organization, as opposed to being distributed to shareholders.

By the same logic that ascribes affection for nonprofits, and given the historic purpose of for-profit firms, there is often skepticism about the ability of for-profits to pursue a social mission. Echoing a quote previously mentioned, economist Milton Friedman famously argued that "there is one and only one social responsibility of business – to use its resources and engage in activities designed to increase its profits."[5] But as a counterpoint, notable economist Michael Porter, in a 2011 article titled "Creating Shared Value" with FSG CEO Mark Kramer, argued that incorporating social mission into a company's value chain is becoming a capitalistic necessity, and that "profits involving a social purpose represent a higher form of capitalism, one that creates a positive cycle of company and community prosperity."[6] As the for-profit SEs in our research illustrate, there are many ways that for-profit firms obtain market value while accomplishing a social mission. In fact, there are a number of successful for-profit firms that incorporate social mission directly into their value proposition. Examples include shoe and eye glass manufacturer, TOMS and Warby Parker,[7] which pioneered a "Buy a Pair, Give a Pair" model, wherein a paying customer underwrites a pair of glasses (Warby Parker) or shoes (TOMS) for nonpaying beneficiaries that lack adequate access to these goods.[8] The social element of this type of business model is central to each organization's value proposition, and is arguably the reason for the success and popularity of these firms' brands. However, if not implemented correctly, it can reap its fair share of criticism too.[9]

One of the principal reasons that SEs elect to adopt a for-profit model has to do with the ability of these types of corporations to raise larger amounts of investment capital in exchange for equity. Our research finds that this is especially important for organizations that require early-stage capital for product development. Some of the SEs in our research that chose the for-profit form for this exact reason include: d.light, Revolution Foods, and Embrace Innovations. According to one of d.light's co-founders, Ned Tozun, "we can get capital from venture investors, from impact investors, commercial banks, and it's a structure that people are comfortable with." Another SE in our sample, Revolution Foods, is also a registered "C" Corporation, but took the additional step to signal its commitment to the environment, employees, customers and communities by acquiring B Lab certification. B Lab certification is a popular and well-regarded private accreditation for companies that meet high social-sustainability and environmental performance standards. Unfortunately, B Lab recently added a requirement that, in order to receive certification, companies must now take the additional step of incorporating as Benefit Corporations, a unique hybrid form discussed in further detail in the next section. As a result of this mandate, and given the costs associated with switching corporate forms, many certified firms are at risk of letting B Lab certification lapse in the coming years.

In this chapter, we introduce the various types of corporate form available to SEs, examine how the organizational structure pursued by each SE affected their ability to scale, and conclude the chapter with an example of one organization that switched forms while staying true to its social mission. We intentionally step away from the view that one corporate form is inherently better than another, and contend instead that each founder should consider which form fits best the mission of the organization, what is normative within a social startup's sector, and the social startup's most likely source of funding.

## FOR-PROFITS AS SOCIAL ENTERPRISES

Unique to SEs is having a choice when selecting corporate form. This is in contrast to pure for-profit entrepreneurial startups, as these companies are almost always founded as Delaware-based "C" Corporations within the US.[10] But incorporating as a for-profit social startup is often normative for a founder seeking outside capital, with the aim of someday filing for an initial public offering (IPO). Battilana et al. (2012) describe the dilemma of the legal structure for SEs: "Areas of corporate law, such as the tax code, were not built for organizations that pursue social and financial value." As argued by these scholars, until recently there was a dearth of standards to guide corporations that wanted to pursue social and environmental change while simultaneously benefiting their shareholders as for-profit firms. Similarly, there was a lack of capital and economic incentives to drive positive corporate behavior, given that capital markets tend to reward short-term growth in shareholder value over long-term economic sustainability. This led to a bifurcation of what remained within the realm of for-profits and nonprofits: "For-profits focus for the most part on shareholder value maximization and are permitted to distribute returns to investors. Nonprofits singularly pursue a charitable purpose, and in return, governments offer substantial tax benefits."[11] Historically, this dichotomy made it difficult for for-profit SEs to set organizational objectives that balanced shareholder demands with social purpose.[12] Additionally, without accommodating legal frameworks, for-profit SEs risked being disproportionately influenced by the demands of paying customers and inadvertently dismissing the needs of their beneficiaries.[13]

In spite of the challenges faced by for-profits having a dual purpose, significant progress has recently been made towards establishing new legal structures. One such structure is the dual-purpose organization, known in some states, such as California, as a "Benefit Corporation,"[14] or in others, such as Delaware, as a "Public Benefit Corporation."[15] In October 2010, the Benefit Corporation emerged as a new type of legal structure to recognize for-profit businesses that desired to embed their social mission into governing documents, such as a company's articles of incorporation and bylaws. In other words, this type of entity is designed to protect every stakeholder, and therefore, permit management of the SE in a way "that balances the stockholders' pecuniary interests, the best interests of those materially affected by the corporation's conduct, and the public benefit or public benefits identified in its certificate of incorporation."[16] Specifically, a Benefit Corporation exhibits three characteristics – purpose, accountability, and transparency – and is organized for the purpose of creating "general public benefit,"[17] which is defined as a "material positive impact on society and the environment, taken as a whole, as assessed against a third-party standard." As a result, the Benefit Corporation allows for the simultaneous maximization of shareholder value and societal value by emphasizing a multiple stakeholder model.

Since 2010 more than 34 states have enacted legislation authorizing Benefit Corporations. As of this writing, there have been close to 5,000 Benefit Corporations registered in the US, with 700 located in Delaware (the most common state for incorporation due to the state's favorable policies towards corporations), and 200 in California. Examples of Benefit Corporations include: Patagonia, Method Home Products (which is a subsidiary of Ecover), Plum Organics (a subsidiary of Campbell Soup Company), and Kickstarter, just to name a few. It is also important to note that Benefit Corporations have been successful in raising venture funds from traditional venture capital firms including Andreessen Horowitz, Founders Fund, First Round Capital, Benchmark, New Enterprise Associates, as well as more socially motivated venture capital firms such as New School Ventures, Omidyar Network, and the Westly Group. As such, Benefit Corporations are a viable option for socially conscious firms. However, as a point of caution, not many Benefit Corporations have successfully held IPOs, and this lack of precedence is a valid point of concern for founders as they consider how to incorporate, given that investors often value the option of having their investees go public.

The Flexible Purpose Corporation (FPC), also referred to as the Social Purpose Corporation (SPC), is another option available within 15 US states, but is used less by SEs relative to either Benefit Corporations or "C" corporations (with or without B Lab Certification). SPCs are required to have one or more social benefit purpose embedded into their governing charters, requiring "boards and management to agree on one or more social and environmental purposes with shareholders, while providing additional protection against liability for directors and management."[18] The definition of the social mission for an SPC is regarded as more flexible than the defined requirements of Benefit Corporations or the 200 possible metrics suggested by B Lab.[19] Less frequently used, the L3C (Low-Profit Limited Liability Company) is another for-profit organizational form with express social benefit "designed primarily to enable companies to access investment from tax-exempt sources such as private foundations."[20] However, venture capital investors typically do not invest in limited liability companies (LLCs), which means that incorporating as an L3C might limit an important source of investment capital to a fledgling SE.

The recent introduction and implementation of new certifications and corporate structures for socially motivated startups are evidence of the fact that dual-purpose organizations are becoming more accepted not only from a societal vantage point, but from a legal one as well. Given the number of new corporate forms now available, it is helpful to consider the main attributes that distinguish for-profits and nonprofits:

- *Access to multiple sources of capital.* For-profit firms can raise money from angel investors, impact investors, and other funding sources such as more traditional venture capital, by giving ownership or equity in exchange for invested capital. Having access to an array of financial resources often gives for-profits an advantage over nonprofits in terms of their ability to raise large amounts of funds quickly. This is especially helpful to firms that require early-stage capital for product development, which was the case for Embrace, d.light and Revolution Foods.
- *Flexibility in earned revenue.* A for-profit business can have flexibility in its revenue sources without regard for various tax implications, since, unlike a nonprofit, all of its income is subject to state and federal taxes, anyway.
- *Equity incentives for employees.* Employees of a for-profit corporation can be granted stock options to align with shareholders' interests. Employee stock options allow for-profit SEs to better compete for talent in the job market against less socially motivated for-profit firms.

In our research, the SEs (see Table 3.1) used a variety of corporate structures (i.e., for-profit, nonprofit and hybrid) to meet their organizational objectives. Three of them – Revolution Foods, Back to the Roots (BTTR) and d.light – elected to adopt a for-profit structure. Additionally, BTTR and Revolution Foods also earned B Lab Certification.[21, 22]

Starbucks, Keurig Green Mountain Coffee, Ben & Jerry's, PepsiCo, Hershey's, Sam's Club, Costco and Whole Foods.

Given the propensity for nonprofits to overrely on charitable donations, FTUSA also serves as a counterpoint, raising most of its funds from certification fees. In fact, FTUSA earns 80 percent of its revenue in certification fees[66] – and is unusual in being operationally funded through a higher percentage of earned versus contributed revenue. Despite FTUSA's success in creating sustainable revenue streams, Gras and Mendoza-Abarca (2014) caution nonprofits against overcommercializing their operations, as that may undermine legitimacy and threaten legal status: "while entrepreneurship may allow NPOs [nonprofit organizations] to rise above the fray inherent in traditional sources of revenue, an overreliance on non-traditional sources of revenue may be detrimental to their survival."[67]

A recent trend amongst donors of nonprofit firms is the increasing demand for more clearly defined social returns in exchange for contributions. Funders are starting to expect significant changes from charities, including being much less institutional and much more entrepreneurial. Klein (2015) advises nonprofits that they must adapt in order to keep up with the changing dynamics of what donors have come to expect: "Nonprofits are losing their monopoly as the most effective agents of social change. Unless they evolve, corporations, B Corps, and SEs that are just as committed to solving social problems and perhaps better able to make a difference will eclipse them." The Founder of Virgin Group, Richard Branson, argues for greater *collective* impact, with nonprofits engaging in collaborative, issues-based problem-solving: "We need collective efforts of countries and companies to step up and play their part – setting strong goals, having clear plans, and openly demonstrating progress."[68] As such, Klein (2015)[69] suggests that nonprofits consider the following types of changes to ensure that their operations are aligned with what funders are looking for:

- Introduce pay-for-performance executive compensation that links salaries and bonuses to specific social change targets.
- Establish an annual review of all programs to identify initiatives that other organizations could better deploy or commercialize, in partnership with the private sector.
- Prioritize innovation by introducing a new "exit strategy" protocol for successful programs, and reduce donor giving requirements as social change outcomes improve.

To the second point above, a key takeaway for nonprofit leaders is that there might be instances where a nonprofit should divest from activities, especially if those operations would be better executed by another organization. This harkens to Jed Emerson's call for additionality: "Simply put, the principle of additionality calls on impact investors to target businesses that would not otherwise be capitalized by private investors."[70] Further, Klein (and the Gates Foundation) argues that nonprofits shouldn't live on past their cause, and that instead, they should "exit", by which he means that "the new imperative for nonprofits that are addressing solvable issues is to plan for their own obsolescence."[71]

In closing, the two nonprofits featured in our research were very passionate about their choice of organizational form and viewed their legal structure as an important statement about their organizations' commitment to their social purpose. Both organizations, FTUSA and Kiva, also managed to scale and raise significant funds despite not having equity to offer in exchange for those funds. Both organizations also felt that their nonprofit status was an important step in culling the trust and goodwill of much larger corporate partners. In the case of both organizations, their nonprofit status also engendered high levels of volunteerism. For FTUSA, the organization was able to gain the support of activists, which was catalytic for many large corporations to certify their products. For Kiva, their unpaid fellows program was foreseen as quite prestigious, attracting highly educated and qualified volunteers. Kiva also attracted high-profile executives to its board of directors, which it felt was in part due to its nonprofit status.

## HYBRID ORGANIZATIONS

As the term suggests, hybrid organizations "unite features of both nonprofit and for-profit configurations or create combinations of these models taken whole-cloth."[72] Dougherty et al. (2014) define hybrids as "structures and practices that allow the coexistence of values and artifacts from two or more [corporate] categories."[73] Put another way, Haigh (2015)[74] describes the organizational forms "on a spectrum. If you imagine a spectrum with pure nonprofit organizations surviving on philanthropy and grants on one end, and pure for-profit organizations with little or no social mission on the other end, hybrids occupy the intermediate points between them."[75] As Kickul and Lyons (2016) outlined, hybrids can take many forms, including for-profits with nonprofit subsidiaries, nonprofits with nonprofit subsidiaries, or nonprofits with for-profit affiliates. Because hybrid models have both nonprofit and for-profit characteristics, they provide entrepreneurs with the unique opportunity to demonstrate "that the capitalist system can be used to create social value and address social ills while at the same time creating economic value."[76]

The market for hybrid structures is growing in part due to the rise in socially responsible investing. As Haigh (2015)[77] noted, the domestic market for socially responsible investing is valued at approximately $3 trillion and represents 12 percent of managed funds. This shift into funding socially and environmentally conscious companies aligns with investors' appetite for financial returns that are paired with social impact (Haigh, 2015).[78] From our sample of firms, Sanergy and World of Good (WOG) were both incorporated as hybrid organizations, allowing them to ensure commitment to their social mission while also enabling them to attract *both* grants and investment capital.

Sanergy co-founder David Auerbach argues that Sanergy's hybrid structure was critical to its rapid expansion. Not only did Sanergy receive grant funding from USAID and other donor funds, such as the Gates Foundation, but they also received equity investments from the Eleos Foundation, the Acumen Fund and SpringHill Equity.[79] Sanergy's organizational model is actually comprised of two distinct businesses: a nonprofit arm that distributes specially designed toilets as an effective method of providing sanitation to urban informal settlements in Kenya, and a for-profit business that converts human waste from those toilets into fertilizer for small and medium-sized farms. Sanergy adopted "a differentiated funding strategy that accesses profit-seeking investors for commercial activities and nonprofit fundraising and public subsidies for social benefit activities."[80] Bifurcating their business in such a way was an important component of the organization's financial sustainability, since Sanergy came to believe that operating toilets in Nairobi's Mukuru and Mathare slums was unlikely to become a profitable operation, and would therefore be dependent on some type of grant subsidy. However, the fertilizer business had the opportunity to become profitable, given that fertilizer was typically imported and quite expensive for Kenyan farmers, making that part of the business attractive to equity investors.

As to Sanergy's social mission, according to co-founder Lindsay Stradley:

> If people are using sanitation, then the entire community is healthier. Children can stay in school, people can hold onto their jobs. More than a million children die every year of sanitation-related diseases in the developing world, which also results in huge health care costs. The impact of proper sanitation cannot be overstressed.[81]

Sanergy's business model was to franchise toilets, and initially, offer franchisees loans through a microfinance partner, Kiva. However, with few roads into the slums, collecting waste was a very labor-intensive process. This meant waste collectors had to travel long distances on foot, using handcarts to transport the waste to a centralized treatment area. From there, the waste went to an off-site processing plant to be converted into fertilizer.

Co-founder David Auerbach comments on Sanergy's strategy to Battilana et al. (2012): "We've found that grant funders are comfortable with the social mission priorities in the non-profit, and that investors like the fact that we cannot fulfill our financial goal without actually providing hygienic sanitation. Both are inextricably linked."[82]

WOG is another example of a hybrid organization that participated in our research. Like Sanergy, WOG was set up from the very beginning as a hybrid organization. The organization sold craft goods created in developing countries to US consumers while ensuring that laborers received a fair wage. Also like Sanergy, WOG established two separate business lines that worked together to meet the company's overall goals. Co-founder Priya Haji saw enormous value in having both a for-profit and nonprofit arm, as WOG scaled. The nonprofit component owned five percent of the for-profit and had a very specific social mission around creating standards for "a living wage." Alternatively, the for-profit part of WOG allowed the company to raise capital through a venture round from a traditional venture capital firm, DFJ,[83] which in turn funded and helped establish WOG as a key distributor of craft goods to many retail stores. For WOG, a hybrid organizational structure allowed the founders to acquire significant upfront investment for its for-profit, product-oriented business, while still pursuing a social mission for fare wage standards through its nonprofit affiliate.

The case of Embrace is one in which the SE started as a nonprofit, but later added a for-profit arm to overcome difficulties the founders faced in obtaining sufficient funding for product development. Embrace began with a product: an infant warmer capable of running without electricity, which mimicked a backpacker's sleeping bag, and used phase change packets to heat the infant warmer "sleeping bag" to safe levels. At its inception, Embrace was set up as a nonprofit because the founders believed that other nonprofits, such as hospitals and large organizations like the Red Cross, would only buy from another nonprofit. They later found this assumption to be incorrect. In fact, the opposite is true, as it is customary for hospitals to buy medical devices from for-profit firms (such as Johnson & Johnson). Furthermore, as a non-profit, funding product development proved especially challenging. Jane Chen, Embrace's CEO and primary fundraiser, would spend six months raising donations, only to have to repeat that fundraising cycle the following year. This fundraising cycle was a huge impediment to the organization's ability to scale in its early stages. Chen and her co-founders reflected: "We were eager to take this product to the disadvantaged communities who desperately needed it. We needed to build an organization by which we could carry out this vision, and inevitably, the question arose: should we be a for-profit or a nonprofit entity?"[84] Ultimately, the founders "came to the conclusion that the fundamental difference between a for-profit and a nonprofit organization is where it can source capital."[85]

In a 2013 interview, the *New York Times* documented how ThinkImpact's CEO, Saul Garlick, also faced fundraising challenges that led the organization to contemplate changing corporate structure from a nonprofit to a for-profit. Garlick added, "a common frustration for nonprofits [is that] … 'many of the aspirational young nonprofit employees become beggars. They are seeking a way out of a tortuous financial reality where they are building the plane while flying it.'"[86] This frustration was aggravated by the organization's constant need to diversify its funding base to ensure that the nonprofit was never too dependent on any single funder.[87] Garlick eventually decided to pivot and have the organization become a for-profit company. Commenting on the rationale behind Garlick's decision, Jones (2013) says:

> the nonprofit/for-profit debate is overestimated and is really just about structure. I believe both structures can work, but they come with different requirements for how people prioritize their time … The notion that nonprofits are the right—or even, better—vehicle for doing good in the world is no longer true.[88]

In summary, as Figure 3.1 shows, there is a spectrum of organizational forms available to social startups. In our research, we had nonprofits, for-profits and hybrid organizations. Two SEs in our research began as hybrids: Sanergy and WOG. Embrace became a hybrid, adding a for-profit organization – Embrace Innovations – to be able to accept investment capital and accelerate both its product development and clinical trial process. Kiva and FTUSA found that being nonprofits was important to their respective missions and cultures, while also providing access to human and financial capital. Revolution Foods, d.light and BTTR had a more traditional for-profit form, but two of these three SEs were also B Lab certified (though none has yet converted to Benefit Corporations). Given the diversity of corporate form among our sample, it should be clear to future founders of social startups that no single legal structure is inherently better than any other, and that the decision of how to incorporate should be predicated on the startup's business model, culture and mission.

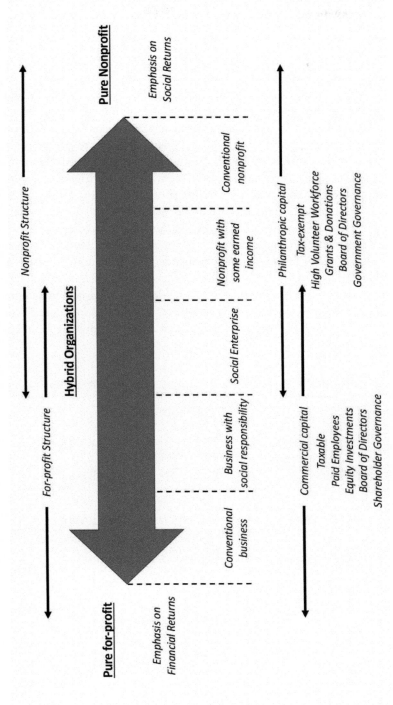

**Figure 3.1** Kathy Brozek's "Spectrum of Social and Financial Returns"

For a summary of the distinctive elements of each organizational type, note the diagram in Figure 3.1, adapted from Kathy Brozek's "Spectrum of Social and Financial Returns."[89]

# CONCLUSION

Kiva and FTUSA are both pure nonprofit organizations. Being a nonprofit had important implications for the stakeholders, and was central to each organization's mission. Even though FTUSA earns much of its revenue, it still wanted a nonprofit structure to reflect its focus on the social mission of laborers' rights. FTUSA's nonprofit status also enabled it to partner more seamlessly with larger for-profit organizations, such as Starbucks, Hershey, Green Mountain Coffee and more recently, West Elm. For Embrace, WOG and Sanergy, a hybrid structure most effectively allowed each organization to take advantage of the benefits of a nonprofit funding structure (which is donor based) for the parts of their businesses that were not likely to be profitable. By incorporating a for-profit business arm, each of these three SEs also established a means to acquire funding from venture capital firms and other equity investors, which ultimately allowed them to scale their businesses and product development more rapidly. For BTTR, Revolution Foods and d.light, a for-profit structure was necessary to get the early-stage capital that these organizations needed to source, produce and deliver their products into the marketplace. Gregory Dees' "Social Entrepreneurship Spectrum" is amended in Figure 3.2 to include the specific benefits inherent to various structures and considerations for founders seeking to scale their SEs.[90]

| | Pure nonprofit | Hybrid Organizations | Pure for-profit |
|---|---|---|---|
| Beneficiaries | Pay nothing | Subsidized rates; some pay and some don't | Market-rate prices |
| Capital | Donations and grants | Below-market capital, donations, investment | Market-rate capital |
| Workforce | Volunteers | Below market-rate wages, some volunteers | Market-rate compensation |
| Suppliers | In-kind donations | Donations, in-kind and full-price | Market-rate pricing |

**Figure 3.2**    Amended Gregory Dees' "Social Entrepreneurship Spectrum"

# KEY TAKEAWAYS

- Given the range of possibilities for organizational structure that are available to SEs, corporate form is a question that founders must consider from the earliest stages of their venture. Considering how expensive and administratively burdensome it can be to change corporate form, we suggest that *there is no reason to incorporate until*:
  - The first check from a purchase, investment or donation needs to be cashed or written.
  - Patents need to be filed for intellectual property protection.
  - Ownership amongst co-founders needs to be determined (for-profits only).
- Instead, we suggest that founders *experiment with the business model that seems to work best for the organization, its product and/or service*. For example, if the organization is unlikely to ever be profitable and its founders anticipate that revenues must be donation-based, perhaps a nonprofit form would best facilitate growth and effective operations. However, if the organization is creating a product that will require a large up-front investment to create physical products, then a for-profit form may be best. It is also important that founders conduct due diligence and check with key stakeholders to see what is normative in a particular sector to prevent ill will or potential public relations troubles.
- Additionally, *founders should seek out legal advice appropriate to the sector/industry/ geography in which they intend to operate*. There are wonderful resources available online, and founders should study them to reduce legal fees. But when it comes time to actually incorporate, there is no substitute for proper legal counsel. This includes working with a law firm that is both knowledgeable and experienced in the various types of organizational forms available to SEs. Experienced counsel will allow management to weigh the pros and cons of each corporate structure (i.e., nonprofit, for-profit or hybrid). In some cases, the best resource might be the law school students and professors on one's campus, or law firms with alumni that are sympathetic to the financial and time resource constraints that startups have. If the SE plans to develop or distribute a product internationally, it's especially important to seek counsel with expertise in those regions.
- Finally, *it is easier to incorporate than to disband a firm*. Shutting down a for-profit company is an involved process, and requires cash reserves to pay off vendors, employees, and so on. Closing down a nonprofit is even more difficult, since the organization is not owned by the founders but registered with the state or government entity in which it was incorporated. While transferring assets from a for-profit to a nonprofit can be done, there are often tax liabilities incurred in the process. Transferring assets from a nonprofit to a for-profit is also a difficult process and is rarely worth the trouble. In fact, the easiest option is often to keep the original entity intact (i.e., the nonprofit) and found a new complementary organization (i.e., a new for-profit) as Embrace did, rather than try to disband the original nonprofit. If an SE pursues a hybrid option that incorporates both for-profit and nonprofit businesses, the founders must be careful to follow the important legal guidelines, including a requirement to have separate boards of directors and separate financials.

## CASE STUDY
## BURNING MAN

In September 2017, as another year of Burning Man drew to a close, Larry Harvey, Burning Man's original founder, looked out at the vast playa while the sun rose over the majestic Black Rock Desert. Over 75,000 people had attended the weeklong Burning Man event, a far cry from its modest origins on Baker Beach in San Francisco in 1986, when Harvey first burned a human effigy with 35 friends. For eight days Black Rock City plays host to an event that has become both a cultural and social movement. The "playa" temporarily becomes the sixth largest city in Nevada state, complete with its own airport and post office, all of which are dismantled in a matter of weeks as part of the event's "leave no trace" ethos. Burning Man's parent organization, Burning Man Project (BMP), is now a nonprofit 501(c)(3), but the event's organizers originally incorporated the venture as a for-profit LLC. The manner in which the founders ultimately elected to transition their enterprise from LLC to 501(c)(3) was a contentious and arduous process, highlighting many of the difficulties that founders face when considering how to incorporate their social venture.

The original impetus for Burning Man to incorporate happened in 1996, after several accidents on the playa catalyzed discussions about the event's future. Although Larry Harvey and two other founders had already established a holding company for the Burning Man trademark (Paper Man LLC), the six main organizers of the event sensed that they needed to establish a new organization that could manage the growing event. Attendance at Burning Man had risen to a point where the founders needed structure to help deal with revenue management, permitting issues, and legal liability. Accordingly, in 1997, the six organizers incorporated as a for-profit Limited Liability Corporation: Black Rock City LLC.

Incorporation as an LLC quickly brought order to a previously disorganized process. Black Rock City LLC was able to file taxes, acquire permits, and the owners were protected from any legal liability in the event that someone might get injured out on the playa.

As Burning Man continued to grow, new affiliated ventures were incorporated, such as the Black Rock Arts Foundation, Black Rock Solar, and Burners Without Borders. Growth also led to event organizers from around the world asking how they could launch their own regional Burning Man events.

Then, in 2004, at which point more than 35,000 attendees were coming to Black Rock City, John Law, one of the original founders of Paper Man LLC, the prior holding

**Figure 3.3**    Burning Man logo

company of the Burning Man trademark, who had parted ways from the other founders many years earlier, brought a lawsuit against Black Rock City LLC. Though the lawsuit was eventually settled, the conflict made the organizers realize that the for-profit structure of their LLC was problematic, as ownership could be passed down through inheritance to those who might not adhere to the principles of Burning Man's social movement.

Accordingly, the founders began to research and debate which organizational form would allow Burning Man to thrive, grow and adapt far into the future. In 2007, after years of debate, the six partners of Black Rock City LLC approved the registration of a nonprofit to serve as the primary home for all of Burning Man's activities. The transition process was not easy though. It was an exhausting administrative task facilitated by a specialized attorney, and the transition came at a great financial cost to the founders (a point they say reflects their commitment to the Burning Man ethos).

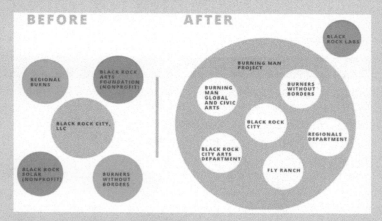

**Figure 3.4    BMP corporate structure**

While BMP's status as a nonprofit aligns well with the overall mission of the social and cultural movement, the transition has also introduced new questions and concerns.

First, despite a robust program of global philanthropic initiatives, organizers of Burning Man have a hard time communicating to donors the impact of their movement beyond what happens in Black Rock City. *If Burning Man is to continue on a growth trajectory, and given the organizers' intent to continue to offer affordable tickets, what role should donations play in the organization's revenue strategy?*

Furthermore, volunteerism has always been a key part of Burning Man's culture, and critical to the event's success. To accommodate the event's growth though, organizers have had to hire more staff than ever before.

| | | 2012 | 2013 | 2014 | 2015 | 2016 |
|---|---|---|---|---|---|---|
| Revenue | Contributions, Gifts, Grants | $539,959 | $7,845,655 | $1,093,008 | $1,329,325 | $8,074,456 |
| | Program Service | $51,680 | $108,219 | $30,696,414 | $34,863,949 | $37,741,207 |
| | Other Revenue | $33 | $15 | $574,587 | $699,656 | $402,808 |
| | Total Revenue | $591,672 | $7,953,889 | $32,364,009 | $36,892,930 | $46,218,471 |
| Expenses | | $259,925 | $984,859 | $30,013,511 | $35,844,236 | $36,975,805 |
| Revenue Less Expenses | | $331,747 | $6,969,030 | $2,350,498 | $1,048,694 | $9,242,666 |

**Figure 3.5**   Burning Man revenues, 2012–2016

## CASE QUESTIONS

1.  As a nonprofit, will transparency of revenues through annual 990 filings deter participants from volunteering their time? With event organizers around the world now hosting affiliated Burning Man events, how should the nonprofit think about licensing in a way that aligns with the organization's values?

2.  Though the history of BMP is unique, the consequences of the founders' choices on how to incorporate emphasize some of the factors that social entrepreneurs must consider as they decide on a legal structure. Fundraising, accountability, and the pursuit of legal revenue-generating activities are just a few of the many factors that social entrepreneurs must consider. Would you choose a nonprofit structure for Burning Man? If yes, why? If not, which one would you choose?

*For more information, see the Berkeley Haas Case Series' title *Burning Man: Moving from a For-Profit to a Non-Profit, the Ultimate Act of Gifting.*

## NOTES

1.  Yunus, Muhammad. *Speech*. 17 January 2008. Social Business Earth, 1 May 2008, socialbusinessearth.org/definition.

2.  All of these organizations were ranked on a top ten list for brand recognition amongst nonprofits by Cone in collaboration with Intangible Business.

3.  List, Andrea. "New Cone Report Values America's 100 Leading Nonprofit Brands." *CONE*, 24 June 2009, www.conecomm.com/news- blog/new-cone-report-values-americas-100-leading-nonprofit-brands.

4.  Weinreich, Marc. "NFL targeted by Oklahoma senator for 'not-for-profit' tax status." *Sports Illustrated*, 18 October 2012, www.si.com/node/411791.

5.  Friedman, Milton. "The Social Responsibility of Business to Increase its Profits." *New York Times Magazine*, 13 September 1970.

6.  Porter, Michael, and Mark Kramer. "Creating Shared Value." *Harvard Business Review*, January–February 2011.

7.  Fitzgerald, Michael. "For Warby Parker, Free Glasses Equals Clear Company Vision." *Entrepreneur*, 10 February 2015, www.entrepreneur.com/article/242437.

8.  Battilana, Julie, Matthew Lee, John Walker, and Cheryl Dorsey. "In Search of the Hybrid Ideal." *Stanford Social Innovation Review*, Summer 2012.

9.  Janzer, Cinnamon, and Lauren Weinstein. "The Buy-One-Give-One Model Might Make You Feel Good, but It Doesn't Make The World Better." *Fast Company*, 22 November 2016, www.fastcompany.com/3053596/the-buy-one-give-one-model-might-make-you-feel-good-but-it-doesnt-make-the-world-better.

10. McGee, Alan. "Why Your Startup Should be a Delaware C-Corporation." *gust Launch*, 15 March 2017, www.gust.com/launch/blog/why-startup-Delaware-c-corporation.

11. Battilana, Julie, Matthew Lee, John Walker, and Cheryl Dorsey. "In Search of the Hybrid Ideal." *Stanford Social Innovation Review*, Summer 2012.

12. Wry, Tyler, J. Adam Cobb, and Howard E. Aldrich. "More than a Metaphor: Assessing the Historical Legacy of Resource Dependence and Its Contemporary Promise as a Theory of Environmental Complexity." *Academy of Management Annals*, vol. 7, no. 1, 2013 439–486.

13. Ebrahim, Alnoor, Julie Battilana, and Johanna Mair. "The Governance of Social Enterprises: Mission Drift and Accountability Challenges in Hybrid Organizations." *Research in Organizational Behavior*, vol. 34, 2014, pp. 81–100.

14. California State, Legislature. CORPORATIONS CODE – CORP. Cal. Corp. Code, section 1. California Legislature Information, 1 January 2012, leginfo.legislature.ca.gov/faces/codes_displayText.xhtml?lawCode=CORP&division=3.&title=1.&part=13.&chapter=4.&article=.

15. Delaware State, General Assembly. GENERAL CORPORATION LAW. Del. Code Ann., section XV. State of Delaware, delcode.delaware.gov/title8/c001/sc15/.

16. Ibid.

17. California State, Legislature. CORPORATIONS CODE – CORP. Cal. Corp. Code, section 1. California Legislature Information, 1 January 2012, leginfo.legislature.ca.gov/faces/codes_displayText.xhtml?lawCode=CORP&division=3.&title=1.&part=13.&chapter=4.&article=.

18. Ibid.

19. "Introduction to the B-Lab Standards." *Certified B Corporation*, bcorporation.net/for-b-corps/resource-library.

20. Battilana, Julie, Matthew Lee, John Walker, and Cheryl Dorsey. "In Search of the Hybrid Ideal." *Stanford Social Innovation Review*, Summer 2012.

21. "B Impact Report – Revolution Foods." *Certified B Corporation*, bcorporation.net/directory/revolution-foods.

22. Tyson, Laura, and Jennifer Walske. "Revolution Foods: Expansion into the CPG Market." *The Regents of the University of California*, 31 July 2015. Berkeley Haas Case Series B5845.

23. Embrace. *990*. 2014, 990s.foundationcenter.org/990_pdf_archive/830/830509261/830509261_201412_990R.pdf.

24. "Back to the Roots." *Crunchbase*, www.crunchbase.com/organization/ back-to-the-roots#section-overview.

25. Sanergy. *990*. 2016, 990s.foundationcenter.org/990_pdf_archive/364/364688468/364688468_201612_990.pdf.

26. "d.light design." *Crunchbase*, www.crunchbase.com/organization/ d-light-design#section-locked-charts.

27. "World of Good." *Crunchbase*, www.crunchbase.com/organization/ world-of-good#section-funding-rounds.

28. "Kiva." *Crunchbase*, www.crunchbase.com/organization/ kiva#section-funding-rounds.

29. "Revolution Foods." *Crunchbase*, www.crunchbase.com/organization/ revolution-foods#section-funding-rounds.

30. FTUSA. *990*. 2014, 990s.foundationcenter.org/990_pdf_archive/262/262780747/262780747_201512_990 .pdf.

31. "Investment Partner Profile: Revolution Foods." *W.K. Kellogg Foundation*, www.wkkf.org/what-we-do/ featured-work/revolution-foods.

32. Led by Acre Venture Partners, Campbell Soup's venture capital fund.

33. "Our Story." *Back to the Roots*, backtotheroots.com/pages/our-story.

34. Zevnik, Neil. "Why We Need To Get 'Back To The Roots'." *Huffington Post*, 6 December 2017, www .huffingtonpost.com/neil-zevnik/why-we-need-to-get-back-t_b_11368478.html.

35. "With Help of $10M Series A, Back to the Roots Poised to Truly 'Undo Food'." *Sustainable Brands*, 6 June 2016, sustainablebrands.com/read/product-service-design-innovation/with-help-of0m-series-a-back-to-the -roots-poised-to-truly-undo-food.

36. "d.light Solar Products." *d.light*, www.dlight.com/products/.

37. "About Us – Learn More About d.light." *d.light*, www.dlight.com/about/.

38. Morris, Susannah. "Defining the Nonprofit Sector: Some Lessons from History." *Voluntas: International Journal of Voluntary and Nonprofit Organizations*, vol. 11, no. 1, 2000, pp. 25–43, doi:10.1023/A: 1008950915555.

39. Gras, David, and Karla I. Mendoza-Abarca. "Risky Business? The Survival Implications of Exploiting Commercial Opportunities by Nonprofits." *Journal of Business Venturing*, vol. 29, no. 3, 2014, pp. 392–404, doi:10.1016/j.jbusvent.2013.05.003.

40. Ibid.

41. Hopkins, B. "Social Entrepreneur's Brief Guide to the Law." *Enterprising Nonprofits: A Toolkit for Social Entrepreneurs*, edited by Gregory Dees et al., Wiley, 2001, Hoboken, NJ.

42. Battilana, Julie, Matthew Lee, John Walker, and Cheryl Dorsey. "In Search of the Hybrid Ideal." *Stanford Social Innovation Review*, Summer 2012.

43. Kickul, Jill, and Thomas Lyons. *Understanding Social Entrepreneurship: The Relentless Pursuit of Mission in an Ever Changing World*, Routledge, 2016, New York, NY.

44. Mishra, Subodh. "Nonprofit Corporate Governance: The Board's Role." *The Harvard Law School Forum on Corporate Governance and Financial Regulation*, The President and Fellows of Harvard College, corpgov.law .harvard.edu/2012/04/ 15/nonprofit-corporate-governance-the-boards-role/.

45. Hopkins, B. "Social Entrepreneur's Brief Guide to the Law." *Enterprising Nonprofits: A Toolkit for Social Entrepreneurs*, edited by Gregory Dees et al., Wiley, 2001, Hoboken, NJ.

46. Jones, Jennifer Amanda. "Social Enterprise: Making the Choice Between For-Profit and Nonprofit." *Nonprofit Quarterly*, 17 July 2013, nonprofitquarterly.org/2013/07/17/social-enterprise-making-the-choice -between-for-profit-and-nonprofit.

47. "We Envision a Financially Inclusive World Where All People Hold the Power to Improve Their Lives." *Kiva*, www.kiva.org/about.

48. Coates, Bethany, and Garth Saloner. "The Profit in Nonprofit." *Stanford Social Innovation Review*, Summer 2009, ssir.org/articles/entry/the_profit_in_nonprofit.

49. Originally, Kiva had a volunteer to employee ratio of 10:1.

50. Ibid.

51. Ibid.

52. *Draper Richards Kaplan Foundation*. www.drkfoundation.org/portfolio/.

53. *Skoll Foundation*. skoll.org.

54. *W.K. Kellogg Foundation*. www.wkkf.org/.

55. SKS Microfinance is a microcredit organization from India and is now known as Bharat Financial Inclusion.

56. Compartamos Banco was founded in Mexico as a nonprofit that turned into the largest for-profit microfinance bank in Latin America.

57. Toyama, Kentaro. "Lies, Hype, and Profit: The Truth About Microfinance." *The Atlantic*, 28 January 2011, www.theatlantic.com/business/archive/2011/01/lies-hype-and-profit-the-truth-about-microfinance/70405/.

58. "Poor People, Rich Returns." *The Economist*, 15 May 2008, www.economist.com/finance-and-economics/2008/05/15/poor-people-rich-returns.

59. Shah, Premal. Interview. By Jennifer Walske. May 2014.

60. Coates, Bethany, and Garth Saloner. "The Profit in Nonprofit." *Stanford Social Innovation Review*, Summer 2009, ssir.org/articles/entry/the_profit_in_nonprofit.

61. Ibid.

62. Ibid.

63. "We Envision a Financially Inclusive World Where All People Hold the Power to Improve Their Lives." *Kiva*, www.kiva.org/about.

64. Rice, Paul. Interview. By Jennifer Walske. 30 April 2014.

65. Walske, Jennifer, and Laura Tyson. "Fair Trade USA: Scaling for Impact." *The Regents of the University of California*, 1 May 2015. Berkeley Haas Case Series B5836, p. 9.

66. Ibid.

67. Gras, David, and Karla I. Mendoza-Abarca. "Risky Business? The Survival Implications of Exploiting Commercial Opportunities by Nonprofits." *Journal of Business Venturing*, vol. 29, no. 3, 2014, p. 403, doi:10.1016/j.jbusvent.2013.05.003.

68. Paul, Klein. "In Search of the Hybrid Ideal." *Stanford Social Innovation Review*, 15 May 2015, ssir.org/articles/entry/are_nonprofits_getting_in_the_way_of_social_change.

69. Ibid.

70. Bugg-Levine, Antony, and Jed Emerson. *Impact Investing*, John Wiley & Sons, 2001, San Francisco, CA.

71. Ibid.

72. Kickul, Jill, and Thomas Lyons. *Understanding Social Entrepreneurship: The Relentless Pursuit of Mission in an Ever Changing World*, Routledge, 2016, New York, NY.

73. Doherty, Bob, Helen Haugh, and Fergus Lyon. "Social Enterprises as Hybrid Organizations: A Review and Research Agenda." *International Journal of Management Reviews*, vol. 16, no. 4, 2014, doi:10.1111/ijmr.12028.

74. Haigh, Nardia. "Understanding Hybrid Organizations." *California Management Review*, vol. 61, no. 2, 2015, cmr.berkeley.edu/blog/hybrid_organizations.html.

75. Ibid.

76. Kickul, Jill, and Thomas Lyons. *Understanding Social Entrepreneurship: The Relentless Pursuit of Mission in an Ever Changing World*, Routledge, 2016, , New York, NY.

77. Haigh, Nardia. "Understanding Hybrid Organizations." *California Management Review*, vol. 61, no. 2, 2015, cmr.berkeley.edu/blog/hybrid_organizations.html.

78. Ibid.

79. http://www.saner.gy/archives/2524.

80. Battilana, Julie, Matthew Lee, John Walker, and Cheryl Dorsey. "In Search of the Hybrid Ideal." *Stanford Social Innovation Review*, Summer 2012.

81. Walske, J., and Laura Tyson. "Sanergy: Tackling Sanitation in Kenyan Slums." *The Regents of the University of California*, 1 July 2016. Berkeley Haas Case Series B5871, p. 3.

82. Battilana, Julie, Matthew Lee, John Walker, and Cheryl Dorsey. "In Search of the Hybrid Ideal." *Stanford Social Innovation Review*, Summer 2012.

83. *DFJ*. www.dfj.com/index.php.

84. Chen, Jane. "Should Your Business be Nonprofit or For-Profit?" *Harvard Business Review*, 1 February 2013, hbr.org/2013/02/should-your-business-be-nonpro.

85. Ibid.

86. Chhabra, Esha. "A Social Entrepreneur's Quandary: Nonprofit or For-Profit?" *The New York Times*, 10 July 2013, www.nytimes.com/2013/07/11/business/smallbusiness/a-social-entrepreneurs-dilemma-nonprofit-or-for-profit.html.

87. Ibid.

88. Jones, Jennifer Amanda. "Social Enterprise: Making the Choice Between For-Profit and Nonprofit." *Nonprofit Quarterly*, 17 July 2013, nonprofitquarterly.org/2013/07/17/social-enterprise-making-the-choice-between-for-profit-and-nonprofit/.

89. "Exploring the Continuum of Social and Financial Returns: When Does a Nonprofit Become a Social Enterprise?" *Community Development Investment Review*, August 2009, pp. 7–17. Federal Reserve Bank of San Francisco, www.frbsf.org/community-development/files/brozek.pdf.
Brozek, Kathy O. "Exploring the continuum of social and financial returns: when does a nonprofit become a social enterprise?," *Community Development Investment Review, Federal Reserve Bank of San Francisco*, no. 2, 2009, pp. 7–17.

90. Dees, Gregory. "Enterprising Nonprofits." *Harvard Business Review*, January–February 1998, hbr.org/1998/01/enterprising-nonprofits.

# 4
# The role of media in building a brand

## BRAND BUILDING

Amazon founder Jeff Bezos once described brands as what people say when you're not in the room.[1] While most people can see the importance of brand building in the consumer space, in the field of social good, brand management can often become an afterthought. In our research, we found that brand management and, relatedly, media management (which should reflect one's brand) are highly correlated with the social enterprises (SEs) that scaled. The most consistent benefit of having impactful media reach, or as we refer to it in our research, becoming a "media darling," was that it allowed the social startup to be perceived in the marketplace as bigger and more established than it actually was, greatly enhancing the startup's credibility. In fact, Kylander and Stone (2012) argue that a strong brand is critical to building operational capacity, galvanizing stakeholder support, and enabling an SE to focus on its social mission.[2] Therefore, throughout this chapter, we suggest that a social startup think carefully about its branding, mission, and alignment to ensure that as the organization expands, its brand value does too.

We suggest that an SE starts by first describing how the organization would like its stakeholders to think about its brand, and how this brand image reflects organizational culture and mission. Kylander and Stone (2012) take an expansive definition of brand, describing it as much more than a visual identity (i.e., beyond the organization's name, logo and graphic design).[3] Instead, these authors define a brand as a psychological construct held in the minds of all those aware of the branded product, person, organization and/or movement. As such, brand management then becomes the work of managing these psychological associations. While in the for-profit world, marketing professionals talk of creating "a total brand experience,"[4] in the nonprofit world, executives talk more about the "global identity" of their organizations. In other words, think of an organization's brand as a promise that conveys: (1) "who" an organization is; (2) "what" the organization does; and (3) "why" it matters. In fact, some describe a brand as the "persona" of an organization, representing the organization's very soul or essence, acting as a "time-saving device" by providing a "shortcut in the decision making of potential investors, customers, clients, and partners."[5]

According to Room to Read's co-founder, Erin Ganju, Room to Read (a girls' literacy nonprofit that has grown to annual revenues now north of $50 million) began with a lot of intentionality around its brand:[6] "Right from the beginning, Room to Read's founders agreed quickly on what the 'personality' or brand of Room to Read would be ... we wanted our brand to be playful, youthful, and fun." As an SE headquartered in San Francisco, near Silicon Valley, it was important for the founders to be known as results-oriented, disruptive, innovative and entrepreneurial.[7] Further, Room to Read's founding team understood that a strong brand would not only help the organization build its earliest resources, but also give the organization more freedom over how to use them.[8] As a result, the founding team came up with the tagline: "World Change Starts with Educated Children." Key to Room to Read's branding was communicating that "large-scale, positive change in the world can be achieved, and that education is a cornerstone solution to helping solve every other problem today."

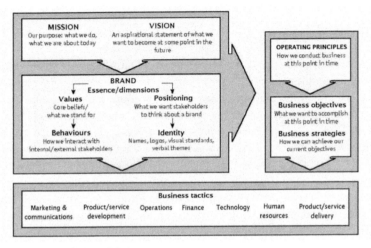

*Source:* Clifton and Simmons (2003).[9]

**Figure 4.1**      Brand organizational context

In keeping with Room to Read's premise, research has shown that strong brands in all sectors help organizations acquire financial, human and social resources, and build key partnerships.[10] A clear brand identity also gives organizations latitude to determine how best to use their resources: "The trust that strong brands elicit also provides organizations with the authority and credibility to deploy those resources more efficiently and flexibly than organizations with weaker brands."[11] This is important for all organizational types, but in the nonprofit sector, there is a sentiment that nonprofits are part of the public trust. As referenced in Chapter 2, nonprofits are organizations specifically set up for public good, and are ultimately (at least in the US) governed by the state in which they operate. Only through public service, are they granted tax-free status. As such, brand value is essential for both internal and external organizational stakeholders to better understand the organization's mission: "Internally, the brand embodies the identity of the organization, encapsulating its mission, values, and distinctive activities ... Externally, the brand reflects the image held in the minds of the organization's multiple stakeholders, not just its donors and supporters but also those it seeks to influence,

out in the news stream, also crowdsourcing the effort to all staff."[37] This means when organizations are young and lean, self-managing media (amongst many other competing priorities) is very important and a key factor in the success of social startups.

Media attention can be accelerated when a nonprofit is attached to a high-profile issue: "One of the most powerful ways to create a sense of urgency is to connect the message to a current issue in the news: in other words, craft a 'news hook' which will also help you immensely with your pitches to get coverage from the media."[38] In Scott Goodson's book titled *Uprising*, about "movement marketing," Goodson explains that instead of having a startup's marketing and advertising focus on an individual, marketers must learn to relate to people in interconnected groups:

> instead of convincing people to believe an ad message, marketers must try to tap into what it is that people already *believe* and care about; instead of being focused on *selling*, the way to connect with movements is to be dedicated to sharing; instead of controlling the message, marketers must learn to relinquish control and let the movement do what it will with that message; perhaps most radical of all, companies and brands must learn to stop talking about themselves and to join in a conversation that is about anything and everything *but* their product.[39]

With FTUSA, news coverage on the coffee crises and the plight of the average coffee farmer drove media attention to the organization: "In 1999 coffee prices plummeted and stayed in a hole for five years. You literally had coffee farmers in Mexico starving or dying in the desert trying to cross to the U.S. escaping the misery of coffee communities."[40] Then juxtaposed against this challenging backdrop was "the exponential profits being reported by all of the specialty coffee companies."[41] Similarly, Room to Read never lost sight of being tied to child development and education in a developing-country context: "At Room to Read we realized early on that we were in the movement-building business and identified different categories of key stakeholders to tailor our message to motivate, engage and inspire action."[42] Kiva also benefited from the increased media focus on microfinance. When Muhammad Yunus won the Nobel Peace Prize for his work in microfinance, the media began looking for case examples of US-based companies that were also in microfinance. Kiva became the US counterpart of Yunus's work in Bangladesh when, in 2010, former US President Bill Clinton mentioned Kiva in his book *Giving: How Each of Us Can Change the World*. This led to many follow-on interviews, including Oprah Winfrey, who featured President Clinton on her show. Oprah not only mentioned Kiva by name,[43] but the show also gave a full demo of the lending platform and featured a testimonial of the product, which gave Kiva incredible visibility across US-based households. Premal Shah, co-founder of Kiva, also spoke about the importance of media in the nonprofit's earliest years:

> It was actually PBS Frontline, as that whole program was funded by the SKOLL Foundation. We weren't a grantee yet, and SKOLL wanted to do more story telling for good. So, you could argue that more important than the grant that they gave us, the one million dollars, was the insanely catalytic media coverage.[44]

BTTR's founders also discovered that early media exposure lent credibility to their startup. In our sample of firms, BTTR's founders were the most media-savvy, being featured in the *Wall Street Journal*, *Fast Company*, *The Rachel Ray Show*, *The Today Show*, *Martha Stewart*, *CBS Evening News* and *PBS Kids*. One of the co-founders was even featured in the reality dating show, *The Bachelor*. This exposure led to greater product exposure within the consumer segment, enlarged distribution channels, and future funding sources. For Sanergy, media attention also helped attract investors. Specifically, as part of winning MIT's $100k competition, Sanergy was featured on PBS radio. This in turn led to a significant investment by USAID. While much of the media attention that BTTR, Kiva, Sanergy and even FTUSA received happened organically, there are lessons that we can learn to help determine the right media strategy for a social startup

## HAVING A COMMUNICATION PLAN

Once the organization has a brand strategy, it's crucial to have a communication plan to implement it. According to Chahine: "Communications includes the exchange of information within your team, other stakeholders, and most importantly your end user."[45] In Room to Read's case, the organization invested in both their employees and volunteers to ensure consistency in external communications and brand management. For example, in Room to Read sponsored events, from salons to larger events in public spaces, they sought out what they called the triple As: Already Assembled Audiences – meaning speaking to groups that were already convening. As such, they said "yes" to every opportunity to speak at corporate events and serve as invited keynotes when corporations were looking for inspirational leaders. These opportunities allowed Room to Read's founders to communicate more broadly why supporting girls' education was important. Additionally, they would hold more informal "lunch and learns" at corporations where they could, in smaller groups, talk about philanthropy and Room to Read's field-building work. Given that both co-founders came from larger organizations, with John Wood from Microsoft and Erin Ganju from Goldman Sachs, they both felt quite comfortable working with executives from corporations in culling financial and other types of support. As Ganju states: "We were constantly pitching to anyone who would listen and said yes to almost every opportunity in those early days to talk about our work." As the organization scaled, the founders began to see more growth from their volunteer-based chapter networks, which made their investment in consistent messaging and branding even more worthwhile: "in the transitional stage of rapid growth, it sometimes felt like we couldn't keep up with the boundless energy of our chapter network."[46] Similarly, many of the social entrepreneurs that we studied took advantage of free media opportunities, such as serving on a panel at important conferences where press, funders or influencers might be present. Such grassroots PR is both costless (except for the founder's time) and often more authentic, as long as the entrepreneur has some minimal type of PR training to execute as well on those opportunities as they arise.

Academic research also shows that having a solid communication plan is quite significant to the success of a startup. Gibbons argues, "If you want your ideas to take hold and win, you need to communicate and communicate well. It's not an option anymore—it's a necessity."[47]

This also includes internal communications, deemed as an essential component for an organization to make progress towards its mission and goals: "Internal communication can take place within team members horizontally and can take place vertically in terms of providing feedback from management to the frontline and vice versa, providing information to the board of directors, and making decisions."[48] In fact, the Communications Matters Research project found that "organizations that excel at communications are stronger, smarter, and vastly more effective."[49] For example, The World Wildlife Fund (WWF) proactively put a communications strategy into action that increased media coverage of illegal poaching by 270 percent, raising visibility to one of the organization's core issues and, therefore, the organization itself. WWF also implemented an "adopt a sea turtle" program, building on the virality of the video showing a plastic straw stuck in a sea turtle's nostril, filmed by marine biologist Christine Figgener.[50]

Chahine advises: "Just like you've tailored your solution and its delivery and pricing around your end user, you'll also need to craft tailored messages to each stakeholder. The trick is to maintain clarity, be concise, be compelling and be *consistent*."[51] Chahine advises one to consider how each message is tailored, and then how it is repeatedly delivered to ensure maximum retention and appropriate association by the receiver. A diagram by Chahine simplifies how to think of an organization's multidimensional messaging (Figure 4.3).

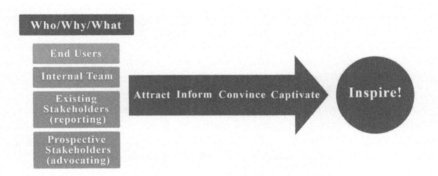

*Source*: Chahine (2016).[52]

**Figure 4.3**      Messaging map

Hootsuite, a social media management platform, emphasizes that traditional media strategies might not work in our current multifaceted media landscape due to the constantly changing platforms and speed of information: "We live in a new era of information … where new tools emerge at a dizzying pace and empower all of us to see and do more."[53] Hootsuite further emphasizes that with a social relationship platform, an organization can not only be "in the room" but also "take an active role in the conversation."[54] Similar to our earlier discussion on branding, Hootsuite suggests articulating one's media strategy by answering first the: *why*, *what*, *who*, *how* and *when*. First answering *why* information needs to be exchanged. Secondly, *what* is the organization hoping to accomplish through its media strategy. Third, *who* the different stakeholders are with which the organization needs to exchange information. And lastly, *how* this messaging reinforces organizational objectives. It's important to close by asking *what* types of media should be used, as well as *how* and *when* the organization will get its various messages across.

As with all communications, it is essential to ask the following: What is the goal (often multifaceted) of a social media strategy? Is it to grow followers? Solicit feedback (in which case someone needs to be actively monitoring company social media channels to respond to as feedback is given), or strategically post to different channels and audiences with more targeted messages (and in some platforms – to what extent is that even possible)?[55] As Mikáčová and Gavlaková (2014) discuss: "Often social media teams will simply delete or block users that leave negative comments on social ads but this data can be very useful in analyzing audience sentiment and refining product positioning."[56] Indeed, the age of social media has led to a blurring of PR and marketing. One of our sample firms, BTTR, has shifted much of their media focus to social media, including Facebook and Instagram, to sustain and build market momentum.

Inspire2Enterprise provides three steps to take to build a social media presence:

1. *Spend time creating a profile page for Facebook and Twitter.* "You'd be surprised how many people visit your Twitter and Facebook profiles. In the last twenty-eight days, for example, the Inspire2Enterpise Twitter profile page has enjoyed hundreds of views, and that means people are proactively seeking information about us."[57] At the most basic level, ensure that there is a logo, header image with the correct dimensions, and basic information such as a website, physical address, and the company's mission/story.[58]
2. *Post daily to keep content current and relevant.*[59] One of the biggest mistakes SEs make is posting irregularly – so that they have no consistent and ongoing messaging – leading to a drop off in widespread engagement.
3. *Make your content a discussion by engaging with others who respond to your posts* – "say 'thanks' – offer your thoughts and ask questions of your own."[60] This also has the benefit of increasing the likelihood that more people will see the company's posts, given that many social media algorithms reward multiuser engagement.

In addition to having an internal communication plan, it is also important to have a feedback loop. Mikáčová and Gavlaková (2014) reinforce this idea of engagement in a social media strategy: "Because social media is receiver-oriented and involves having two-way conversations, it is diametrically opposite of the traditional one-way, sender-oriented concept of advertising and marketing communications." A feedback loop allows the organization to ensure that the initial goals for each communication strategy are being met, and if not, to show why not. Feedback is often garnered through surveys, focus groups, and other more formal feedback mechanisms. It is also helpful to encourage informal feedback that is often given directly through an organization's users, donors, employees and partners. In order to ensure this feedback loop works, stakeholders must be encouraged to share feedback. While most people can generally agree with sharing feedback in concept, a way to ensure it in practice is through regular company meetings, internal surveys, and importantly, communicating ongoing management objectives up and down the organization through such processes as annual, semiannual and/or quarterly 360 degree reviews. In sum, the organization needs to be open culturally to feedback to allow more organic communication. There also needs to be

operations that were intended to help cut back on consumer waste (a model based on their original coffee grounds mushroom farming operations), but by 2014, the company's vision had shifted more broadly towards creating innovative DIY products that help consumers to connect more thoughtfully with the food they eat and provide to their families.

In deciding what to call their company, the founders reflected on some of their marketing classes at Berkeley Haas, and they knew that the name needed to part of a compelling story. Velez and Arora also knew that they wanted the company story to represent sustainability, innovation, and social responsibility – a "better" way of doing business. "Back to the Roots" reflected not only the values they emulated, but also the nature of their mission to bring customers closer to their food.

A decade after founding the company, Arora writes that:

> story-telling is everything, because it represents an opportunity to talk about your "why." Why this mission? Why you? Why this product? Ultimately, that story outlines the purpose of your company and the mission you're on. It is critical to building a brand, and garnering support from partners, employees, investors, etc. But that story has to be authentic – authentic to you and your team – that's where the magic lies.

Nine years after Nikhil Arora and Alex Velez watched themselves on TV during that first BBC segment, the founders note that[77] "media is a great friend for social entrepreneurs. Coverage can drive traction, momentum and serve as 'proof of concept'." Importantly however, they also underscored that media should not be viewed as a desired outcome, but merely as one step towards achieving longer-term impact:

> Media is a tool to drive awareness. And like any tool it's not an "end," but a means to achieve another goal. That goal can be sales, financing, finding new partners, etc. So each piece of press should be thought of as a tool in your toolbox to accomplish your larger strategic goals. One thing we have learned is that media itself isn't what's important, it's what you do with it – leveraging each feature to drive maximum momentum for your brand – for all stakeholders.[78]

## CASE QUESTIONS

1. Other than generating sales, what are the potential outcomes of media coverage for SEs? Does its importance differ by what industry the SE is in?
2. What specific marketing opportunities and challenges do SEs face when attempting to communicate the story of their brand?

*For more information, see the Berkeley Haas Case Series' title *Back to the Roots Ventures (BTTR)*.

# NOTES

1.  Bezos, Jeff. "10 brand stories from Tim Leberecht's TEDTalk." *TEDBlog*, October 2012, https://blog.ted.com/10-brand-stories-from-tim-leberechts-tedtalk. Accessed 20 May 2021.

2.  Kylander, Nathalie, and Christopher Stone. "The Role of Brand in the Nonprofit Sector." *Stanford Social Innovation Review*, Spring 2012, ssir.org/articles/entry/the_role_of_brand_in_the_nonprofit_sector. Accessed 26 April 2019.

3.  Ibid.

4.  Ibid.

5.  Ibid.

6.  *Room to Read*. www.roomtoread.org.

7.  Ganju, Erin, and Corey Heyman. *Scaling Global Change: A Social Entrepreneur's Guide to Surviving the Start-Up Phase and Driving Impact*. Wiley, 2018, Hoboken, NJ, p. 50.

8.  Kylander, Nathalie, and Christopher Stone. "The Role of Brand in the Nonprofit Sector." *Stanford Social Innovation Review*, Spring 2012, ssir.org/articles/entry/the_role_of_brand_in_the_nonprofit_sector. Accessed 26 April 2019.

9.  Clifton, Rita and John Simmons. *Brands and Branding*. The Economist, 2003. Profile Books, London.

10. Ibid.

11. Ibid.

12. Ibid.

13. Ibid.

14. Ibid.

15. Kylander, Nathalie, and Christopher Stone. "The Role of Brand in the Nonprofit Sector." *Stanford Social Innovation Review*, Spring 2012, ssir.org/articles/entry/the_role_of_brand_in_the_nonprofit_sector. Accessed 26 April 2019.

16. Ibid.

17. Brunsman, Barrett J. "P&G Cuts Annual Ad Spend by $350M as it Targets 'Smart Audiences'." *Cincinnati Business Courier*, 8 August 2019, www.bizjournals.com/cincinnati/news/2019/08/08/p-g-cuts-annual-ad-spend-by-350m-as-it-targets.html.

18. "Session on Marketing: Building Consumer-Brand Relationships in Social Media." *YouTube*, uploaded by MIT Sloan Alumni, 21 June 2016, www.youtube.com/watch?time_continue=2&v=fM6xv6kJai8&feature=emb_title.

19. Ibid.

20. Douglas, S.P., C. Samuel Craig, and Edwin J. Nijssen. "Integrating Branding Strategies Across Markets: Building International Brand Architecture." *Journal of International Marketing*, vol. 9, no. 2, 2001, pp. 97–114.

21. Miltenburg, Anne. "Building Brand as Your Organization Grows." *Stanford Social Innovation Review*, 8 September 2017, ssir.org/articles/entry/building_brand_as_your_organization_grows. Accessed 26 April 2019.

22. Keller, Kevin Lane, and Sanjay Sood. "Brand Equity Dilution." *MIT Sloan Management Review*, vol. 45, no. 1, 2003, p. 1.

23.  Miltenburg, Anne. "Building Brand as Your Organization Grows." *Stanford Social Innovation Review*, 8 September 2017, ssir.org/articles/entry/building_brand_as_your_organization_grows. Accessed 26 April 2019.

24.  Ibid.

25.  Ibid.

26.  Ibid.

27.  Anand, Mridula, Anand Nandkumar, and Charles Dhanaraj. "Embrace (A): Opportunity Identification." *Harvard Business Review*, 16 April 2013, p. 3.

28.  Chu, Michael, David E. Bloom, and Alison Berkley Wagonfeld. "Embrace." *Harvard Business School Publishing*, 18 July 2013. Harvard Business School Case Series 9-814-001.

29.  Ganju, Erin, and Corey Heyman. *Scaling Global Change: A Social Entrepreneur's Guide to Surviving the Start-Up Phase and Driving Impact.* Wiley, 2018, Hoboken, NJ, p. 103.

30.  Ibid.

31.  Flannery, Matt. "Kiva and the Birth of Person-to-Person Microfinance." *Innovations: Technology, Governance, Globalization*, vol. 2, no. 1–2, 2007, pp. 31–56.

32.  Ibid.

33.  Ibid.

34.  Ibid.

35.  Interview. By Jennifer Walske. 30 April 2014.

36.  Rice, Paul. Interview. By Jennifer Walske. 30 April 2014.

37.  Janus, Kathleen Kelly. *Social Startup Success*. De Capo Life Long Books, 2017, New York, NY, p. 194.

38.  Janus, Kathleen Kelly. *Social Startup Success*. De Capo Life Long Books, 2017, New York, NY.

39.  Manzo, Peter. "Branding Social Change?" *Stanford Social Innovation Review*, Fall 2012, ssir.org/book _reviews/entry/branding_social_change. Accessed 26 April 2019.

40.  Rice, Paul. Interview. By Jennifer Walske. 30 April 2014.

41.  Ibid.

42.  Ganju, Erin, and Corey Heyman. *Scaling Global Change: A Social Entrepreneur's Guide to Surviving the Start-Up Phase and Driving Impact.* Wiley, 2018, Hoboken, NJ, pp. 50–51.

43.  "How We Got to 1 Billion: A Look at Kiva's History." *Kiva*, www.kiva.org/blog.

44.  Shah, Premal. Interview. By Jennifer Walske. 22 February 2014.

45.  Chahine, Teresa. *Introduction to Social Entrepreneurship*. CRC Press, Taylor & Francis Group, 2016, Boca Raton, FL.

46.  Ganju, Erin, and Corey Heyman. *Scaling Global Change: A Social Entrepreneur's Guide to Surviving the Start-Up Phase and Driving Impact.* Wiley, 2018, Hoboken, NJ, pp. 50–51.

47.  Gibbons, Sean. "The Case for Communications." *Stanford Social Innovation Review*, 24 February 2016, ssir .org/articles/entry/the_case_for_communications. Accessed 26 April 2019.

48.  Chahine, Teresa. *Introduction to Social Entrepreneurship*. CRC Press, Taylor & Francis Group, 2016, Boca Raton, FL, p. 234.

49.  Ibid.

50.  "Sea Turtle with Straw up Its Nostril." *Bing*, www.bing.com/videos/search?q=sea+turtle+with+a+straw+ video&docid=608004877366265738&mid=3E5144AC4EFF2351A5923E5144AC4EFF2351A592&view= detail&FORM=VIRE.

51. Chahine, Teresa. *Introduction to Social Entrepreneurship*. CRC Press, Taylor & Francis Group, 2016, Boca Raton, FL, p. 238.

52. Ibid.

53. Hootsuite. *8 Tips for Building a Social Business*, p. 3. https://www.hootsuite.com/resources/8-tips-for-social-business. Accessed 20 May 2021.

54. Ibid.

55. Chahine, Teresa. *Introduction to Social Entrepreneurship*. CRC Press, Taylor & Francis Group, 2016, Boca Raton, FL.

56. Mikáčová, Lenka, and Petra Gavlaková. "The Role of Public Relations in Branding." *Procedia – Social and Behavioral Sciences*, vol. 110, 2014, pp. 832–40, doi:10.1016/j.sbspro.2013.12.928.

57. "3 of the most effective social media strategies for social enterprises." *Inspire2Enterprise*, 27 February 2017, www.inspire2enterprise.org/3-effective-social-media-strategies-social-enterprises/. Accessed 26 April 2019.

58. Ibid.

59. Ibid.

60. Ibid.

61. Mikáčová, Lenka, and Petra Gavlaková. "The Role of Public Relations in Branding." *Procedia – Social and Behavioral Sciences*, vol. 110, 2014, pp. 832–40, doi:10.1016/j.sbspro.2013.12.928.

62. Janus, Kathleen Kelly. *Social Startup Success*. De Capo Life Long Books, 2017, New York, NY.

63. Ganju, Erin, and Corey Heyman. *Scaling Global Change: A Social Entrepreneur's Guide to Surviving the Start-Up Phase and Driving Impact*. Wiley, 2018, Hoboken, NJ, p. 56.

64. Ibid.

65. Janus, Kathleen Kelly. *Social Startup Success*. De Capo Life Long Books, 2017, New York, NY, p. 190.

66. Janus, Kathleen Kelly. *Social Startup Success*. De Capo Life Long Books, 2017, New York, NY.

67. Ibid., p. 199.

68. Ibid., p. 199.

69. Blickley, Leigh. "How Brands Are Shifting Ad Campaigns amid the COVID-19 Outbreak." *HuffPost*, 9 April 2020, www.huffpost.com/entry/coronavirus-commercials-advertising-brands_n_5e8df008c5b670b4330a059d.

70. "Every Covid-19 Commercial Is Exactly the Same." *YouTube*, uploaded by Microsoft Sam, 15 April 2020, www.youtube.com/watch?v=vM3J9jDoaTA.

71. "One Team." *YouTube*, uploaded by Budweiser, March 2020, www.youtube.com/watch?v=3_t9niMNkdg.

72. "Best Video Ads for Covid-19." *YouTube*, uploaded by Broadcast2World, 27 March 2020, www.youtube.com/watch?v=NbMPbnSx7D8.

73. Taylor, Derrick Bryson. "Professor Fired After Joking that Iran Should Pick U.S. Sites to Bomb." *New York Times*, 11 January 2020, www.nytimes.com/2020/01/11/us/Babson-professor-fired-Iran-trump.html.

74. "1 Year Later Feature by the BBC." *YouTube*, uploaded by Back to the Roots, 17 November 2020, www.youtube.com/watch?v=2rnmposUN4A&feature=youtu.be.

75. Arora, Nikhil. Interview. By Jennifer Walske. 2019.

76. *Back to the Roots*. www.backtotheroots.com.

77. Arora, Nikhil. Interview. By Jennifer Walske. 2019.

78. Ibid.

cataracts in the population); market knowledge (the lack of affordable solutions in India); and operational acumen (the benefits of specialization and productivity optimization).[10] In fact, he often cited McDonald's as a source of inspiration for the model, stating: "Just as fast food is affordable to many lower-middle-class families in the West, in developing countries we can organize to provide affordable cataract operations."[11]

*Evaluation and Judgment* is the third dimension and contribution made by Tang et al. to the research on entrepreneurial alertness. After searching, collecting and connecting information in the previous stages, Tang et al. argue that the final element of alertness is an evaluation of the options to determine whether a commercial opportunity exists, either for the individual or for someone else. "For there to be an entrepreneurial opportunity, action needs to evolve from the cues, gathered information, and evaluations."[12] The entrepreneur's judgment and evaluation may ultimately lead her back to scanning and searching for further information in order to adapt or better assess the business opportunity (as indicated by the link from *evaluation and judgment* back to *scanning and search* in Figure 5.1). In this last stage of the process, judgment and evaluation helps entrepreneurs choose the business opportunity that seems most viable given their capacity to capitalize on it, as well as their vision of future market developments.[13] Returning to the example of the entrepreneur exploring a learning solution for students affected by school closures, he might come up with the idea of a virtual tutoring program for children. At this stage, he would evaluate whether the idea has profit potential (or is financially sustainable, in the case of a nonprofit) and whether this venture opportunity is available to him (i.e., does he have the time, resources, skill-set, and connections to realize the idea) in order to decide whether to move forward in the entrepreneurial journey. Entrepreneurial alertness theory, though seemingly complex, is grounded in the same concepts and practices that we'll discuss throughout this chapter: the role of knowledge gained through study and direct experience, the practice of creating hypotheses and connecting the dots, and the continued importance of listening for and acquiring actionable information.

## PATTERNS IN IDEA GENERATION

By examining nonprofit and startup origin stories, it is possible to pull out clear patterns in how and where entrepreneurs build the knowledge and connections that lead to their eureka moments. For some entrepreneurs, their ideas are inspired by personal passions or frustrations.[14] Not only does this intimate familiarity with the problem position the entrepreneur to identify a market need, it can also be a strong motivating factor for seeing the venture through, despite the inevitable setbacks and sacrifices along the way. Angela Benton, the founder and CEO of NewME Accelerator, advises aspiring entrepreneurs to "start your brainstorming with problems that you are personally invested in. Building a business is hard as hell and takes the kind of relentless dedication that comes from personal passion."[15] Paul Rice, the founder of Fair Trade (FT) USA, became passionate about advancing more effective approaches to poverty alleviation after spending 11 years living in Nicaragua and working with local farmer cooperatives. When he returned to the US to pursue an MBA, he remained committed to launching a fair trade organization to boost farmers' incomes, despite having to live off of a meager salary for years until the organization had enough traction to secure significant grant capital.[16]

Entrepreneurs also find inspiration by analyzing innovations taking place in other countries, industries, cultures, or periods in history.[17] While attending a guest lecture at UC Berkeley, the co-founders of Back to the Roots (BTTR) learned about and were inspired to launch a startup using a method for growing mushrooms from coffee grounds common in Columbia and parts of East Africa.[18] The explosive growth of ride-hailing startups in the US has inspired entrepreneurs in other countries to launch similar models elsewhere (i.e., Bolt, DiDi, Ola Cabs),[19] as well as very region-specific versions such as SafeBoda in Uganda, a successful ride-hailing company for the motorcycle-taxis, known as bodas, used to get around Kampala.[20] When we think about innovation, we often think about old methods making way for new ones, yet historical approaches sometimes go on to inspire the next wave of entrepreneurs. According to Sam Calagione, founder and president of Dogfish Head Craft Brewery Inc.,

> In the mid-'90s, some beer enthusiasts and experts called us heretics for brewing beers with ingredients outside of the "traditional" water, yeast, hops and barley. So, I started researching ancient brewing cultures and learned that long ago, brewers in every corner of the world made beer with whatever was beautiful and natural and grew beneath the ground they lived on.[21]

For Revolution Foods (RevFoods), a key innovation was to return to what could be considered more traditional cooking, by serving fresh, "real" food, as opposed to the artificial ingredient-rich, bland meals that had become the status quo in school cafeterias throughout the US.[22]

The lack of alternative options for earning a living wage has long been a catalyst for many individuals to start their own businesses as well. This is especially true in economies where unemployment rates might be high, startup costs low, and where there is a lack of big business presence to ensure employment. The desire for independence more broadly (financial or otherwise) is another strong motivator: in Turkey, one study found that "female entrepreneurs are mostly intrinsically motivated and are driven by the desire to achieve and to become independent."[23] Small businesses created for these reasons might not be driven to scale or have outsized impact, but they are vital parts of the economy, creating new jobs and contributing to the tax base.[24] Their importance and the challenges they face have been underscored even further by the COVID-19 pandemic.[25]

Finally, many social entrepreneurs are inspired to launch SEs based on problems they've seen in the world but have not directly experienced, a common but sometimes problematic starting point. For example, research has described the Dunning–Kruger effect, a cognitive bias we have wherein, rather than feeling less confident about our grasp of a subject we know little about, we feel more confident because our ignorance leads us to believe the subject is simple. It is only when we start to learn about the issue more deeply that we recognize its complexity, and ultimately moderate our confidence more appropriately.[26] Another concern is that the lack of familiarity with a problem often goes hand in hand with a lack of awareness of the solutions that already exist. While a competitive landscape analysis is a good start, this often just touches the surface of the market and rarely captures the variety of stakeholders involved in addressing social challenges, such as governments, nonprofit organizations, advocacy groups, labor groups, and so on. In a 2016 interview, Christy Remey Chin of Draper Richards Kaplan Foundation said, "People who don't understand the problem they are trying to solve also don't have the relationships they need to get the work done. Their actions can end up being paternalistic at worst and at best will end up wasting funds or fueling duplication."[27] This quote drives home the point that most people already have a product they're using, so what is it about the novel solution that would compel these individuals to switch to a new product? For example, there are many examples of cookstove innovations (more fuel-efficient, less pollutive) that have been introduced in rural communities globally, sometimes at no cost, which remain unpopular compared to the more familiar, locally made charcoal-burning stoves. The lack of user uptake for these cookstoves indicates that there are overlooked or undervalued factors that go into new product adoption beyond fuel efficiency and price.[28] Finally, the practical reality is that lived experience and deep expertise matter just as much as technical skills. Consider the likely difference it makes to an entrepreneur launching an education startup if he doesn't have experience as a teacher or a school administrator, or further, lacks a network within school districts. As Maya Winkelstein, CEO of the impact investing fund Open Road Alliance, emphasized, "If you want to go into finance and you haven't worked in the sector yet you wouldn't ever say 'Oh, I want to start a bank!' You'd know you needed to learn first!"[29]

This is not to say that those who are passionate about an issue and have come up with a promising idea cannot become great social entrepreneurs. Where individuals have terrific technical skills, they should certainly use them to achieve impact, but we advise that budding entrepreneurs put in the time to build a nuanced and holistic understanding of the issue and consider joining an established organization before launching their own. Daniela Papi-Thornton, formerly of the Skoll Centre for Social Entrepreneurship at Oxford, suggests that individuals evaluate their readiness to become entrepreneurs by reflecting on three areas: self-awareness (understanding your skills, risk tolerance and personal strengths); understanding of the problem (living or "apprenticing" with the problem and deeply understanding it); and skills and inspiration (the soft and technical skills, as well as the motivation to deliver).[30] In the end, no matter how "ready" a social entrepreneur is, he can never fathom all the roadblocks that lie ahead, and if he did, the social entrepreneur might not start at all. Therefore, more important than knowing everything is the recognition that launching an SE requires flexibility and resilience, and entrepreneurs must be prepared to ask questions, bring a large dose of humility to the process, and surround themselves with people who can supplement their limitations.

## CUSTOMER DISCOVERY

To quote Thomas Edison, "Genius is one percent inspiration and ninety-nine percent perspiration."[31] Once a social entrepreneur has formulated an initial idea, the hard work begins. As we stated at the beginning of this chapter, entrepreneurship is a journey of continuous learning and the first major step in that journey is to test whether your idea holds promise. This involves not only conducting secondary research (such as reading books and reports) but also garnering regular and highly focused feedback from potential customers. In our research, we have yet to hear of a social entrepreneur whose initial concept was the same one that ultimately achieved scale. Getting feedback early and often is critical, especially before taking the leap to fully invest oneself and potentially others' resources into building the SE. An authority on early-stage entrepreneurship, Steve Blank, calls this part of the process "customer discovery."[32]

An increasingly common method of testing entrepreneurial ideas is to use lean innovation principles, popularized by Eric Ries in 2008 and inspired by the lean manufacturing approach pioneered by the Toyota Production System in Japan in the middle of the twentieth century. Ries considers the defining characteristic of a startup to be "its environment of extreme uncertainty,"[33] and therefore centers his methodology on reducing uncertainty through rapid, low cost, hypothesis testing that enables a business to iterate its product, adjust its strategy, and achieve PMF while minimizing the resources utilized.[34] There are three main uncertainties for early-stage entrepreneurs: (1) technical risk: will the technology ultimately work?; (2) customer or market risk: are there customers who will use or buy it?; and (3) business model risk: is there a way to deliver and generate revenue from the solution? Determining the feasibility of the technology can be resource-intensive as it may involve building prototypes, hiring technical staff, or running time-intensive field tests or clinical trials. Business model risks are not always possible to mitigate in the near term and can take time to work through (consider Google's eventually successful but not immediately obvious revenue model of selling search-related ads for those who used its browsers). For this reason, it is often best to start by reducing the risks associated with the customer, which can be done by extracting actionable insights from potential customers and beneficiaries.[35] As Sarah Milstein of Lean Startup Company put it: "At this stage, you'll likely discover, as startups commonly do, that your basic idea holds little appeal for your target customers, or that a key assumption about customers' needs was simply wrong. Excellent. You've just saved yourself thousands of dollars and months of time."[36]

Customer discovery is the first of four steps in Steve Blank's customer development model, the other three being: (1) customer validation, when the entrepreneur achieves PMF and validates the business model; (2) customer creation, when the entrepreneur drives user growth; and (3) company building, when the entrepreneur scales the team and operations.[37] In her book, *Lean Customer Development*, Cindy Alvarez writes that customer development is critical to an organization's success because "We're biased towards our own great ideas."[38] The first months, if not years, for an SE are spent going back and forth between customer discovery and validation, so it is important to talk to the right people, ask the right questions, and ask questions in the right way.

1. *Ask the right people.* Talk to people who really are potential customers or users of the product. Perhaps they use a competitor's product, or they've expressed frustration with the problem you're trying to solve. If you are intending to charge money for your product, screen out those who don't spend money on your product category, or in the case of social solutions, where there is not a salient need. Sometimes this means asking hard questions: If the beneficiary is not able to pay for the product, then who will? How do you then test your product/service idea with that funder or slate of funders? If local

government is the primary target funder of your solution to a social problem, what is the right way to engage the government early in your test cases?

2. *Ask the right questions.* Some questions are unlikely to produce accurate data, even when the customer is trying to be honest. A common example is asking someone how much they would pay for your product. The answer is likely to be wrong, so get creative: Is there a product that they already use that provides similar value or is a competing product? If so, ask how much they spend on that product and how often. Lastly, remember that "why" a customer feels or thinks a certain way is always more interesting to understand than "what" they think or feel.

3. *Ask questions in the right way.* Make sure that the people you're speaking with feel comfortable being candid. If they're being polite or giving exaggerated responses, they're not helping you. Sometimes Yes/No type questions provide few valuable insights because they don't give you a sense of the degree of positive or negative sentiment the individual feels. In those circumstances, you can ask for open-ended responses, or have people rank their needs, or ask them to make trade-offs between solution options.[39] Further, it might be best to let them know you are doing market research for an entrepreneur but not identify yourself as that entrepreneur; people are less likely to be honest if they believe it's your idea.

Though the co-founders of RevFoods, Kirsten Tobey and Kristin Richmond, already had professional experience in education, they made sure to interview principals, students and parents from over 30 schools when they began exploring their idea of bringing fresh, healthy food to school cafeterias. As highlighted in Chapter 2, Tobey and Richmond actively engaged the community and gathered helpful insights about what would be appealing to students, such as the importance of both taste and presentation of the food.

Another important principle of the lean innovation method is to be sure that as you gather feedback, you categorize the respondents into "customer archetypes" or market segmentations. These archetypes describe the characteristics common to different subsets of your target market.[40] For example, RevFoods' potential customers – schools – differed widely in size, administrative structure, facilities, funding sources and culture, and therefore had different needs and positions on meal programs. Ultimately, RevFoods' initial customers were charter schools in the Bay Area that were too small to secure contracts with large food service management companies but wanted high quality lunches that were "ready to heat" or "ready to eat" due to limited kitchen space.[41] These characteristics probably informed RevFoods' initial positioning and helped it secure its first clients.

Another approach to organizing customer discovery insights is to think about what "jobs" individuals are trying to accomplish and which products they "hire" to do those jobs, an idea introduced by management scholars, including the late Harvard Business School professor, Clayton Christensen. Christensen advised entrepreneurs to focus on understanding the situations in which customers hire a product and then put together "job descriptions" that crystallize their customers' goals. To use a hypothetical example to illustrate this point, perhaps during customer discovery, the RevFoods co-founders observed a school principal talking to a parent about why the school was the right fit for his child, and she mentions the after-school tutoring program, the new computer lab, and the championship-winning soccer team. The tutoring program, lab and soccer team all serve additional purposes but in this specific situation, they are "hired" by the principal to convince the parent to send his child to the school. This insight could then help the RevFoods team consider how the meal program could also be hired for this job, as serving higher quality meals could make a school stand out from the crowd.

Clearly, the customer discovery process cannot be done by keeping your ideas to yourself, which leads some entrepreneurs to worry that their concept will be stolen.[42] Cory Levy, co-founder at One, Inc., shared how he and his team thought about this issue: "Ideas are a dime a dozen; it's the execution that will set you apart from the rest ... We plan to compete not by keeping our idea secret, but by building the best possible team and by creating the best solution to the problem we are solving."[43] Withholding all business details prevents entrepreneurs from getting actionable feedback and from focusing on the importance of the actual execution of their idea.

> By sharing your idea with people you trust, you might become aware of competitors you did not know about, challenges you were unaware of, or maybe even fundamental flaws in the possible go-to-market strategy ... In the early days of building a venture, feedback is key, and by keeping your idea hush-hush, you are basically preventing yourself from accessing this important step.[44]

For BTTR co-founders, Alejandro Velez and Nikhil Arora, their first idea was to be a distributer of coffee waste to mushroom farmers. According to Velez, input from potential customers led to an early pivot: "We definitely wanted to find a market before spending a dime, which has been our philosophy all along, so we went to farmers' markets, asking mushroom growers how much they paid for their growing mediums and if they would pay for our coffee growing medium."[45] Going straight to the farmers allowed Velez and Arora to discover quickly that farmers' willingness to pay for the growing medium was low and that BTTR's initial idea would not make for a profitable and scalable business. So, the co-founders shifted their thinking to growing the mushrooms themselves from the coffee waste they collected at local coffee shops. "At that point, our business model changed 180 degrees," Velez said.[46] In fact, this was only the beginning of BTTR's product evolution (Figure 5.2).

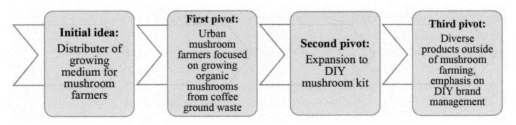

*Source:* Calderon and Bagadia (2015).[47]

**Figure 5.2**      BTTR's product evolution

# BUSINESS MODEL DEVELOPMENT

The next stage of the entrepreneur's journey is defined by an emphasis on experimentation. By investing the time to build a deep understanding of their target customers' challenges, "jobs" and characteristics, social entrepreneurs already are in a much better position to build a product that achieves the social or environmental impact they seek. However, conducting dozens or hundreds of interviews, observations and surveys does not ensure PMF and scale. Customer development and product development are processes that happen simultaneously and collaboratively and feed into what is ultimately the development of a robust business model. In this section, we'll outline the most important hypotheses to test, the components of a business model, business model development methodologies, and how to run experiments using MVPs, prototypes and pilots.

## Validating Value, Growth and Impact Potential

For social entrepreneurs, there are three dimensions to test and validate during the business model development process: (1) the value hypothesis; (2) the growth hypothesis; and (3) the impact hypothesis. The *value hypothesis*, also first introduced by Eric Ries, is focused on determining whether the product or service is something that customers really want or need. Some indicators of value might be evidence of strong interest in the product (i.e., sign-ups, purchases, etc.) and high engagement with the product (i.e., daily usage, retention, etc.). The *growth hypothesis* tests the drivers that fuel the organization's growth, such as a customer's willingness to pay and the virality of the product. In Ries's words, "Given that we've got one customer who finds our product valuable, how are we going to get more?"[48] Finally, the *impact hypothesis*, a new term introduced by Ann Mei Chang in her book *Lean Impact*,[49] considers whether the use and growth of the product will result in the intended positive impact. The degree of impact an organization has often takes years to determine, making it much harder to validate, but it is still possible to perform early tests by focusing on what Chang calls "linkages in the theory of change."[50] We'll discuss how to develop a theory of change in Chapter 8, but a simple example can illustrate what Chang means. Consider an organization that seeks to reduce malaria infection rates by distributing mosquito nets. While it might take years to prove out the long-term impacts of this intervention, in the near term, the organization can check whether the mosquito nets are being used properly. If they are not even being used or are being hung up incorrectly, then clearly the intended long-term goal of malaria reduction will not be achieved. This learning gives the organization the opportunity to resolve this linkage issue early by adapting a component of the delivery model.[51] Value, impact and growth should underlie the experimentation process throughout an SE's life cycle.

## The Business Model

The term "business model" may only seem relevant to profit-seeking businesses, but the term and the ingredients that make up a business model apply just as well to nonprofits. Many scholars and management professionals describe the business model as the set of assumptions

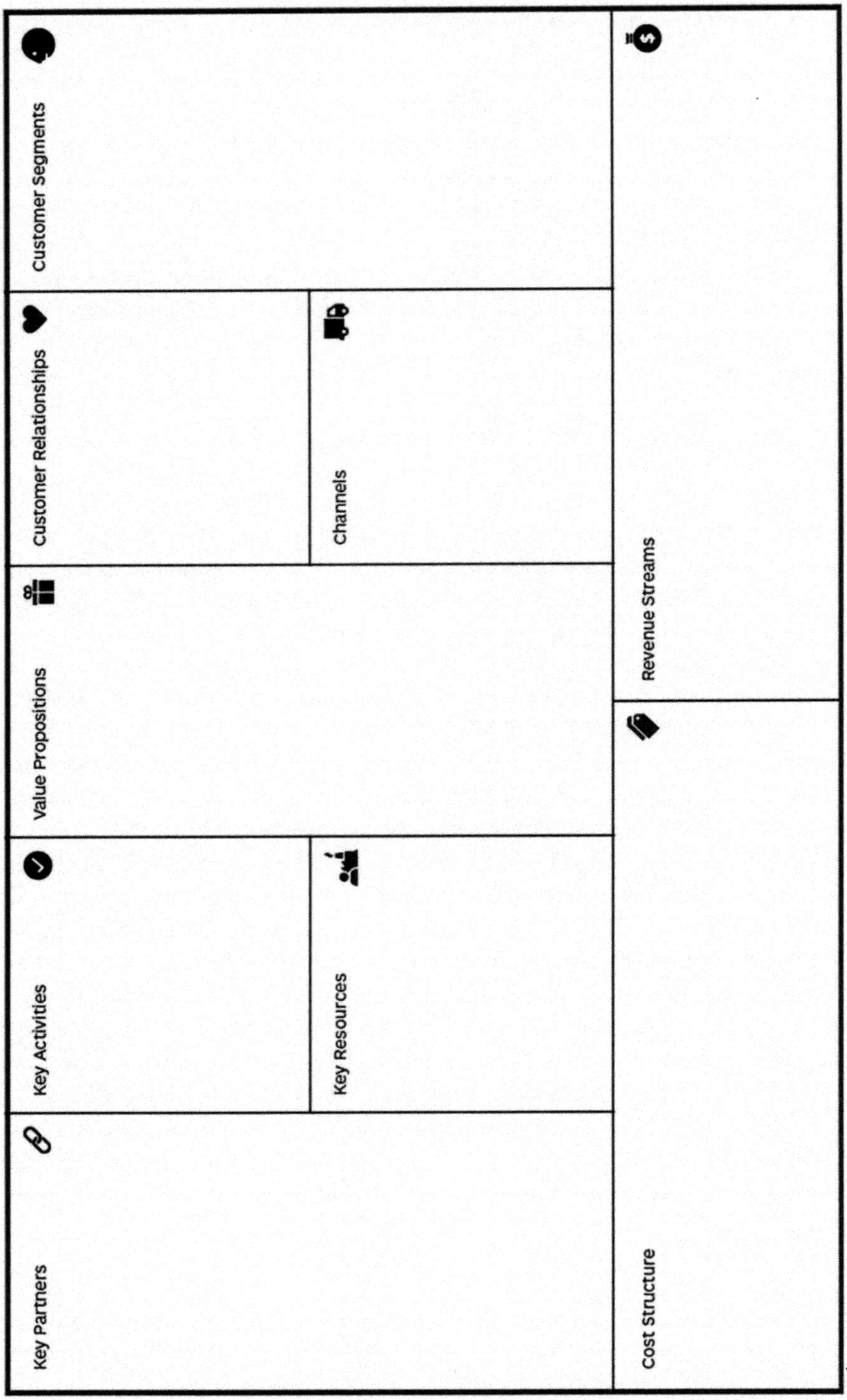

*Source:* Osterwalder, *Strategyzer.*[52]

**Figure 5.3**     The business model canvas

or logic that underlies how an organization delivers value to its customers at an appropriate cost.[53] Former strategy editor of the *Harvard Business Review*, Joan Magretta, breaks down the business model into two parts: "Part one includes all the activities associated with making something: designing it, purchasing raw materials, manufacturing, and so on. Part two includes all the activities associated with selling something: finding and reaching customers, transacting a sale, distributing the product, or delivering the service."[54] Business theorist Alex Osterwalder builds on Magretta's value chain orientation and incorporates the customer perspective; Osterwalder's well-known "business model canvas" (see Figure 5.3) breaks down the business model into nine elements: customer segments (those for whom you're creating value); value proposition (the value and differentiation you're providing); channels (the touch points for delivering this value); customer relationships (the kind of relationship you're building); revenue streams (how you capture value); key resources, key activities, and key partners (all three are part of the infrastructure for creating value), and finally, cost structure (the costs of delivering value).[55]

As a takeaway, social entrepreneurs should recognize that validating their solutions does not mean simply coming up with a great product that a handful of people find helpful; they must take into account the full value chain and the economics that delivering the product entails. While continuing to study at MIT, the Sanergy team was able to make significant progress on the product itself, the Fresh Life toilet, but learned quickly that a truly holistic solution would be necessary in order to deliver impact and achieve sustainability as an organization. They wrote in their original business plan from 2011: "Solving the sanitation crisis requires more than just building toilets … We combine these novel technologies with a realistic deployment strategy in our sustainable sanitation cycle."[56] Given the full value chain approach, they had to validate three core elements of their business model alongside the technology itself: the Fresh Life Network of micro-franchises spread throughout Nairobi's informal settlements, the waste collection process for that network, and the process for converting that waste into a commercial product. Regarding the Fresh Life Network, which grew to include a residential and a school model as well, co-founder Lindsay Stradley stated:

> In thinking about the three different distribution models [that we have now], we need to think about: "What is the problem [each customer is] trying to solve?" "How do we help [each customer] understand that problem?" and "How to help solve for their problem?" We think that there is a different learning curve for each model.[57]

The complexity of Sanergy's overall business model clearly demonstrates the importance of looking beyond the product itself and understanding what else is required to bring value to customers in a financially sustainable and scalable way.

## Development Methodologies

When it comes to testing the value, impact and growth hypotheses across these business model elements, there are numerous methodologies available. The exact business model development process will differ depending on the nature of the product, but the overarching theme is that customer input should be solicited throughout. The most widely applicable framework is Steve Blank's "Hypothesis–Design Experiment–Test–Insights" cycle. It starts with an entrepreneur identifying key business model assumptions and prioritizing which to test first based on where the biggest risks lie. Next, the entrepreneur designs an experiment to test this hypothesis effectively, without expending too many resources, and then runs the experiment using an MVP. Finally, the entrepreneur reviews the results of the test and derives insights that then feed into the business model, leading to the next experiment cycle (Figure 5.4).[58]

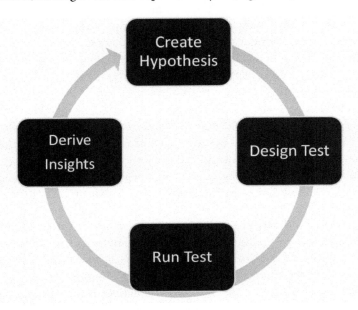

*Source:* Blank (2015).[59]

**Figure 5.4**     Development cycle

Blank developed his four-step process by adapting Ries's "build–measure–learn" framework for lean product development (itself based on the scientific method), and both approaches capture the cyclical nature of running experiments while developing the product and business model. Blank's approach can stand alone or be incorporated into other, more industry-specific or technologically required development cycles. For example, in software development, agile methods, which rose in popularity and use in the 1990s and 2000s, share a similar focus on customer feedback loops and rapid product development "sprints." Agile represents a marked evolution from the waterfall method that preceded it, which focused on gathering customer requirements as an initial step but limited further customer input during the remainder of the product development process. Because of the waterfall method's linear, asynchronous process, companies would find that customers were often dissatisfied with the product, leading to a lengthy and expensive product redesign before getting it right. In contrast, agile methods "implement adaptive planning, evolutionary development, early delivery, and continuous improvement."[60]

Kiva's experience also demonstrates another benefit of running a pilot: it can give social entrepreneurs a sense of what it actually means to run an organization, whether it is worth the risks involved, and whether they have what it takes (i.e., passion, skill-set, resources, etc.) to see their startup through to success.[79] After the second pilot succeeded in funding all 50 micro-businesses, Flannery, who had been fully employed elsewhere at the time, quit his job and committed to Kiva full-time. These two small pilots demonstrated that the idea was worth pursuing but also underscored that a part-time commitment would be insufficient. The information and results gathered through running a pilot can also demonstrate traction, such as early revenue, user uptake, or partnership agreements, that indicates progress to potential funders and adds credibility to both the idea and the entrepreneurs behind it. This is especially important for social entrepreneurs, who often find it more difficult to secure funding than their commercially driven counterparts, because they are proving models in challenging markets that serve overlooked or low-income customers.[80] Traction can also help SEs attract qualified talent to support their next stage of growth. After Kiva was featured in DailyKos, it brought on several skilled professionals who were interested in volunteering to support the team's mission, and it led an early contact at PayPal, Premal Shah, to join the Kiva team.[81]

Running a pilot can be difficult in industries that are heavily regulated or require licensing. Because person-to-person microfinance in the US was a new concept, Kiva faced intimidating regulatory hurdles and unclear tax implications, but Flannery and Jackley eventually took a leap of faith to pilot with the first seven businesses previously mentioned. As Flannery recounted:

> We decided that it would be extremely difficult, if not impossible, to get much traction on the business unless we figured out a way to just start. True, there were several open questions about this model. However, there's no more powerful way to resolve debates than to actually test and see. So we resolved to "just start" and see how things would play out over time.[82]

For other types of regulated products, it is critical to ensure that you do no harm while testing your product with customers. As mentioned earlier in the chapter, Embrace had to run dozens of carefully designed clinical trials in order to get its product in the market. CellScope used the standard diagnostics approach alongside its technology until there was sufficient evidence that its innovation performed just as well or better than existing diagnostic products.[83] And both Embrace and Global Water Labs decided to set higher standards than required by their pilot countries in case standards eventually became stricter or they decided to scale into other markets, to ensure their technology would still meet safety requirements.[84]

## FINDING PRODUCT–MARKET FIT (PMF)

PMF is the term used in entrepreneurship to describe the stage at which an organization's product (more broadly, "solution") delivers a compelling value proposition to its target market. Ries described PMF as "the moment when a startup finally finds a widespread set of customers that resonate with its product."[85] Reaching PMF is a key milestone for a social entre-preneur but also one that too many do not sufficiently validate before investing resources in growth. Startup Genome found that startups typically take two to three times longer to validate their market than expected and face pressure to scale prematurely: "In our dataset we found that 70% of startups scaled prematurely along some dimension. While this number seemed high, this may go a long way towards explaining the 90% failure rate of startups."[86] In fact, CB Insights' postmortem survey of the causes for startup closure found that the number one reason was "no market need," cited by 42 percent of startups. One of those startups, Treehouse Logic, shared its experience:

> We were not solving a large enough problem that we could universally serve with a scalable solution. We had great technology, great data on shopping behavior, a great reputation as a thought leader, great expertise, great advisors, etc., but what we didn't have was technol-ogy or a business model that solved a pain point in a scalable way.[87]

For the d.light team, their journey to PMF required them to travel far beyond the Stanford classroom of "Entrepreneurial Design for Extreme Affordability," where they first came up with the idea for their product. While being based at Stanford provided unique resources for engineering their prototypes and access to a multidisciplinary team, launching the SE outside the US was challenging. Due to political instability in Myanmar, the team made an early market pivot to India and this change, even at the prototype stage, was significant as they had to adjust the product design to reflect consumer behavior and needs specific to India. Early team member Erica Estrada-Liou recollected: "We went to India and retested all of our assumptions. Do LEDs[88] make sense? Is there anything about the Indian household that we need to know in order to inform our design? And in general, how do people like our light?"[89]

There are a number of metrics to monitor in order to determine whether or not you've achieved PMF. Andy Rachleff, CEO of Wealthfront, finds the Net Promoter Score (NPS), which captures how likely users are to recommend the product and produces a score ranging from −100 to +100,[90] to be a good option, with a score of 40+ indicating that "you're on the right track."[91] Another key metric is confirmed purchases, which validates customers' "willingness to pay" and "ability to pay," but be cautious as the initial influx of purchases can also be a temporary blip, driven by first adopters and not the larger target market. When word-of-mouth marketing takes off, this is also a good sign that there is PMF. As Rachleff put it: "You know you have fit if your product grows exponentially with no marketing. That is only possible if you have huge word-of-mouth. Word-of-mouth is only possible if you have delighted your customer."[92] This is also proof of market "virality," that is, the growth hypoth-esis, as discussed earlier. Finally, Alex Schultz, an early employee of Facebook and now its VP of Product Growth, stresses retention as the most important metric to monitor. Retention, or ongoing use, suggests that customers are receiving value and that the product meets their needs. While retention numbers might naturally fall over time, this drop-off could also be an early indication that a product is not delivering its intended value. It's then important to reassess what product features warrant further testing and ensure performance benchmarks are met, before scaling up and bringing the wrong product to market.[93]

Retention became a key innovation in Kiva's model: the SE was able to shift the experience of donating from a onetime event to a continued connection with loan recipients. When people made loans on the Kiva website, they had reasons to continue to engage with the platform, as they could relend any returned funds to new businesses (the profiles for which they could explore on the website), donate the repayment to Kiva directly, or withdraw the funds. Donor engagement with the Kiva website became quite different from the typical donor experience of making a onetime grant to a small business, where the relationship with the online platform usually was brief. In fact, from its early days, two tenets of Kiva's "product philosophy" were:

> Lending is connecting. At Kiva.org, lending money is all about information exchange … Lending to someone else creates an ongoing communication between two individuals that is more binding than a donation.

> Things are always changing. Every time you load our website, it should be different. Every minute, loans are being purchased and repaid, and stories are being told about the borrowers. This can lead to a dynamic where philanthropy actually becomes addictive.[94]

PMF is not the end of the product development or iterative process, but if at a small scale an SE has not yet demonstrated that there is a ready market for its solution, then the startup will almost certainly struggle during the scaling process and will likely make costly mistakes along the way.

> PMF is not a magic elixir. It signifies an important milestone that is necessary but not sufficient for success. Once a company has PMF it still must find a sustainable growth model and create a moat against competitors and so on. What PMF does do is help prevent businesses from spending money trying to grow a business (often inorganically) in a way that is doomed to fail.[95]

Once an SE understands how to deliver value to the customer or beneficiary, it is tempting to go out and hire sales or field staff, move into larger facilities, and purchase higher capacity equipment. However, it is critical to review the whole business model and validate replicability before investing in growth. Even when SEs start delivering a validated value proposition to customers, it might be through a highly inefficient business model or rest on relationships and delivery channels that cannot sustain scale. There is a common misperception that growth will lead to sensible unit economics due to economies of scale, but startups like WeWork, Uber and many others in recent years have shown that growth does not inherently create a sustainable model.[96] In fact, an unprofitable model will only be exaggerated during rapid growth, either calling into question the business model altogether, and/or in the short term, increasing a startup's need for capital. Even for nonprofits that can access grant capital, well-planned and effective service delivery is important not only for the financial sustainability of the program (by reducing its reliance on grants), but more importantly, for the impact the program can achieve with the available resources. Therefore, it is also worth testing at a modest scale whether you can repeat the model in a new geography or with different customers. As the team at the failed startup, Meetra, found in scaling to a second market, "having hundreds of active users in Chicago didn't mean that you would have even two active users in Milwaukee, less than a hundred miles away, not to mention any in New York or San Francisco. [Our] software and concept simply didn't scale beyond its physical borders."[97]

RevFoods eventually scaled to work with many different types of schools throughout the US, and by 2015 it was serving one million meals a week in almost 1,000 schools, had seven commercial kitchens and employed over 1,000 workers.[98] Yet, its expansion into new states had a rocky start. In the first few years, the company approached growth organically through word of mouth, and RevFoods' first expansion out of Oakland was to nearby Los Angeles. In considering where to scale from there, the co-founders received mixed messages: some advisors told them to expand gradually across the country, while others felt that launching in an East Coast city would prove that they weren't just a "regional" company. They decided in 2010 to launch in both Denver and Washington DC, where they faced a number of unforeseen challenges: the need to double local capacity in a matter of days to accommodate the school districts' catering decision timeline, find a new facility, update the menu, bus staff to and from the new facility (in Baltimore, as a DC facility could not be located), and recruit management positions. Co-founder Richmond called the DC launch "one of the hardest moments for the company."[99] Since then, entering new states has been much smoother, as the company was forced to really understand which pieces of its business to replicate and which to customize based on the local school population. Richmond continued: "Although we were ultimately successful in DC in 2010 and beyond, the experience forced us to lock down every facet of our replication approach and focus even more on recruiting world-class operational talent across our team." Years later, once the company had established operations in nine regions, they focused on scaling more deeply where the company already had adjacent operations. For example, in 2012, RevFoods was awarded a contract to serve lunches to San Francisco public schools' 55,000 students, thereby doubling the number of meals it served within the Bay Area and demonstrating significant scale only miles away from its initial customer schools in Oakland.[100]

## KEY TAKEAWAYS

Over the course of this chapter, we've covered the critical first steps to take to ensure that your SE delivers value to its chosen customers and/or beneficiaries, has growth potential, and will ultimately lead to the desired impact outcomes. Below are some key takeaways:

1. *Customer discovery*: Get out there and talk to potential customers and/or beneficiaries. Further, take the time to identify the people who can provide you with real insights, such as potential customers, subject matter experts, and competitors. Ask questions in a way that makes people comfortable with sharing candid feedback, not just telling you "what you want to hear."
2. *Test hypotheses*: Starting an SE is risky. By testing hypotheses around the value of the product or service, the impact it has when used, and the growth potential of the business model, you can reduce key risks dramatically, and the SE can be resourced more efficiently. Make sure to design your tests carefully to maximize insights and differentiate between actionable and "vanity" metrics when reviewing test results.

3. *Be creative with your MVPs*: MVPs can take any form. They are not early prototypes that are carelessly put in front of customers for feedback. Well-designed MVPs are focused on validating or invalidating specific hypotheses. Over time, the entrepreneur can produce prototypes and run pilots that more closely reflect the product and business model.

4. *Look at the business model holistically*: Developing the business model is multifaceted and will take time to refine. Remember to look at all elements of the model, not just the product itself. No matter how terrific a product is, the SE cannot scale without looking at the complete value chain, stakeholder set, and cost structure holistically.

5. *Find PMF _before_ scaling*: Social entrepreneurs are often disrupting mature markets or creating new ones, so finding PMF takes time and numerous iterations. Trying to scale a business before PMF has been validated is likely to result in product failure in the marketplace, which could ultimately be the downfall of the company as well.

## CASE STUDY
### EMBRACE

Jane Chen and Rahul Panicker, two of the co-founders of Embrace, sat in the organization's Bangalore office in 2012, reflecting on how far their SE had come since they first conceived of the idea for an affordable infant warmer as part of a graduate school class at Stanford University in 2007. The SE had made steady progress towards achieving its mission to "give all infants an equal chance for a healthy life through a low-cost infant warmer."[101] By 2012, the company had launched its first product, had taken on a hybrid corporate structure to enable greater scale, and had reached thousands of babies with its innovative warming device.[102] Still, the founders recognized that they were not yet addressing the problem that had first motivated them to create Embrace: the lack of access in rural areas to warming technology for vulnerable infants.

The idea for Embrace came out of a class at Stanford University called "Design for Extreme Affordability." The course that year was focused on tackling a devastating global statistic: almost three million babies die annually within the first 28 days of their life (the neonatal period). Hypothermia is one of the major risk factors, especially for preterm babies, but the traditional incubators utilized to warm vulnerable infants are costly, require ongoing maintenance, and depend on reliable electricity, leading to a severe shortage of incubators in many of the regions where the devices are most needed.

**Figure 5.5** Embrace Innovations logo

As part of the Stanford class, Jane Chen, Rahul Panicker, and fellow classmates Linus Liang and Razmig Hovaghimian were tasked with developing an incubator that cost less than one percent of the price of a traditional incubator, which could run up to $20,000 each.[103, 104]

As part of the course, Liang traveled to Nepal for a fact-finding trip so he could better understand the problem and meet stakeholders treating or affected by the issue. His customer discovery interviews led to a radical change in the team's initial product concept. Though they had been told to design a lower-cost incubator, the team saw that cost was not the only barrier to increased access. They found that most of the infants requiring treatment were in rural areas where incubators were not available or were left unused. According to co-founder Jane Chen,

> When Linus [Liang] was in Nepal, he saw that there were actually incubators sitting in these city hospitals with no babies in them. That's because the babies were dying in the villages. And so that really helped us reframe the problem to focus on home usage ... We realized we needed a solution that works without electricity, was portable, and easy enough for a mother or midwife to use.[105]

The team reconsidered what kind of product would be appropriate for a rural setting: simple and safe to use, electricity-independent, culturally appropriate, and inexpensive.[106] By the end of the term, the team had developed a prototype of an infant warmer that used phase change material and could provide heat at a constant temperature for up to four hours using hot water. Embrace incorporated as a 501(c)(3) nonprofit[107] the following term to move the idea forward. The founding team brought on Naganand Murty (who had been in another student group in the same Stanford course). Razmig Hovaghimian decided to pursue another venture and left the team.

While still in school, the founders continued to create many prototypes. They were able to work out of the d.school, and the Stanford University community overall provided early support via financial capital, in-kind donations, and advice. The team brought on board Dr Bhutani, a neonatologist at Stanford Hospital, first as an advisor and later as a member of the board of directors.[108] Critically, the team secured $35,000 from Stanford's BASES (Business Association of Stanford Entrepreneurial Students) competition, giving them the initial capital (combined with an Echoing Green Fellowship) to continue working on the venture postgraduation.[109]

The nature of the business and the focus on markets outside of the US meant that hypothesis testing played an even more critical role in getting the SE from idea to PMF. After early product testing in the US, the team moved to Bangalore, India (their initial target market) in mid-2009 to be closer to the communities that would be using the warmer, and to more affordably modify and manufacture the product.[110] While market testing became easier, going from the prototype to market launch was a lengthy process. According to Panicker:

> It is very easy to make a prototype, but to make a safe medical device in line with all the regulatory acts is an uphill task. India at that point didn't have

guidelines ... We had the choice of not sticking to any guidelines since India didn't need them, but it wasn't a good idea for scaling.[111]

As the team was refining the technology and navigating the regulatory system, they also continued seeking feedback from customers and beneficiaries to validate their impact and growth hypotheses. They interviewed midwives in small villages and uncovered that the midwives' product use depended on recommendations from the village doctor. The team traced the line of influence from the village to the town to the city physicians, and realized that they needed to take a top-down approach by first getting the medical community on board. The team made the decision to go to market first with *Embrace Nest*, an infant warmer that used electricity as the heating source, while still working on a version that used boiling water (which they called *Embrace Care*) and was therefore more suitable for the rural setting and at-home usage.[112]

Jane Chen explained: "Embrace initially launched a version of our warmer that could be used by doctors in hospitals and clinics, thinking this would allow us to safely introduce the product in a controlled environment with trained professionals."[113] Getting buy-in from physicians also proved difficult despite positive market feedback. But eventually, by running clinical trials, the team was able to share data that showed the product was as effective as the current standards of care, and that there were no adverse events.[114] For Embrace, demonstrating initial traction and impact was critical for unlocking further customer growth, navigating regulatory hurdles, and securing financing for the organization.

Now three years later, back in the Embrace office in Bangalore, the co-founders were pleased to see their flagship product, *Embrace Nest*, was helping thousands of infants, and that they had already expanded outside of India through the organization's nonprofit arm. Still, they had not yet launched a product for at-home use in villages, where mortality rates were the highest, and which had been the original catalyst for their idea. While good progress had been made on *Embrace Care*, it was not yet ready for sale. The team reflected on their decision to first launch *Nest* instead of persisting with their original concept for a warmer independent of electricity.

## CASE QUESTIONS

1.  What role did early market testing play in leading Embrace to launch with *Nest* instead of with *Care*?
2.  Was launching with *Nest* the right decision in order to achieve the impact, value and growth they had envisioned?

# NOTES

1. Kirzner, Israel M. "Creativity and/or Alertness: A Reconsideration of the Schumpeterian Entrepreneur." *The Review of Austrian Economics*, vol. 11, nos. 1–2, 1999, pp. 5–17, doi:10.1023/A:1007719905868. Accessed 15 January 2020.

2. Kaish, Stanley, Benjamin Gilad. "Characteristics of opportunities search of entrepreneurs versus executives: sources, interests, general alertness." *Journal of Business Venturing*, vol. 6, no. 1, 1991, 45–61.

3. Tang, Jintong, K. Michele Kacmar, and Lowell Busenitz. "Entrepreneurial Alertness in the Pursuit of New Opportunities." *Journal of Business Venturing*, vol. 27, no. 1, 2012, p. 77, doi:10.1016/J.JBUSVENT.2010.07 .001. Accessed 4 December 2019.

4. Ibid.

5. Ibid, p. 80.

6. Ibid., p. 79.

7. Ibid.

8. Ibid.

9. Ibid., p. 80.

10. Govindarajan, Vijay, and S. Manikutty. "What Poor Countries Can Teach Rich Ones About Health Care." *Harvard Business Review*, 23 July 2014, hbr.org/2010/04/how-poor-countries-can-help-so.

11. Mehta, Pavithra K., and Suchitra Shenoy. *Infinite Vision: How Aravind Became the World's Greatest Business Case for Compassion.* Berrett-Koehler Publishers, 2012, San Francisco, CA.

12. Tang, Jintong, K. Michele Kacmar, and Lowell Busenitz. "Entrepreneurial Alertness in the Pursuit of New Opportunities." *Journal of Business Venturing*, vol. 27, no. 1, 2012, p. 79, doi:10.1016/J.JBUSVENT.2010.07 .001. Accessed 4 December 2019.

13. Ibid., p. 81.

14. Spaly, Brian. "How Entrepreneurs Come Up with Great Ideas: There Is No Magic Formula. But That Doesn't Mean There's No Formula At All." *The Wall Street Journal*, 29 April 2013, www.wsj.com/articles/SB1 0001424127887324445904578283792526004684. Accessed 4 December 2019.

15. Benton, Angela. "How Entrepreneurs Come Up with Great Ideas: There Is No Magic Formula. But That Doesn't Mean There's No Formula At All." *The Wall Street Journal*, 29 April 2013, www.wsj.com/articles/ SB10001424127887324445904578283792526004684. Accessed 4 December 2019.

16. Walske, Jennifer, and Laura Tyson. "Fair Trade USA: Scaling for Impact." *The Regents of the University of California*, 1 May 2015. Berkeley Haas Case Series B5836, p. 124.

17. Benton, Angela. "How Entrepreneurs Come Up With Great Ideas: There is No Magic Formula. But that Doesn't Mean there's No Formula at all." *The Wall Street Journal*, 29 April 2013, www.wsj.com/articles/SB1 0001424127887324445904578283792526004684. Accessed 4 December 2019.

18. Calderon, Jorge, and Nishant Bagadia. "Back to the Roots Ventures (BTTR)." *The Regents of the University of California*, 10 June 2015. Berkeley Haas Case Series B5834.

19. "Top Uber Competitors You Didn't Know About." *Business Strategy Hub*, 9 February 2020, bstrategyhub .com/top-ubers-competitors.

20. "SafeBoda – Your City Ride." *Welcome to SafeBoda – Your City Ride*, safeboda.com/ng.

21. Calagione, Sam. "How Entrepreneurs Come Up with Great Ideas: There Is No Magic Formula. But That Doesn't Mean There's No Formula At All." *The Wall Street Journal*, 29 April 2013, www.wsj.com/articles/ SB10001424127887324445904578283792526004684. Accessed 4 December 2019.

22. Tyson, Laura, and Jennifer Walske. "Revolution Foods: Expansion into the CPG Market." *The Regents of the University of California*, 31 July 2015. Berkeley Haas Case Series B5845, p. 2.

23. "Patterns of Female Entrepreneurial Activities in Turkey." *Gender in Management: An International Journal*, vol. 32, no. 3, 2012, pp. 166–182, www.emerald.com/insight/content/doi/10.1108/GM-05-2016-0102/full/html.

24. "The Foundation for Economies Worldwide Is Small Business." *IFAC*, 9 June 2020, www.ifac.org/knowledge-gateway/contributing-global-economy/discussion/foundation-economies-worldwide-small-business-0.

25. "Coronavirus (COVID-19): SME Policy Responses." *OECD*, 2020, oecd.org/coronavirus/policy-responses/coronavirus-covid-19-sme-policy-responses-04440101.

26. Papi-Thornton, Daniela. "Tackling Heropreneurship." *Daniela Papi-Thornton*, June 2016, http://tacklingheropreneurship.com/wp-content/uploads/2016/07/tackling-heropreneurship-daniela-papi-June2016.pdf.

27. Ibid.

28. *Market Research in the Clean Cooking Sector: Tools and Tips*. www.cleancookingalliance.org/resources/411.html.

29. Papi-Thornton, Daniela. "Tackling Heropreneurship." *Daniela Papi-Thornton*, June 2016, http://tacklingheropreneurship.com/wp-content/uploads/2016/07/tackling-heropreneurship-daniela-papi-June2016.pdf.

30. Ibid.

31. "Genius is One Percent Inspiration and Ninety-Nine Percent Perspiration." *Dictionary.com*, www.dictionary.com/browse/genius-is-one-percent-inspiration-and-ninety-nine-percent-perspiration.

32. *Steve Blank*. www.steveblank.com.

33. Ries, Eric and Jim Euchner. "What Large Companies Can Learn from Start-Ups: An Interview with Eric Ries." *Research-Technology Management*, vol. 56, no. 4, 2013, pp. 12–16, doi: 10.5437/08956308X5604003.

34. Ibid.

35. Milstein, Sarah. "Lean Startup 101: The Essential Ideas." *Lean Startup Company*, https://leanstartup.co/lean-startup-101-the-essential-ideas.

36. Ibid.

37. Blank, Steven G. *The Four Steps to the Epiphany: Successful Strategies for Products That Win*, K&S Ranch Publishing Inc., 2007, Pescadero, CA.

38. Alvarez, Cindy. *Lean Customer Development*. O'Reilly Media, Inc., 2014, p. XV (preface), Sebastopol, CA.

39. Alvarez, Cindy. "10 Things I've Learned About Customer Development – Cindy Alvarez: Blog." *Cindy Alvarez*, 10 July 2019, www.cindyalvarez.com/10-things-ive-learned-about-customer-development.

40. Blank, Steven G., and Bob Dorf. *The Startup Owner's Manual: The Step-by-Step Guide for Building a Great Company*. Wiley, 2020, Hoboken, NJ.

41. Tyson, Laura, and Jennifer Walske. "Revolution Foods: Expansion into the CPG Market." *The Regents of the University of California*, 31 July 2015. Berkeley Haas Case Series B5845, p. 2.

42. Siskar, Kevin. "Why You Should Tell Everyone Your Startup Idea." *Medium*, 25 June 2015, medium.com/swlh/why-you-should-tell-everyone-your-startup-idea-4b8372f31ca0. Accessed 4 December 2019.

43. Ibid.

44. Fuld, Hillel. "You Have More to Gain than to Lose by Sharing Your Idea with Others." *Inc.*, 27 August 2018, www.inc.com/hillel-fuld/why-keeping-your-startup-idea-to-yourself-is-a-horrible-move.html. Accessed 4 December 2019.

45. Calderon, Jorge, and Nishant Bagadia. "Back to the Roots Ventures (BTTR)." *The Regents of the University of California*, 10 June 2015. Berkeley Haas Case Series B5834.

46. Ibid.

47. Calderon, Jorge, and Nishant Bagadia. "Back to the Roots Ventures (BTTR)." *The Regents of the University of California*, 10 June 2015. Berkeley Haas Case Series B5834, pp. 2–7, 11–12.

48. Ries, Eric and Jim Euchner. "What Large Companies Can Learn from Start-Ups: An Interview with Eric Ries." *Research-Technology Management*, vol. 56, no. 4, 2013, pp. 12–16, doi: 10.5437/08956308X5604003.

49. Chang, Ann M. *Lean Impact: How to Innovate for Radically Greater Social Good*. Wiley, 2018, Hoboken, NJ.

50. Ibid.

51. Ibid.

52. Osterwalder, Alex. "Business Model Canvas – Download the Official Template." *Strategyzer*, www.strategyzer .com/canvas/business-model-canvas.

53. Ovans, Andrea. "What Is a Business Model?" *Harvard Business Review*, 6 December 2017, hbr.org/2015/01/ what-is-a-business-model.

54. Ibid.

55. "Business Model Canvas Explained." *Vimeo*, uploaded by Strategyzer, 2013, www.vimeo.com/78350794. Accessed 4 December 2019.

56. Walske, J., and Laura D. Tyson. "Sanergy: Tackling Sanitation in Kenyan Slums." *The Regents of the University of California*, 1 July 2016. Berkeley Haas Case Series B5871, p. 3.

57. Ibid.

58. Blank, Steve. "Steve Blank Why Build, Measure, Learn – Isn't Just Throwing Things against the Wall to See if They Work – the Minimal Viable Product." *Steve Blank*, 21 August 2015, steveblank.com/2015/05/06/build -measure-learn-throw-things-against-the-wall-and-see-if-they-work/.

59. Ibid.

60. "Infographic: A Brief History of Software Development Methodologies." *Intetics*, intetics.com/blog/a-brief -history-of-software-development-methodologies.

61. Graves, Eric. "Applying Agile to Hardware Development (Part 1)." www.playbookhq.co/blog/agile-hardware -development.

62. "A/B Testing." *Wikipedia*, Wikimedia Foundation, 28 July 2020, en.wikipedia.org/wiki/A/B_testing.

63. Fletcher, Dan. Interview. By Jennifer Walske and Elizabeth Foster. 16 July 2020.

64. Chu, Michael, David E. Bloom, and Alison Berkley Wagonfeld. "Embrace." *Harvard Business School Publishing*, 18 July 2013. Harvard Business School Case Series 9-814-001.

65. Ries, Eric and Jim Euchner. "What Large Companies Can Learn from Start-Ups: An Interview with Eric Ries." *Research-Technology Management*, vol. 56, no. 4, 2013, pp. 12–16, doi: 10.5437/08956308X5604003.

66. Chang, Ann M. *Lean Impact: How to Innovate for Radically Greater Social Good*. Wiley, 2018, Hoboken, NJ.

67. The Bridgespan Group. "Using Innovation to Accelerate Your Impact." *Zoom Video*, 18 June, 2020, zoom.us/ rec/play/up0qIeispzo3HYaS5ASDBKQsW467K6is1CAW_KdZzxqxV3RQM1eiYbdAZbOORVfdjSR28L HsxLtoWs81?continueMode=true&_x_zm_rtaid=g-EJAzPZQISJ5saL88WOTQ.1595711307162.0a c967fc88ee80a116dd65ac05d6d9ab&_x_zm_rhtaid=403.

68. Ibid.

69. Ibid.

70. Milstein, Sarah. "Lean Startup 101: The Essential Ideas." *Lean Startup Company*, https://leanstartup.co/lean -startup-101-the-essential-ideas.

71. Ibid.

72. Gothelf, Jeff. *Lean UX: Applying Lean Principles to Improve User Experience.* O'Reilly Media, 2013, Sebastopol, CA, Ch. 5.

73. Ibid.

74. Fletcher, Dan. Interview. By Jennifer Walske and Elizabeth Foster. 16 July 2020.

75. Ibid.

76. Schrage, Michael. "The Right Way for an Established Firm to Do an Innovation Pilot with a Startup." *Harvard Business Review,* 30 May 2018, hbr.org/2018/05/the-right-way-for-an-established-firm-to-do-an -innovation-pilot-with-a-startup.

77. Cherukumilli, Katya. Interview. By Jennifer Walske and Elizabeth Foster. 10 July 2020.

78. Ibid.

79. "Researching and Piloting a New Idea." *SSE,* www.the-sse.org/resources/idea/researching-and-piloting-a -new-idea/.

80. Bugg-Levine, Antony, Bruce Kogut, and Nalin Kulatilaka. "A New Approach to Funding Social Enterprises." *Harvard Business Review,* 1 August 2014, hbr.org/2012/01/a-new-approach-to-funding-social-enterprises.

81. Flannery, Matt. "Kiva and the Birth of Person-to-Person Microfinance." *Innovations: Technology, Governance, Globalization,* vol. 2, no. 1–2, 2007, p. 45.

82. Ibid.

83. Fletcher, Dan. Interview. By Jennifer Walske and Elizabeth Foster. 16 July 2020.

84. Cherukumilli, Katya. Interview. By Jennifer Walske and Elizabeth Foster. 10 July 2020.

85. Griffin, Tren. "12 Things about Product-Market Fit." *Andreessen Horowitz,* 15 April 2019, a16z.com/2017/ 02/18/12-things-about-product-market-fit.

86. Marmer, Max, Bjoern Lasse Herrmann, Ertan Dogrultan, and Ron Berman. "Startup Genome Report Extra on Premature Scaling." *Innovation Footprints,* 29 August 2011, http://innovationfootprints.com/wp -content/uploads/2015/07/startup-genome-report-extra-on-premature-scaling.pdf.

87. CB Insights. "Why Startups Fail: Top 20 Reasons." *CB Insights Research,* CB Insights, 17 July 2020, www .cbinsights.com/research/startup-failure-reasons-top.

88. LED stands for Light Emitting Diode, which is considered more energy efficient.

89. Kennedy, Michael, Gina Jorasch and Jesper Sorensen. "d.light, Selling Solar to the Poor." *Harvard Business School Publishing,* 20 August 2012, Stanford Graduate School of Business Cases Series IDE-03, p. 18.

90. The Net Promotor Score asks the question: *How likely is it that you would recommend our company/product/ service to a friend or colleague?* It follows a specific calculation that leads to a score ranging from −100 to +100.

91. Griffin, Tren. "12 Things about Product-Market Fit." *Andreessen Horowitz,* 15 April 2019, a16z.com/2017/ 02/18/12-things-about-product-market-fit.

92. Ibid.

93. "Lecture 6 – Growth (Alex Schultz)." *YouTube,* uploaded by How to Start a Startup, 9 October 2014, https:// www.youtube.com/watch?v=n_yHZ_vKjno&feature=emb_logo.

94. Flannery, Matt. "Kiva and the Birth of Person-to-Person Microfinance." *Innovations: Technology, Governance, Globalization,* vol. 2, no. 1–2, 2007, p. 40.

95. Griffin, Tren. "12 Things about Product-Market Fit." *Andreessen Horowitz,* 15 April 2019, a16z.com/2017/ 02/18/12-things-about-product-market-fit.

96. Shameen, Assif. "Tech: WeWork Fiasco and the Growth-At-All-Costs Model." *The Edge Markets,* 16 October 2019, www.theedgemarkets.com/article/tech-wework-fiasco-and-growthatallcosts-model.

97. CB Insights. "Why Startups Fail: Top 20 Reasons." *CB Insights Research*, CB Insights, 17 July 2020, www.cbinsights.com/research/startup-failure-reasons-top.

98. Tyson, Laura, and Jennifer Walske. "Revolution Foods: Expansion into the CPG Market." *The Regents of the University of California*, 31 July 2015. Berkeley Haas Case Series B5845, pp. 2–3.

99. Ibid.

100. Ibid.

101. Chu, Michael, David E. Bloom, and Alison Berkley Wagonfeld. "Embrace." *Harvard Business School Publishing*, 18 July 2013. Harvard Business School Case Series 9-814-001, p. 8.

102. Ibid., pp. 6, 9.

103. Chen, Jane. "Opinion: How to Save the Life of a Baby." *CNN*, Cable News Network, 18 September 2013, edition.cnn.com/2013/09/18/opinion/chen-saving-babies.

104. Center for the Protection of Intellectual Property. "Embrace Infant Warmers Help Save Lives of Preterm Babies in Developing Countries." *Medium*, Innovate4Health, 27 February 2018, medium.com/innovate4health/embrace-infant-warmers-help-save-lives-of-preterm-babies-in-developing-countries-bf3fd45cb193.

105. Chu, Michael, David E. Bloom, and Alison Berkley Wagonfeld. "Embrace." *Harvard Business School Publishing*, 18 July 2013. Harvard Business School Case Series 9-814-001, p. 3.

106. "Embrace." *Design for Extreme Affordability*, extreme.stanford.edu/projects/embrace.

107. It later converted into a hybrid structure in order to attract the capital they needed to accelerate product development and achieve scale.

108. Chu, Michael, David E. Bloom, and Alison Berkley Wagonfeld. "Embrace." *Harvard Business School Publishing*, 18 July 2013. Harvard Business School Case Series 9-814-001, p. 4.

109. Sinha, Snigdha. "Combating Neonatal Hyperthermia with Embrace Innovations' Affordable and Portable Baby Warmers." *YourStory.com*, 22 July 2015, yourstory.com/2015/07/embrace-innovations.

110. Chu, Michael, David E. Bloom, and Alison Berkley Wagonfeld. "Embrace." *Harvard Business School Publishing*, 18 July 2013. Harvard Business School Case Series 9-814-001, p. 4.

111. Sinha, Snigdha. "Combating Neonatal Hyperthermia with Embrace Innovations' Affordable and Portable Baby Warmers." *YourStory.com*, 22 July 2015, yourstory.com/2015/07/embrace-innovations.

112. Chu, Michael, David E. Bloom, and Alison Berkley Wagonfeld. "Embrace." *Harvard Business School Publishing*, 18 July 2013. Harvard Business School Case Series 9-814-001, pp. 4–5.

113. Chen, Jane. "Opinion: How to Save the Life of a Baby." *CNN*, Cable News Network, 18 September 2013, edition.cnn.com/2013/09/18/opinion/chen-saving-babies.

114. Chu, Michael, David E. Bloom, and Alison Berkley Wagonfeld. "Embrace." *Harvard Business School Publishing*, 18 July 2013. Harvard Business School Case Series 9-814-001, pp. 5–6.

# 6
# Defining and refining one's value chain

So far in our book, we have discussed a range of topics including the founding team, building and curating a stakeholder network, and implementing both a product and brand strategy, but we have yet to address an organization's value chain. Ned Tozun, founder of d.light, underscores the challenges in building a social startup and how its value chain is often overlooked:

> My experience in talking to entrepreneurs coming out of business school programs … is that there tends to be a lot of focus on the product idea. That's just one small fraction of the real challenge and I think the implementation side, like how do you manufacture it, how do you get the cost right, how do you get the quality right, how do you distribute, how do you market. Those are the things that, at least when I was in business school, they never talked about.[1]

In this chapter, we hope to right this wrong, by delving into the startup's value chain, referring to Michael Porter's classic definition: "The value chain disaggregates a firm into its strategically relevant activities in order to understand the behavior of costs and the existing and potential sources of differentiation."[2] This includes assessing the organizational inputs (i.e., supplier based) and outputs (i.e., distribution channels, and after-purchase support) that can build the best competitive advantage. This is no less true in a social enterprise (SE), than it is with a more traditional and larger business; as Porter describes, regardless of size, an organization must develop a strong relationship with the suppliers, contractors and distributors who are significant to the delivery of the SE's product or service. Porter warns: "If you neglect these crucial components, your social venture could fail. Ideally, these partners are aligned with your organization for business reasons, social reasons or both."[3] A picture of Porter's "Generic Value Chain" is featured in Figure 6.1.

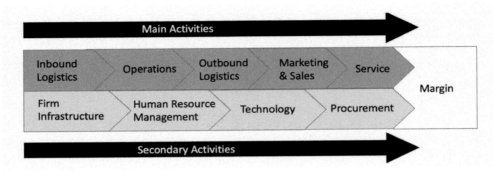

*Source:* Porter (1985).[4]

**Figure 6.1    Generic Value Chain**

In the field of social entrepreneurship, the subject of an organization's value chain is often overlooked. Yet, as Porter emphasizes: "Every firm is a collection of activities that are performed to design, produce, market, deliver, and support its product."[5] In larger, more traditional firms, establishing close supplier relationships can create a key competitive advantage. As McKinsey research shows: "Companies that build effective, collaborative partnerships with suppliers are outsmarting their competitors on cost, quality, innovation and agility."[6] The key difference for any startup, though, is to decide which pieces of a value chain are going to be vital to building the organization's point of differentiation, and alternatively, which areas the organization is content with being "good enough." In its earliest years, a startup will most likely need to outsource some or all of its products' subcomponents, given the startup's limited resources, its lack of scale, and in some cases, insufficient expertise. In fact, even for larger companies, it is not uncommon to lack the expertise and resources to develop all of the necessary subcomponents of their more sophisticated products, and some organizations find it difficult even to trace their supply chain and map the interdependencies of their supply chains.[7] As Pinkert, Ton-that and Soopramanien point out: "In conflict mineral chains, for example, seven to eight layers can exist between the mine and the customer, and the gap can reach over 50 layers for electronic components."[8] As such, the challenges of just building a value chain can be overwhelming for startups that produce physical products. While there is a promise that the use of blockchain technology can increase the traceability of components within supply chains, the use of blockchain technology is still emerging.[9]

Another constraint for startups in building their value chains is that it can be difficult to access materials inexpensively, as startups often lack both the reputation and volume to command low prices. These challenges are further exacerbated by the fact that most startups also lack economies of scale, making the price point at which they buy materials much higher than larger competitors from day one. Finally, for social startups, founders are often trying to get the highest quality products into the marketplace at the most affordable price points, while ensuring minimal environmental impact and that laborers are earning a living wage. In other words, the social mission of the organization extends to its value chain, too, and the complexities and trade-offs are not only cost and efficiency driven, but mission driven as well.

To illustrate this point, let's use a fictitious example: Conscious Capital Clothing Company [C⁴]. C⁴ is a socially conscious clothing brand, and its mission is to provide budget-based consumers with organic clothing, adopting the tagline "fairly traded fashion forward." By being at a lower price point, C⁴'s goal is to make fair trade clothing accessible to younger consumers, as the antidote to "fast fashion," which has received heavy criticism for its labor and environmental abuses.[10] Given C⁴'s mission, it's not enough for C⁴ to pay fair wages to its seamstresses, if those creating the fabrics are not also earning a living wage, which involves a deeper approach to tracking and verification within C⁴'s supply chain. Similarly, this ethos extends through C⁴'s value chain to the sellers of C⁴'s clothing (i.e., their distribution channels), by ensuring that a retailer's workers are also being fairly compensated. Yet, at the end of the day, if the cost of material acquisition, production and distribution are so high that C⁴ cannot break even, and/ or their clothing moves to the high end of pricing to cover their costs (and therefore, outside of their original target segment of budget buyers currently purchasing fast fashion), one of two outcomes are likely to occur: (1) C⁴ goes out of business due to its affordable price point and costly supply chain due to ongoing financial loses; (2) it isn't able to fulfill its social mission because it has to "cut corners" by "looking the other way" in some parts of its value chain in which workers are not being fairly compensated.

In reality, many SEs have to make trade-offs, especially when initially launching their businesses, as the cost of both their supply chains and distribution channels are simply too high at the outset. For startups, operational costs are often high, as they have yet to ramp their revenues, and also lack the volume to ensure meaningful economies of scale. The question then becomes how to make judgment calls within one's value chain with intentionality, so that the startup can know where justifiable concessions can be made, and then, have a plan to continue to upgrade the supply chain as the organization scales. For example, Revolution Foods (RevFoods), one of the companies highlighted in our research, has a mission to deliver healthy school lunches to K-12 populations. RevFoods chose to emphasize fresh ingredients-based meals in its school lunches but did not restrict itself to all organic sourcing, as that would have driven costs above the threshold necessary for government reimbursable meals.

When d.light first started, the founders erred when estimating the costs of their first solar light product. As co-founder Tozun states:

> essentially [we] got these memorandums of understanding saying: "Yeah, if you have this product at this price, we'll buy it." Of course, we totally didn't estimate the pricing right – we got everything wrong essentially, but we validated to ourselves that the market was big, there were partners there we could work with, and it was the right place to start.[11]

They ultimately decided to manufacture their solar lights in Shenzhen, China, to both minimize price and maximize quality. While manufacturing its lights in China and selling them in India and Africa (and now globally) creates a larger carbon footprint than the founders initially wanted, d.light simply couldn't make its lights for the price point that it needed to otherwise. As Tozun explains: "we got an operations person in China who actually had experience in that area … kind of our age and an entrepreneurial woman." She in turn had an uncle with a factory in Shenzhen, and one of the d.light co-founders spoke Mandarin well enough to create "some semblance of communication with the manufacturing team," which allowed them collectively to manufacture their lights in China. Centralized manufacturing also gave them flexibility in global distribution, with their sights first set on distributing their product to India and later in Africa where they had greater demand for their product.[12] Now, d.light's lights are available in developed markets as well, through Amazon, for a tertiary customer base of those in disaster relief situations where they are forced to be off the grid, and those that simply choose to be "off grid" by enjoying camping in remote areas.

Another example of supply chain evolution is exemplified by Embrace. Embrace began by first manufacturing its infant baby warmers in China, also for cost reasons, but as its product progressed through the clinical trial process, it made more sense to relocate final manufacturing and assembly to India where Embrace's personnel could more easily manage product iterations. Ultimately, Embrace chose to integrate its supply chain vertically to get the highest quality control necessary, given its vulnerable population of users (i.e., fragile premature infants). According to co-founder Jane Chen: "While we initially planned to outsource everything, we later realized that we either had to make it in-house or really micromanage the process, mainly because of quality concerns."[13] The team hired further in-house expertise to manage partial manufacturing, final assembly, and quality testing, and took product quality one step further by ensuring it met ISO (International Standards Organization) certification standards.

When RevFoods first launched its school lunch program, its goal was to provide a healthier alternative to most school lunches, which meant the co-founders wanted to adhere to government guidelines for nutrition. However, they also had to manage their costs, as RevFoods' meals needed to be reimbursable through the US government lunch program, which meant they had to stay below a certain pricing threshold. This is where a relationship with the Northern California division of Whole Foods became important; Whole Foods supplied key ingredients to RevFoods at wholesale prices, treating the organization as if it were one of its stores. Accordingly, co-founder Kirsten Tobey states: "Initially, we could order from their bake house, produce distribution center and other suppliers, and the Whole Foods truck would come and deliver things to us."[14] Executives at Whole Foods also helped advise the co-founders, Tobey and Kristin Richmond, on how to set up their first kitchen. They further made introductions to other companies, such as Stoney Brook Farms, for discounted pricing on cheese, yoghurt and other items. Through its partnership with Whole Foods, RevFoods was able to garner economies of scale in its supply chain, critical to getting its meals priced at the point where they could be part of government subsidized lunch programs. This supports what scholars state, that: "As with traditional for-profit businesses, developing and leveraging key external relationships can improve the delivery of the product or service and over time should lead to lower costs for SEs."[15] Unlike traditional business relationships, partnerships, like the one between RevFoods and Whole Foods can be more meaningful for both entities if the organizations are mission-aligned; as one scholar notes: "Alignment around social goals can lead to favorable economic terms but if this is the primary basis for the partnership, make sure the commitment from your partner is long-term."[16]

Setting up sales and distribution for the social startup is similarly fraught with issues that are particularly challenging. Most startups lack the volume and the name brand recognition to create market pull for their products. As a result, any independent distributors they might use must then engage in "missionary sales" for the startup's products by having to educate customers about the products they are trying to sell them. This is especially true if the product is a novel product. As Martin Fisher, co-founder of KickStart International (a nonprofit that innovates affordable irrigation pumps used in rural farming across Sub-Saharan Africa) states: "We spend all of our time in the field talking about irrigation and how much money they [rural farmers] can make ... Then we have to sell them a big-ticket item they've never seen before."[17] KickStart created simple pedal pumps, enabling rural farmers, who often lack sources of electricity, to pump water from local rivers much more efficiently rather than having to carry water to their fields and watering by hand. Fisher goes on to explain that eventually, the reputation of KickStart pumps spread regionally, and it became known that the pumps worked, increasing agricultural yields by 500 percent on average and moving many farmers out of poverty. By proving the efficacy of the products, KickStart was then able to build out a partnership-based distribution model, with training and advocacy remaining core to its social mission. Now its products are made available to buyers both at local retail shops as well as by NGO and government partners running programs that reach farmers living in regions at income levels that otherwise would make KickStart's irrigation pumps financially out of reach. This dual strategy of commercial and NGO distribution partnerships has allowed KickStart to grow its presence to over a dozen countries in Sub-Saharan Africa, without having to build extensive and difficult-to-manage sales teams directly.[18] In sum: "Management of a direct sales force poses significant challenges for recruitment, training, monitoring/control and retention, all of which are critical for success in developing an effective direct selling channel."[19] In the rest of this chapter, we elaborate on important elements for building and maintaining one's value chain through the lens of a social startup.

## SETTING UP THE SUPPLY CHAIN

A supply chain "refers to all those activities associated with the transformation and flow of goods and services, including their attendant information flows, from the sources of materials to end users."[20] A more recent addendum to this supply chain analysis is understanding the environmental impact of post-consumption disposal and recycling, as well as post-use standards for collection, dismantling and decomposition. For example, in the single-serve coffee area, a big challenge for the market leaders is determining the appropriate recycling and/or compost uses for coffee pods after the cup of coffee has been consumed. Global leader Nespresso allows consumers to mail in or drop off their used coffee pods as part of their recycling program. For other types of beverage companies, there is now an expectation that drinks will be sold in recyclable plastic or glass. Danone yoghurt went one step further by experimenting with edible yoghurt packaging and has made a commitment "for every piece of packaging – from bottle caps to yoghurt cups – to be reusable, recyclable, or compostable" by 2025.[21]

As research reminds us, the supplier–producer relationship is a two-way street, and in order to build a collaborative relationship with one's supplier, the social startup's mission alignment is a core point of mutual collaboration: "Make sure to try and research your potential partner through your contacts or on-line to see if there is a cultural fit and to see if they've worked with ventures like yours in the past."[22] Also, remember, that in the early years, you are not only getting to know and build trust with your suppliers, your suppliers are also gauging your organization, and assessing if there is a potential for a good long-term relationship. Reiss (2010) outlines four actions a business can do to build a better relationship with its suppliers including: paying bills for orders on time; providing as much lead time as possible – most particularly around design changes; making the relationship personal so there is a sense of connection; and sharing of other types of information (i.e., global trends, competitors, etc.) to encourage true collaboration.[23] We add to Reiss's findings, suggesting that suppliers can impact a business by aiding: quality, timeliness, competitiveness, innovation, and financing, as described in more detail as follows:[24]

- *Quality*: A supplier's components can positively or negatively affect the perceived quality of the product; the perception of higher quality, for example, increases customer satisfaction and decreases defects, which can be very important when deploying into a developing-country context. In fact, in these contexts, where servicing a product can be more difficult than delivering the initial product, durability of a product becomes a key consideration.
- *Timeliness*: How quickly a supplier delivers either key components or the completed product (when product manufacturing is completely outsourced), is crucial to how customers might view a company's reliability. Quick fulfillment of components by a supplier can become the key to minimizing an SE's inventory, which in turn translates into less risk of inventory obsolescence and lower cash needs (which in turn also impacts a startup's working capital). Alternatively, a slowdown in a supplier's essential goods can become a big problem if one has increased customer demand but has gaps in product availability. Today, with COVID-19, inventory fulfillment has become a big issue for many of those with production facilities in another country. In many cases, not only has overseas production shut down, but global transportation has been stalled as well. As such, scholars advise: "It's not prudent to rely on one supplier. If that supplier has a strike or a fire, you don't want to be in a position where you'd be shut down too. So, keep a second or multiple suppliers on hand, and don't be embarrassed to tell your key supplier that you're doing so."[25] During this current pandemic, many companies are now considering adding a local supplier, just to create less dependency on global manufacturing and transportation.
- *Competitiveness*: A supplier can be crucial to helping a startup bolster its competitive advantage, by enabling the SE to deliver better pricing, quality and reliability, while potentially passing along technological breakthroughs and meaningful industry trends. Through close collaboration with manufacturers, a startup can also better understand how to reduce costs for both materials and production.
- *Innovation*: Suppliers can also make major contributions in product development. A close relationship with a supplier might help a startup's leadership team better comprehend its industry and customers' needs, adding important suggestions to tweak a product idea. In fact, many SEs concentrate on designing the product to be suitable

for the local market but rely on skilled and innovative manufacturing partners to work through the specifications required to realize that localized design on a global scale.

- *Financing*: A supplier can be a source of working capital for a startup once it hits growth mode, preventing a cash crunch.[26] That financing may take the form of extending payment terms for goods, a loan, or even an investment in the startup itself. All of these can potentially improve a startup's cash position, critical to the successful scaling of an organization; most organizations have a lag in their revenue to cash conversion cycle, meaning that a cash crunch can catch an organization off-guard, even when the organization is doing very well and ramping its sales. So, working on a financially beneficial working relationship with a supplier, especially a larger supplier that might not be as cash strapped, could really boost a startup's working capital.

For larger companies, McKinsey has found that a close supplier relationship is key to improved financial performance: "among those [of the 100 companies in the study] who did collaborate [with their suppliers], the EBIT[27] growth rate was double that of their peers."[28] McKinsey's 2013 report outlines four principles for successful partnerships with suppliers that can apply to social startups as well:[29]

- *Prioritize suppliers with a focus on collaboration-based capabilities.* As the new venture gets off the ground, it is important to focus on a select group of suppliers where there are unique opportunities to create and retain significant mutual value. As part of this exercise, it is important to set mutually defined joint targets and improvements that might play out over several years. For some suppliers, there might be a longer-range focus on achieving cost improvements, while with others, long-term planning might revolve around jointly developed points of innovation.[30]
- *Be aspirational.* This means getting the right tone with the supplier to create a demanding but collaborative, trust-based partnership. This includes setting targets in terms of both financial impact and timing. Without clear targets, there can be little sense of urgency or commitment to actively pursue continuous improvement opportunities and resolve issues that might arise in a transparent, objective, and fact-based way.[31] Additionally, for SEs, setting mission-aligned targets is important, too.
- *Don't just monitor from afar: Engage.* McKinsey suggests: "Trust but verify," taking a "go and see" approach. McKinsey further suggests that best-in-class companies put dedicated "boots on the ground" at key suppliers, ensuring a broader set of cross-functional team members that have regular on-site presence, to test both progress and capabilities, while being there to solve issues proactively: "Without a deep understanding of supplier operational processes—and the opportunities to close the gap to best-in-class companies—it is very difficult to design the program and set the right milestones to meet overall goals."[32] In the social entrepreneurship space, this becomes very important as suppliers can have social or environmental objectives that in practice are not consistently applied. In terms of reputation, this could be disastrous for a social startup, if its supplier were in breach of environmental or social targets that the SE depends on as part of its mission and/or reputation.

To go back to our C⁴ example, suppose it's discovered that the "organic" clothing line was not produced by organic material. Or that its factory where the products were sewn was not truly adhering to fair labor laws. While this would be a supplier issue, it could greatly damage the reputation of the social startup. Working with certification companies, such as Fair Trade (FT) USA, can give a social startup an external stamp of approval in ensuring that fair labor practices are being met. Specifically, FTUSA requires all of its certified companies to follow strict standards, with mechanisms for ongoing auditing: "Rigorous standards are the way we fulfill our mission and deliver full benefits to producers and businesses we work with. They are tailor-made for each industry to ensure that we're all working together toward the same goal."[33] To deepen its engagement with the laborers themselves, in 2012, FTUSA acquired a nonprofit subsidiary, Good World Solutions, which enables workers to provide direct feedback via mobile phones on labor practices at their workplace. By 2015, this text-based technology had been used to survey more than 125,000 farmers and workers at co-ops and factories in nine countries, and FTUSA made Good World Solutions' technology available to organizations to embed into their supply chain practices, such as Cisco, Disney, Vodafone, and Marks & Spencer.[34]

- *Build internal competency.* "Outsourcing" doesn't mean outsourcing all ability to plan and manage the production process. As the report states: "Companies need to put in place a robust, integrated supplier collaboration process with the right supporting tools, and they need to ensure it is executed consistently." Ultimately, it is critical to define the right internal roles and responsibilities within the organization to drive accountability as well as collaboration and – as Embrace found – that sometimes results in moving critical pieces of the production process in-house. Additionally, an internal change agent needs to be responsible for driving continuous improvements in select categories and keeping in mind supplier dependencies and alternatives.[35]

Because not everything will go smoothly, it is important to think of how to work through conflict that will likely arise between one's supplier(s), as constructively as possible: "With these considerations in mind, negotiation can be viewed not as a discrete segment of the supply chain process but instead as embedded throughout it."[36] A key point is to ensure that you have someone managing the supplier relationship that is capable of navigating this type of conflict, and to be prepared to manage up, bringing in your CEO, if necessary, when major problems surface, which they undoubtedly will give the ongoing shifts and disruptions to supply chains due to a variety of factors (i.e., unexpected climate impacts, change in tariffs or labor practices, etc.). Figure 6.2 shows how to think of the supplier/company ongoing relationship, which emphasizes that negotiation (and conflict resolution) isn't necessary just at the front end of contract negotiation, but instead holds pretty much constant in managing the supplier relationship throughout the contract period.

*Source:* Rogers, (2012).[37]

**Figure 6.2**    The buyer–supplier negotiation process

In a study of Ghana-based startups, three of the four key factors identified for startup success centered on its supply chain, specifically calling out relationship building, relationship sharing, and the quality of information sharing. In fact, strategically managing one's suppliers "allows both parties to collaborate and work towards reducing stock-outs, minimizing waste, reducing costs and meeting delivery schedules."[38] As companies begin to scale, it is important to think about how to engender a better relationship with one's suppliers, including how to handle the bumps in the road that will inevitably be encountered along the way. Rogers and Fells (2012) outline three types of factors that are important in building relationships with suppliers including: (1) ongoing cooperation; (2) open lines of communication; and (3) professional respect and concern for each other's financial health. Specifically: "Buyer-supplier transactions are becoming increasingly driven by technological processes, but relationships between buyer and supplier are dynamic and are subject to a range of pressures as the contract is being fulfilled."[39] These authors underscore the importance of having a contract – as a formal contract bounds the buyer–supplier relationships, reducing the transaction costs associated with ongoing negotiations.[40] But there is also an understanding, as mentioned previously, that relationship management doesn't end with the initial contract negotiation (see Figure 6.3).

| Enablers |
| --- |

- open – and two-way – communication and information exchange;
- trust based on personal integrity;
- organisational trust shown in the clarity and stability of the contract;
- all resulting in trust that, in the first instance, is calculus-based;
- actively looking beyond contract compliance to broader relationship opportunities.

Practicalities
- actively seeking face-to-face contact with the supplier – opportunistic rather than only in response to problems having arisen;
- an increasing exchange of commercial and strategic information beyond the requirements of the contract;
- personal integrity (and that of the organisation) is maintained;
- trust builds into a clear identification and understanding of each other's interests and aspirations;
- objective performance management, representing the supplier when necessary;
- investment beyond words into mutual activities.

Relationship repair
- recognising the important role of line management in building proactive relationships;
- a rapid, objective, face-to-face response when adverse situations arise;
- encouraging a mutual problem-solving approach to addressing difficulties.

*Source:* Rogers (2012).[41]

**Figure 6.3**      Key elements in negotiating buyer–supplier relationships

As we write this book, we are currently living in unprecedented times with the COVID-19 pandemic, which has been disruptive to most companies' abilities to deliver products to fulfill customer demand, most especially for those companies that outsourced manufacturing abroad and held low inventory levels, optimizing for just-in-time inventory management. As an analysis by Deloitte emphasizes:

> China's dominant role as the "world's factory" means that any major disruption puts global supply chains at risk. Highlighting this is the fact that more than 200 of the Fortune Global 500 firms have a presence in Wuhan, the highly industrialized province where the outbreak originated, and which has been hardest hit.

According to Bain & Company: "Once the pandemic passes and the global economy begins to function normally, many senior executives might assume they should manage their global supply networks as in the past, with the lowest-cost supply and minimal inventory levels. While that approach worked in a stable global economy, it now brings increased risk."[42] As such, there is now renewed emphasis on regional (not just centralized) supply chains. According to Sunil Chopra, professor of operations at Kellogg:

> The additional cost of a large company operating plants in different locations is often not more than the cost of having one huge plant … you may reach the limit of your economies of scale at half the size, so by running two plants, you don't give up much in efficiency, but you gain a lot in resiliency.[43]

And finally, McKinsey also chimes in, noting that having another supplier needn't be a source of conflict, as long as the company is transparent in its communication with the initial supplier: "They will appreciate your honesty. If your supplier is savvy, they'll also know that you need backup suppliers on key products and services if you ever plan on raising money (lenders are sure to ask that question)."[44] For a visual representation of McKinsey best practices guidelines from its 2012 report, see Figure 6.4.

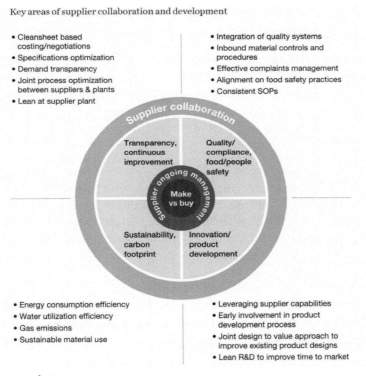

Key areas of supplier collaboration and development

- Cleansheet based costing/negotiations
- Specifications optimization
- Demand transparency
- Joint process optimization between suppliers & plants
- Lean at supplier plant

- Integration of quality systems
- Inbound material controls and procedures
- Effective complaints management
- Alignment on food safety practices
- Consistent SOPs

Supplier collaboration

Transparency, continuous improvement

Quality/ compliance, food/people safety

Supplier ongoing management

Make vs buy

Sustainability, carbon footprint

Innovation/ product development

- Energy consumption efficiency
- Water utilization efficiency
- Gas emissions
- Sustainable material use

- Leveraging supplier capabilities
- Early involvement in product development process
- Joint design to value approach to improve existing product designs
- Lean R&D to improve time to market

*Source:* McKinsey analysis.

**Figure 6.4**     Key areas of supplier collaboration and development

During the current pandemic, typically profit-motivated companies also pivoted to being social first, which they could only achieve through their sophisticated supply chains:

The Covid-19 crisis has thrown a spotlight on companies that already have flexible production lines. The fashion industry couldn't be further removed from the production of disinfectants and medical gear. But when the spread of Covid-19 overwhelmed the French and Italian healthcare system and medical supplies ran short, nimble luxury goods manufacturers overhauled operations to make the urgently needed items. Within 72 hours of the French government's call for business to pitch in, LVMH's perfume factories were producing hand sanitizer. Giorgio Armani, Gucci and Prada repurposed their designer clothing factories in Italy to churn out medical overalls, and Burberry harnessed a trench coat plant to make face masks and nonsurgical gowns. It was more than a feat of factory retooling. Flexible supply chains played a critical role, including rapid raw material sourcing, product design, development and testing, and distribution.[45]

Buyers and suppliers were only able to negotiate delivery of important goods during unprecedented times through mutual trust and ongoing discussion, as the current COVID-19 pandemic dictated. While the longer-term implications of this pandemic are unclear, there is evidently a greater desire for companies to create redundancy within their supply chains while balancing the best and least expensive manufacturing between local and more immediate supplier locations. Even during conventional times, the notion of trust (a company's approach to handling issues), fairness (such that both parties are getting something out of the relationship) and transparency (in going above and beyond, sharing information that can lead to the fulfillment of mutual goals) is central to healthy buyer–supplier relationships.[46] Bain & Company outlines the following learned lessons from the most successful companies to manage the pandemic:[47]

- *Network agility.* Reacting quickly to disruption requires a flexible ecosystem of suppliers and partners that can handle sudden shortfalls, or pivot to produce new products.
- *Digital collaboration.* This includes better insights into suppliers' supply chains, to understand interdependencies and potential impact throughout.
- *Real-time network visibility.* Technology and the use of blockchain might help companies understand vulnerabilities in their network of suppliers, based on weather-related events or other global disruptions.
- *Rapid generation of insights.* This is the leadership team's ability to pivot quickly based on new and evolving data to create better forecasting and timely decision-making.
- *Empowered teams.* In times of uncertainty, learning and gleaning insights from distributed teams becomes only more important.

While the lessons learned from large, global companies might seem a bit removed from the daily lives of smaller, social startups, one can conceptualize why some smaller firms have greater flexibility, while others have less. Clearly, smaller startups are less likely to have several layers of redundancy for manufacturing sources, as their volumes are likely to be small such that multiple manufacturing sites are not needed and even difficult to secure. However, by leaning on and learning through partnerships, smaller firms could potentially shift manufacturing sources quickly with less customized parts. Further, real-time network visibility and having empowered teams are often considered essential for any startup and therefore are likely to be an asset – not a liability – during uncertain times. Finally, any startup team should think of how to build and curate a network of alliances, as discussed in Chapter 2, regardless of the global environment. Strong alliances can: (1) build credibility with potential suppliers; (2) reinforce an organization's commitment to quality and social values; and (3) give access to new customer sources. For example, Stonyfield Farm, producer of organic ice cream and yoghurt, has formal relationships with other like-minded and "earth-friendly" partners, including Newman's Own. These alliances serve as endorsements of each organization's environmental practices and commitment, while at the same time building consumer trust and exposure to their environmentally oriented customer bases.[48] Similarly, organizations that become B Certified, as referenced in Chapter 3, have access to a jointly promoted platform of B corporations that want to do well (financially) while doing good (socially).

# DETERMINING DISTRIBUTION CHANNELS

Echoing Fisher's comments stated earlier in this chapter, when the founders of d.light were launching its solar lighting product in India, d.light's co-founder Tozun experienced hesitancy from d.light's target market, in trusting a new company: "Rural customers are inundated with marketing and they are very skeptical about new things." This in turn negatively impacted d.light's ability to attract established distributors, as Tozun states:

> the partners we work with now, they would have never worked with us when we were small. For one thing, with one product, no one is going to work with you. If you have no ability to support them with marketing, they are not going to want to work for you either.[49]

These distribution challenges are amplified by the fact that resource-constrained social start-ups often lack the bandwidth to train their distributors on their products with field visits. Tozun elaborates:

> For the first four of five years, we were really proving ourselves in the market. Effectively, we were managing our own distribution, selling directly to retailers, getting proof of concept in the market. The economies [of scale] were horrible ... because having one or two products and building a whole distribution network around that is very difficult.

Now, d.light has a range of products and has further collaborated with M-KOPA to provide financing to its customers, making the purchase of its products that much easier.[50] d.light has also joined, in conjunction with its investor, Acumen Fund, an off-grid alliance organization that can help build recognition, funding and best practices as d.light tackles distribution challenges across geographically dispersed regions.[51] Additional examples of channel challenges in our set of companies are illustrated as follows:

- Embrace forged a partnership with a well-established global medical device company, that also sold established (and more expensive), high-end products/incubators to hospitals. But, due to the price difference between Embrace's product and the company's more expensive products, this channel resulted in very few sales, as commissions were too low to attract the more established company's sales team.
- RevFoods distributed its "Jet Pack" pre-packaged lunches through Target, yet RevFoods didn't have the advertising budget that its main competitor, the Kraft Heinz Company, had through its Lunchables product line. As a result, the product didn't have great "sell-throughs," and Target both dropped (and returned) the product, eliminating Target as a viable channel partner.

In the first example, Embrace had a relationship with General Electric (GE), but this channel proved ineffective in producing meaningful revenue. This is because Embrace's product was far less expensive than GE's other products. As a result, this translated into lower potential commissions for its sales representatives, such that Embrace's infant baby warmer failed to capture the interest of GE's sales teams. Co-founder Chen emphasizes that product-based startups must invest in their own direct sales force in their early years, as the product is still being proven in the marketplace. As Chen states: "we initially thought we could rely on third parties to sell the product, but we realized that, in the early stages, you have to do it yourself, because no one can promote your product as well as you can."[52] This led to Embrace hiring 11 sales representatives to cover the three Southern states in India: Kerala, Tamil Nadu and Karnataka. Another surprise for Embrace was the importance of urban-based physicians' endorsements, even though Embrace's target beneficiaries were the rural poor. As a result, Embrace's team had to "get the medical community to buy in first from the top down,"[53] leading them to embark on clinical trials that proved Embrace's product was as effective in treating premature babies as more expensive traditional incubators. Ultimately, the product's novelty (and therefore lack of track record), affordability (making it lucrative on a commission basis for MedTech salespersons), and lack of physician endorsement delayed widespread product acceptance and created a major setback for the company. Embrace's findings also match our own observations across the other firms in this study: that only after some initial customer success can a social startup really successfully engage distributors.[54]

In RevFoods' earliest years, retail distribution was not its main distribution channel, as the startup's healthy school lunches were sold directly to schools and school districts. In fact, RevFoods benefited most from "word of mouth" between school districts, making sales easier and easier as the organization's reputation grew. While RevFoods' first customers were charter schools that lacked kitchens, the organization soon moved to selling to complete school districts based in California, Texas, Washington DC, Boston, New York, New Jersey, and other states. Each new area required some adaptation, as food tastes differed by region. For example, in DC the local team conducted dozens of school tastings to create a baked chicken wing with spicy sauce that would be "child-approved."[55] Later in its development, when RevFoods moved into consumer packaged goods (CPG) with its family meal product lines, it had to employ a different distribution strategy. Instead of taking a more "business to business" approach to expansion and becoming reliant on referrals, RevFoods was now in a "business to consumer" market segment, which was reliant on in-store demonstrations and a large advertising budget to create and maintain consumer interest. Working with large retailers meant investing in food brokers to increase their reach into grocery stores. After three attempts to enter the CPG market, RevFoods finally exited CPG and returned its core focus back to healthy school meals for school districts, offering not only lunch, but also breakfast, snacks and meals throughout the day. A key challenge for RevFoods moving into CPG was ultimately not its supply chain, which the organization did adapt to; in the end, channel management proved to be the biggest barrier to successfully staying in the CPG market.

One way to think of your startup's product delivery model is to engage in process mapping, incorporating both the service and product elements needed to deliver one's solution into the field: "Process mapping refers to the clarification of how exactly the moving parts of your product or service will flow between these different components to get to your end goal. The result is a step-by-step description of your core operations, similar to a recipe or instructions for your team."[56] The goal is to map out the entire product/service delivery value chain, including both the point of delivery and post-delivery customer service. Doing so can also ensure that nothing "falls through the cracks" in one's delivery model and that the organization has the right resources in place when considering scaling. This is especially important if one of the main ways an organization is scaling is through a franchise or distributed model, where others are expected to emulate a proven process model. An example of a modified process map for a health clinic, as originally depicted by Chahine,[57] can be seen in Figure 6.5.

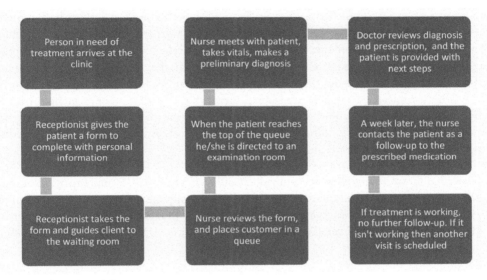

*Source:* Chahine (2016).[58]

**Figure 6.5**     Chahine process map

In the developing-country context, distribution challenges can sometimes be exacerbated by reaching the "last mile," a catchphrase used to describe the difficulty of getting products to customers located in remote areas. Some of the challenges laid out by USAID include: inadequate information systems; shortage of trained personnel to manage supply chains; lack of appropriate cold storage for medicine; poor roads and infrastructure, making routes inaccessible for cars/trucks; limited collaboration with the private sector; and poor public financing.[59] As Melinda Gates pointed out in her TED Talk,[60] nonprofits can learn a lot from Coca-Cola, given that the Coca-Cola company has managed to get its product to some of the most remote villages globally for decades (i.e., Coca-Cola has been in Africa since 1928). Initially, Coca-Cola also experienced problems in reaching customers, but solved this distribution problem by tapping into local entrepreneurial talent. The company realized that a large truck couldn't roll down streets as they do in the developed world, so it set up micro distribution centers to get its products to regions where transportation and infrastructure were not as industrialized and where locals were willing to use a wheelbarrow, motorcycle, boat, or whatever means of transportation was necessary, to get Coca-Cola's products to remote villages. As such, the Gates Foundation and USAID partnered with Coca-Cola to see if medicines could be distributed by packaging them alongside Coke products,[61] laying the groundwork for large company and nonprofit collaboration. Within a seven-year period from 2005 to 2012, this partnership benefited nearly 20 million people and reduced the lead time for medicine deliveries to Tanzanian health facilities by as much as 25 days (from 30 days to just five days).[62]

Another issue with distribution, as pointed out by USAID, is localized support and training, so that when products do arrive at their target destination, they are successfully deployed and used. As Melinda Gates referenced in her TED Talk: training local people in basic healthcare has been critical to "last mile" care. Specifically, in Ethiopia, child mortality has been reduced by creating, through training, local frontline heath care workers.[63] Much of this thought is rooted in Max-Neef's "barefoot economics,"[64] wherein he refers to the working lives and practices of individuals who live in communities (rural or urban) that are marginal or peripheral to mainstream economic systems; this is where the poor often are forced to carve out a living in order simply to survive. In such circumstance, there is a real need for employment, providing a win–win in those communities when local talent is trained to deliver products and provide services (such as localized frontline healthcare). Having local distributors also leads to product reach and growth. As authors Chu and Segre state:

> Informal direct selling, in which individuals independent of any formal organization purchase products and resell them at higher prices, is among the most common and intuitive ways that consumer products are distributed across the developing world. In fact, informal trade represents half of overall trade GDP and over 90% of employment in several developing countries.[65]

Another benefit of training and employing locals to serve as frontline product representatives, is that it creates greater buy-in for the product and/or service, and also creates meaningful feedback loops for further product enhancements. However, there is a dark side to this model as well. In some cases, selling representatives are forced to buy products outright – and carry inventory risk, in the hope that they can resell their inventory later. To offset this risk, the sales representative might then inflate the price of a product when reselling in local communities, above the level that the SE's founders had envisioned. And then, there might even be local competition for those resellers, depending on how aggressively the SE recruited and developed its distributor channel: "The ease of entry and difficulty of exiting the business can trap these sellers, increasing competition such that five or more individuals may sell the identical product on popular street corners. The pattern repeats itself in several other geographies and product areas."[66]

This naturally leads to the topic of how your distribution channel can be scaled. There are several ways to scale your channels, including a dissemination or franchising, as briefly touched on before. These are more cost-effective and preserve greater capital compared to organically growing a dedicated sales force – which is the most expensive way to scale. Dissemination is sharing best practices and letting other like-minded organizations mimic your organization's product or service, without any financial benefit to your organization. Social entrepreneurs are more likely to employ dissemination in comparison to traditional startups, as the goal is often not market dominance, but instead, collective commitment to addressing global crises. However, dissemination also provides the least control over quality and impact. Franchising is a way to scale reach with fewer resources, in comparison to other forms of expansion, while still controlling product/service quality. However, in our experience, this form of expansion is less frequently employed by SEs.

One of the companies in our sample of firms that has used franchising effectively is Sanergy. Sanergy moved from being a US-based startup team to a Kenyan-based company, with over 93 percent of its 251 employees being local Kenyans, as mentioned in the Case Study at the end of Chapter 1. In fact, the employees that service the Fresh Life Toilets are often from the same Kenyan slums that Sanergy serves. Sanergy's seven-member government relations team is completely staffed by Kenyans. Sanergy has also grown its Fresh Life Toilets with a franchise model, such that entrepreneurs within slums are motivated to purchase a toilet, with the help of microfinancing, and then operate it in accordance with standards set and enforced by Sanergy. As a further example of agility, Sanergy also built a robust and trusted logistics network that became a resource when COVID-19 hit Nairobi, and the city was confronted with the challenge of getting sanitation supplies into its crowded, informal settlements. In partnership with Safe Hands Kenya, Sanergy began distributing free soap and hygiene products through its established network while continuing to operate its waste collection services as an "essential business."[67]

Like Sanergy, RevFoods found that one unintended and important social benefit of its employee base was in hiring local, inner city talent to serve in its operations as they expanded in each city. This meant that RevFoods grew through expansion by its own employees fueling its reach into new cities. This had the additional benefit of also creating buy-in within the community for their lunch programs, as children in the school might have a relative or family friend working for the organization. The company also extended its impact beyond employment by helping its employees learn financial literacy, often opening their first savings or checking account, which represented their very first formal banking relationship. RevFoods also found itself in a position to support COVID-response efforts by leveraging its community network. The National School Lunch Program provides free and reduced-cost meals to 22 million children in the US. However, when COVID-19 prompted schools to close across the country, millions of children were left without a steady source of nutritious meals, even as school districts worked diligently to develop creative solutions for distributing these meals. During the first four months of the pandemic, RevFoods supplied two million meals per week to children outside of school, across 18 states, adapting to meet the districts' needs. For example, in San Francisco, RevFoods provided all five-days' worth of meals in a one-day-per-week service model and expanded its collaboration with community partners to combat food insecurity, serving thousands of additional children and adults across six sites.[68]

# VALUE CHAINS DURING A PANDEMIC

Due to COVID-19, we are now moving into very different types of company–employee and employee–community relationships. Many employees are working at home, giving them more opportunities to deeply embed and serve their local communities. But this is also creating stressors, as employees are expected to participate in a more "elastic digital workplace,"[69] and for those working remotely, this means an absence of more organic learning and mentoring through co-workers. For those working – as usual – by showing up to an office, store or factory, this means potential exposure to a life-threatening disease through co-working spaces or direct client engagement. For example, the Los Angeles-based apparel company, LA Apparel, which pivoted from making clothes to making masks, had 300 confirmed COVID-19 cases and four deaths due to close work proximity – even with safety measures in place.[70] Globally, in meat-packing facilities, outbreaks have been rampant due to the close proximity of work spaces, the cold working environments (i.e., working in refrigerated areas), and the fact that many workers live in cramped company housing, which can also lead to the spread of the disease.[71] Furthermore, some workers continue to work, even when showing symptoms of COVID-19, as their sick pay is worth a fraction of their normal salaries, making them less likely to report their illness.[72] One of the worst examples of such an outbreak was in Germany, where 360,000 people working in a meat plant had to be quarantined in one of its western states.[73] This is true of larger distribution channels as well, such as retail. As reported by the *New York Times*, in an interview with Liz Dunn, founder of Pro4ma, a retail analytics company: "this crisis is shining a light on the inequality across our nation and economy … a lot of people can't [work from home], and it's likely they're a lot more vulnerable in terms of what an economic downturn will do to their ability to keep their family and keep themselves housed."[74] Similarly, fulfillment centers from larger companies, such as Amazon, have also reported outbreaks of the virus.[75] Even when workers want to work, outbreaks may force shutdowns of factories, fulfillment centers, and retail stores, unfortunately shutting out those that remain healthy and able to work. Additionally, consumers might be less inclined to go to retail stores for fear of being infected. All of this has accelerated a shift to e-commerce and other forms of product fulfillment and delivery,[76] altered jobs, and created a need for training outside of peer-to-peer and in-person training programs, developing trends that are likely to outlive the pandemic.

COVID-19 has also highlighted the fact that for startups dependent on outsourced fulfillment and delivery, through e-tailers such as Amazon, a delay in fulfillment and delivery could result in both revenue shortfalls and customer dissatisfaction. For those startups that distribute through retail stores, many have been negatively impacted due to COVID-19, given that retail stores have been shuttered due to local health mandates. However, there could also be a positive impact, depending on the company. For example, World of Good (WOG) originally sold its goods through yoga studios and grocery stores, such as Whole Foods. During the pandemic, more people were cooking at home, which could have potentially boosted WOG's jewelry sales at Whole Foods. However, simultaneously, there could have also been a complete drop-off in business through other channels, as yoga studios remained closed. WOG's e-commerce platform, though, could have done quite well given that more people are shopping online, and a low-cost jewelry item that benefits the poor in developing countries could have been a very appropriate purchase during these uncertain times. While drone delivery has been an important development in hard-to-reach rural areas for the delivery of medicines and other necessary health or food products, it could also prove to be the solution for "contactless" delivery even in urban areas, for necessary products as well, given the highly infectious nature of the COVID-19 disease.

For some SEs, the pandemic has been catalytic towards SEs digitizing their distribution channels. In addition to offering more e-commerce options for delivering physical products, SEs that previously conducted training or collected payments in-person are accelerating their efforts to continue their work by leveraging mobile phone technology and the web. For example, the agriculture nonprofit, myAgro, offers a package to farmers of quality inputs, fertilizer, agronomy advice, and a layaway savings platform. The SE began using WhatsApp, YouTube, and radio transmission to disseminate safe planting information when face-to-face training became unsafe. In reality, the pandemic accelerated its planned pilots for using mobile money (rather than cash) for layaway payment collection. Using these digital channels is also more cost-efficient, causing the organization now to evaluate which distribution channels should continue, even when the pandemic is over.[77] Chapter 7 goes into more detail about the potential of technology solutions that support SEs in scaling their work, through cost-efficient and far-reaching digital distribution channels, employed by organizations such as Grameen America.

In closing, we have the following key takeaways when considering building and managing one's supply chain:

- Building a value chain for SEs is a different challenge compared to less mission-driven organizations, as the social startup needs to be mindful of cost efficiencies, operational excellence, having a secure supply chain management, *and mission alignment.*
- Since COVID-19, most organizations are now building redundancies into their supply chains, and reducing their dependency on geographically distant suppliers. However, nascent SEs often have less economies of scale, making it more difficult to incorporate redundancies in their supply chain. As a result, we suggest that SEs engage in joint partnerships with other SEs to mutually secure supply chain redundancies and consider building products with as many "standard parts" as possible, mitigating the need for the sourcing and stocking of specialized parts.
- Often, new SEs must build their first distribution channels while demonstrating a "proof of concept." Our research shows that this is best done by creating a growing number of satisfied and engaged customers, likely to be hand-built by the startup instead of its distributors. In sum, distributors are more likely to engage with SEs that have proven customer traction and a clearly demonstrated value proposition with its target customers, and the only way for the startup to do this in the early years is by doing so itself. This means that a social startup should consider having someone on its founding team with experience in customer sales and fulfillment.

## CASE STUDY
### d.LIGHT

The genesis for the founding of d.light came from Stanford's graduate-level course called Design for Extreme Affordability. In this class, teams composed of students with technical and business expertise, both professionally and educationally, were presented with a design challenge. In d.light's case, based on the team's travels through Burma, the team was inspired to provide safe, affordable and durable lighting as an alternative to the commonplace candles and kerosene lamps as: "Such fuel-based sources are often expensive, very dim and dangerous."[78] In fact, according to the United Nations, "The ingestion of kerosene is the leading cause of childhood poisonings, and a large fraction of the severe burns and injuries occurring in low- and middle-income countries are linked to household energy use for cooking, heating, and/or lighting."[79] Even as late as 2012, six years after d.light's founding, 25 percent of the world's population was still living without electricity, with the most impacted region being the continent of Africa: 57 percent of its population, 600 million people, still lacked access to electricity. India also had poor electrical infrastructure and accounted for another 300 million people living without access to electricity. This split of have and have nots, when it comes to energy access, is often amplified when comparing those in urban versus rural areas. For example, in India, 97 percent of those living in urban areas have access to electricity, whereas in rural areas, only 67 percent do.[80] The concentration of off-grid populations in rural areas has important distribution implications for those SEs that seek to reach them with their products.

Even with these compelling case statements as to why customers should want d.light's off-grid lighting products, it was difficult – in the beginning – for d.light to attract distributors. As Tozun states, "For the first four or five years, I would say, we were really proving ourselves in the market. Effectively, we were managing our own distribution, selling directly to retailers, getting proof of concept in the market."[81] The SE did ultimately attract distributors, but according to Tozun:

"What'll often happen is a distributor will get excited, they'll put it [the product] out there, it won't sell, and then they won't buy again … making a product available is not sufficient." Now, d.light has a global network of distribution partners including: Total, Unilever, Orange, PEG, the World Bank, UNHCR, Oxfam, BRAC, and World Vision.[82] The organization credits three important aspects of its distribution strategy: importers (to ensure the

**Figure 6.6**      d.light logo

product gets to the end location on time, and is not held up in customs), a network of distributors, and retailers. The company now also has a robust e-tailing strategy, with products available through Amazon.[83]

As to the supplier side of their value chain, the founders made a decision early on to manufacture their solar lights in China, optimizing both cost and quality. As stated earlier in the chapter, d.light's products had to be both affordable and durable, given the population the founders aimed to serve – individuals at the base of the pyramid, earning less than $2,000 (USD) a year in income.[84] As Tozun jokes, while some software-based startups have to worry about "software bugs," the d.light team had to worry about actual "bugs" getting into, and ruining, their product in the field. Tozun explains their production process:

> We really believed in the human-centered design method, prototyping a lot in the field ... the other component of that, that I think differentiated us a lot, especially in those early days, is the fact that we felt that had to be done in close collaboration and coordination with the supply chain, which is why we had our engineering development team and me in China.[85]

Given that d.light's products are still made in China, which has caused some criticisms from outsiders that question the company's commitment to being carbon neutral, all products are shipped from China to its locations around the world. However, the company counters that its products offset its transport-related $CO2$ emissions given that solar lights are a cleaner electricity source than kerosene. Further, as mentioned previously, durability in the field is important to the SE, which matters both from a customer value and a product life-cycle perspective; d.light promotes that all of its products come with a warranty good for up to two years, and that claims can be made from any of the 25,000 retail outlets that sell d.light's products, worldwide.[86]

As we look forward, what suggestions do you have to improve d.light's value chain? Should the company, in keeping with recommendations coming out of COVID-19, diversify its supply chains to have local production centers? What would be the social and environmental benefits of doing so? What should d.light be mindful of, with respect to its distribution channels? In closing, and as a prelude to Chapter 8, which addresses social impact measurement, how does d.light seem to measure its social impact?

# NOTES

1.  Tozun, Ned. Interview. By Jennifer Walske, April 2014.

2.  Porter, Michael. *Competitive Advantage: Creating and Sustaining Superior Performance*, Free Press, 1985, New York, NY, p. 36.

3.  "Suppliers, Distributors & Partners for Social Ventures: Social Enterprises (SE) & Social Business: Entrepreneur's Toolkit." *MaRS Startup Toolkit*, 2013, www.marsdd.com/mars-library/suppliers-distributors -and-partners-for-social-ventures-social-enterprises-se-and-social-business/.

4.  Porter, Michael. *Competitive Advantage: Creating and Sustaining Superior Performance*. Free Press, 1985, New York, NY, p. 37.

5.  Porter, Michael. *Competitive Advantage: Creating and Sustaining Superior Performance*, Free Press, 1985, New York, NY, p. 37.

6.  Goel, Ankur, et al. "Supplier Collaboration and Development." *McKinsey & Company*, January 2012, www .mckinsey.com/practice-clients/operations/supplier-collaboration-and-development. Accessed 6 May 2019.

7.  Ridley, Matt. "When Ideas Have Sex." *TED*, July 2010, https://www.ted.com/talks/matt_ridley_when_ideas _have_sex.

8.  Pinkert, Dean, James Ton-that, and Ravi Soopramanien. "How Blockchain Can Make Supply Chains More Humane." *Stanford Social Innovation Review*, 18 January 2019.

9.  Ibid.

10. Schlossberg, Tatiana. "How Fast Fashion Is Destroying the Planet." *New York Times*, 3 September 2019, www .nytimes.com/2019/09/03/books/review/how-fast-fashion-is-destroying-the-planet.html.

11. Tozun, Ned. Interview. By Jennifer Walske, April 2014.

12. Ibid.

13. Chu, Michael, David Bloom, and Alison Wagonfield. "Embrace." *Harvard Business School Publishing*, 18 July 2013, Harvard Business School Case Series 9-814-001, p. 5.

14. Walske, Jennifer and Laura Tyson. "Revolution Foods: Expansion into the CPG Market." *The Regents of the University of California*, 31 July 2015, Berkeley Haas Case Series, p. 4.

15. "Suppliers, Distributors & Partners for Social Ventures: Social Enterprises (SE) & Social Business: Entrepreneur's Toolkit." *MaRS Startup Toolkit*, 2013, www.marsdd.com/mars-library/suppliers-distributors -and-partners-for-social-ventures-social-enterprises-se-and-social-business/.

16. Ibid.

17. Lesle, Tim. "The Simple Water Pump that's Changing Lives Across the World." *Wired*, 5 December 2013, www.wired.com/2013/12/2112kickstart/.

18. "FY18 KickStart Annual Report." *KickStart International*, 2018, http://kickstart.org/wp-content/uploads/ 2019/05/FY18_KickStart_Annual_Report.pdf.

19. Chu, Michael, David Bloom, and Alison Wagonfield. "Embrace." *Harvard Business School Publishing*, 18 July 2013, Harvard Business School Case Series 9-814-001, p. 3.

20. Kainuma, Yasutaka, and Nobuhiko Tawara. "A Multiple Attribute Utility Theory Approach to Lean and Green Supply Chain Management." *International Journal of Production Economics*, vol. 101, no. 1, 2006, p. 99.

21. "Circular Economy Model." *Danone*, 24 October 2019, www.danone.com/impact/planet/packaging-positive -circular-economy.html.

71. Reuben, Anthony. "Coronavirus: Why Have There Been So Many Outbreaks in Meat Processing Plants?" *BBC News*, BBC, 23 June 2020, www.bbc.com/news/53137613.

72. Stewart, Anna, and Ivana Kottasová. "Why Meat Processing Plants Have Become Covid-19 Hotbeds." *CNN*, Cable News Network, 27 June 2020, www.cnn.com/2020/06/27/health/meat-processing-plants-coronavirus -intl/index.html.

73. Ibid.

74. Maheshwari, Sapna, and Michael Corkery. "Plight of Retail Workers: 'I'm Scared to Go to Work'." *The New York Times*, 18 March 2020, www.nytimes.com/2020/03/18/business/coronavirus-retail-workers.html.

75. "Coronavirus Strikes at Amazon's Operational Heart: Its Delivery Machine." *Los Angeles Times*, 17 March 2020, www.latimes.com/business/story/2020-03-17/amazon-coronavirus-delivery.

76. "Accenture COVID-19 Consumer Goods Rapid Response." *Accenture*, March 2020, https://www.accenture .com/_acnmedia/PDF-121/Accenture-COVID-19-Consumer-Goods-Rapid-Response.pdf.

77. "myAgro FY20 Q3 Report." *myAgro*, 2020, https://www.myagro.org/wp-content/uploads/2020/08/myagro -fy20-q3-report-2.pdf.

78. Kennedy, Michael, Gina Jorasch, and Jesper Sorensen. "d.light, Selling Solar to the Poor." *Harvard Business School Publishing*, 20 August 2012, Stanford Graduate School of Business Cases Series IDE-03, p. 1.

79. https://www.who.int/news-room/fact-sheets/detail/household-air-pollution-and-health.

80. Lindemin, Todd. "1.3 Billion Are Living in the Dark." *Washington Post*, November 6, 2015, https://www .washingtonpost.com/graphics/world/world-without-power/.

81. Tozun, Ned. Interview. By Jennifer Walske, April 2014.

82. According to d.light's website accessed on 17 September 2020, https://www.dlight.com/partners/.

83. Its S30 solar light is available for "camping" and is an "Amazon choice" for solar lighting. Amazon website accessed on 17 September 2019, https://www.amazon.com/d-light-S30-Solar-Rechargeable-Lantern/dp/ B00BJELHS0/ref=sr_1_5?dchild=1&keywords=d.light+solar+lantern&qid=1600647920&sr=8-5.

84. Prahalad, C.K., and A. Hammond. "Serving the World's Poor, Profitably." *Harvard Business Review*, vol. 80, no. 9, 2002, pp. 48–57.

85. Tozun, Ned. Interview. By Jennifer Walske, April 2014.

86. According to d.light's website accessed on 17 September 2020, https://www.dlight.com/partners/.

# 7
# The pivotal role of technology in scaling

We first started writing this chapter in late 2019, in a "pre-COVID-19" world. Teachers educated students in lively classrooms, meetings with colleagues took place at the office, and gatherings with friends and family happened over dinner at a local restaurant. Within a few weeks of the first confirmed cases in the US, small businesses, nonprofits and large corporations alike were confronted by debilitating disruptions and had to make rapid adjustments to their operations. For many organizations, these adjustments were not enough to save them from closing, leading to an unemployment rate in the US not seen since the Great Depression.[1] As of this book's publication, it is still too early to understand just how much will permanently change as a result of the multifaceted impacts of the COVID-19 pandemic; but even at this early stage, most people believe that whenever and however a full recovery does take place, our society will not go back to operating as it did before.

One almost certain long-term effect of the pandemic will be the acceleration of technology adoptions by organizations as a necessary step towards building resilience and adaptability to withstand future shocks. While social entrepreneurs may understand that a digital transformation is inevitable, our research shows that they often adopt new technologies without clear goals and leave opportunities untapped and risks overlooked. In this chapter, we give social entrepreneurs a guide for considering how and where to capitalize on the growing number of technological resources available to them. We begin by considering how technology innovations have been changing the entrepreneurial landscape long before the COVID-19 outbreak. Then we return to themes covered in the book, such as hiring a team with diverse and complementary skill-sets, keeping the target user central to product development, and diligently measuring impact performance, to develop a set of six principles for evaluating the role technology can play in organizational growth. We wrap up the chapter by highlighting some of the challenges associated with technological progress that social entrepreneurs should monitor.

## TECHNOLOGY AND INNOVATION

The steady advancement of technology since the mid-twentieth century has upturned long-standing business models and industries,[2] diminished the advantages of economies of scale, and placed a premium on the ability to adapt and stay nimble. Technology life-cycles are becoming shorter, leaving businesses less time to plan for strategic investments, and even shorter timeframes to benefit from them.[3] The average tenure of S&P 500 companies decreased from 61 years in 1958 to just 18 years by 2012, and the return on assets of public companies has been declining since 1965, an indication of the uncertainty and pressure to invest, perform and scale that businesses face.[4] While such companies look to new technologies to remain relevant, these innovations also provide a pathway for small businesses, startups and young nonprofits to achieve outsized impact and success.[5]

In the mid-1990s, the late Harvard Business School professor, Clayton Christensen, introduced the concept of "disruptive innovation." According to Christensen, disruption occurs when a company offers previously overlooked consumers a product or service that is simpler and cheaper than the market alternatives. That company then gradually moves up-market to eventually challenge industry leaders for their customers. Industries can experience disruptive innovation even when incumbents consistently innovate and invest in R&D, in part, because market leaders tend to focus resources on improving their existing products for their most demanding or profitable customers.[6] These "sustaining innovations" are "a critical component in the growth engine of most organizations and are important for economies to remain vibrant and competitive"[7] yet they often leave the lower end of the market underserved.

Research by the Christensen Institute has shown a connection between organizations investing in disruptive or market-creating innovations and increased economic prosperity. By focusing on meeting the needs of overlooked market segments and offering solutions for a lower price, disrupters have the potential to unlock access for marginalized populations and spur economic development and job creation.[8] Building on his earlier work, Christensen later put forward a subset of the disruptive innovation concept called "catalytic innovation," which shares the same qualities as disruptive innovation, but with a focus on creating "systemic social change through scaling and replication."[9] It is a term that could be applied to many of the solutions social entrepreneurs are developing today, including those of the eight social enterprises (SEs) researched in this book.

Developing solutions that are accessible and affordable to overlooked populations presents difficulties that deter many entrepreneurs from pursuing catalytic innovations; and for those entrepreneurs that do, the challenges can seriously jeopardize financial sustainability and scale. Technological advancements over the last few decades have altered this calculus. The tools that exist today, and the promise of what will be developed in the years ahead, have transformed the opportunities for reaching "last-mile" customers, for offering products at a price point low-income consumers can afford, and for connecting a broader set of stakeholders to an organization's mission.

## SIX PRINCIPLES FOR USING TECHNOLOGY TO SCALE

That technology can serve as a powerful tool for SEs is not a revolutionary idea (as the COVID-19 pandemic has certainly made even clearer), and yet all too often, organizations invest in technology solutions without clear goals or preparation. According to Salesforce. org, the nonprofit arm of the technology company, Salesforce, "Leadership vision, budget constraints, change management, and adoption difficulties continue to challenge nonprofits attempting to successfully implement technology that provides actionable data. Not many are planning ahead for the digital revolution that is already well underway."[10] Only 23 percent of the 725 nonprofits Salesforce.org surveyed had a long-term vision for how to use technology within their organization.[11] Rather than using technology for technology's sake, social entrepreneurs should consider how it can enable them to better deliver on performance targets that are foundational to the sustainability, growth and ultimately the impact of their organization. To this end, we offer the following six principles to help social entrepreneurs consider the ways in which they can leverage technology to deepen their impact, improve their resilience, and achieve scale.

## #1: Don't Start From Scratch

According to CB Insights, it now costs less than $5,000 to launch a startup. As such, high barriers to entry are now almost entirely irrelevant in many industries due to the rich ecosystem of available open-source software and cloud-based tools.[12] In the past, enterprises needed to build business functions like payroll, hosting and client relationship management (CRM) systems from scratch, whereas startups today can purchase or lease turnkey options, keeping costs low and giving entrepreneurs the flexibility to add or change tools over time.[13] A 2016 survey conducted by Tech City UK and Stripe identified a set of approximately 200 cloud-based tools that are transforming industry by offering cost-effective and easily integrated building blocks for organizations. The survey, which had over 300 respondents from early-stage startups, found that companies used an average of six to 15 of these tools, with 85 percent of respondents saying that they had made the launch and scale-up process cheaper and 89 percent saying they had made the process simpler.[14] New catalytic innovations are in part possible because these earlier disruptors have developed more accessible startup tools.

While the full suite of startup stack tools referenced in the survey is likely not present or functional everywhere, the trend towards increasingly accessible, user-friendly and affordable technology options for lean startups globally is clear. Executive Director of IT for Change, Parminder Jeet Singh, reported that worldwide, "Vastly improved connectivity is shifting the dominant computing paradigm towards remotely managed applications." This has produced numerous advantages including lower up-front costs and faster upgrading of systems. According to Singh, "Companies can therefore be agile in shifting to newer digital modes and applications, rather than be stuck for years with expensive on-premise IT infrastructures and systems. Such flexibility is most important in the current times of rapid digital evolution."[15]

Such technology tools don't only benefit startup models. The multitude of solutions available means that rarely should there be a need for a nonprofit to invest heavily in developing new systems themselves or to absorb certain overhead costs. At Grameen America (GA), a US-based microfinance institution, the organization originally used the custom-built software of Grameen Bank. When GA was looking to advance the organization's technological capabilities, it actually chose an off-the-shelf banking platform. GA's VP of Technology and Innovation, Marcus Berkowitz, states, "It's hard to go from a custom software to an out-of-the-box software ... because people say 'Wait a minute. Why would you give up on something that's custom?'"[16] The new platform, called Mambu, not only had inherent capabilities that were valuable (it was a cloud-based system for example), but it could also still be customized to fit GA's unique needs, and importantly, allow for future API integrations and tweaks as the organization evolved.

Nonprofits can also frequently take advantage of high discounts due to their nonprofit status. Kiva, for example, was able to benefit from significant cost savings because PayPal provided its transaction processing service for free, rather than charging the typical three percent of every transaction.[17] The nonprofit TechSoup has also been distributing free or discounted technology products to other nonprofits on behalf of leading technology companies such as Microsoft, Adobe, Intuit and Hewlett Packard since the 1980s.[18] Autodesk, the design and engineering software company, offers its products for free to nonprofits and early-stage social startups, and Google provides nonprofits with numerous resources such as discounted access to Google Workspace, grants for AdWords, and the use of Google Earth and Maps to illustrate organization impact.[19, 20]

These technology products have been transformative for resource-constrained social startups and nonprofits that are just getting started. Later on, when organizations secure grants or venture capital investment that support dramatically increased operating budgets, these fundamental technology tools remain important. Spending resources wisely, avoiding reinventing the wheel, and driving towards healthy unit economics are important all along the scaling journey.

## #2: Keep Customers Central

As Meera Chary of the consulting firm, The Bridgespan Group, and Christopher Keefe of the Omidyar Network wrote, "For social entrepreneurs today, the potential is clear for technology to transmit solutions faster, further, and more cost effectively to populations that need them. But converting that potential into reality starts with putting beneficiaries at the center of the scaling process."[21] As we discussed in Chapter 5, rapidly prototyping and continuously gathering stakeholder feedback are critical steps for arriving at product–market fit for core products and services. Product development does not end with version 1.0 though; it is a process that should be viewed as a long-term endeavor, which is where feedback loops and data collection come into play.[22]

As Room to Read states, having the right data platforms to track progress was critical as they expanded overseas: "Key to success was customizing the database and using it consistently over the years to track our program outputs and outcomes."[23] This went beyond just buying and entering data; this also meant an expensive investment in training their field staff in program monitoring and measurement. "This staffing structure was becoming complex and expensive. But it was what we believed – and still believe – to be the necessary infrastructure to sustain quality concerns."[24] Indeed, experts in the field of social entrepreneurship suggest that "robust data management is essential to assess both operations delivery and impact. Having access to such information helps social enterprises diagnose next steps to improve their impact" by determining first, whether the solution was delivered as intended, and second, whether the solution created the impact intended.[25] In the 2020 Salesforce.org Nonprofit Trends Report, more than half of the nonprofit respondents did not measure their impact and 73 percent said that they "can't tell if their programs are effective or reaching the populations they want to serve."[26]

Fortunately, there are now better surveying and data analytics options to support social entrepreneurs. SurveyMonkey, SurveyGizmo, Typeform, Qualtrics and many other surveying platforms can help entrepreneurs gather feedback efficiently. Even in low-resource settings, startups like M-Shule and mSurvey, both based in Nairobi, and Viamo, which works globally, can help organizations ask questions and gather information from individuals who have basic feature phones or live in hard-to-reach locations. Social entrepreneurs can also pull data from their products or services directly. For digital programs, entrepreneurs can uncover customer and beneficiary insights by looking at usage data, completion rates and product ratings, amongst many other metrics. For hardware products, sensors can feed valuable data back to the SEs in real time. Nexleaf Analytics, a nonprofit that designs sensor and remote monitoring technologies to produce data-driven insights to global challenges, offers its solutions to help nongovernmental organizations (NGOs) and governments keep vaccines safe and advance clean cooking designs.[27] These feedback and monitoring methods enable SEs to understand the impact of their solutions and the decision-making of customers on an ongoing basis.

For Fair Trade (FT) USA, the leadership team saw how technology could help them make their core certification business process more timely, rigorous and farmer-driven. According to FTUSA founder, Paul Rice, "The certification business is a clipboard and pencil industry, where an auditor comes in and writes up reports. It's top-down, not bottom-up." FTUSA eventually acquired Good World Solutions in order to launch a mobile, voice-based platform called LaborLink, through which the organization could survey farmers directly and get timely feedback on three areas: "1) monitoring and evaluation of certification and capacity building impact; 2) real-time performance measurement and return on investment of training activities; and 3) meta-analysis to track trends and changes over time, across products and countries."[28]

Strong feedback loops should lead to ongoing product improvements, but technology lends itself to an improved user experience in other ways as well. Amit Phadnis, now the Chief Digital Officer at GE Healthcare, observes that in education, technology allows the "creation of content that is localized, relevant, and consumable in different regional languages, improving learning outcomes."[29] In other words, technology does not just facilitate educational content distribution through digitization, it also allows for the customization that leads to improved learning for students. It is now easier to translate content and cater subjects to the local context, classes can be shared on a laptop, smartphone or feature phone in both written and audio formats, and AI-powered assessments and exercises can adapt to focus on where students are struggling. These are just a few examples within one sector of how technology facilitates solution delivery and increased impact for the target beneficiary or customer.

In our research on GA, we found that its move to a cloud-based software system and digital payments platform not only produced numerous advantages for the nonprofit's internal processes but also led to a better client experience. Clients used to have to pay in cash at the weekly group meetings, which led to time-consuming payment reconciliations as well as safety concerns for clients walking to the meetings. Switching to a digital payment system mitigated such security risks and minimized the time spent during group meetings to complete the reconciliation process. This allowed GA to reimagine how the additional time during weekly meetings could be used for supplemental services such as small business training and peer-led workshops.[30]

## #3: Communication Is Key

Management consulting firm, A.T. Kearny, and Ashoka, a leading network for social entrepreneurs, published a joint report in 2016 outlining the challenges social entrepreneurs in India face when attempting to scale. SEs, especially those with significant field operations, high-touch models, or large geographic scopes often struggle to grow high-quality and well-integrated operations without absorbing significant ongoing costs. "For some social enterprises setting up extensive field operations can be as difficult as setting up a new organization, as one needs to establish new personnel, map out towns and villages, and invest more capital."[31] These operational challenges are exacerbated in areas where the infrastructure is poor and where the target beneficiaries and customers live in remote areas but they can be greatly reduced through strong communication systems.[32]

Information and communication technology empowers geographically dispersed teams. Many of the SEs researched in this book had international reaches from the beginning and had to develop systems for working effectively across such a broad footprint. d.light, for example, was headquartered in San Francisco, manufactured its lights in China, and sold its products across Asia and Africa.[33] Other organizations like Sanergy and Embrace were able to work across markets while remaining efficient in a way that would have been impossible for SEs just 20 years ago. Still, setting up more extensive field teams was important for their models to work. As Sanergy began deploying its toilets in Kenya, its team became mostly Kenyan, with 60 percent of its 250+ staff coming from the informal settlements Sanergy served. Similarly, as Embrace conducted expensive clinical trials in India, it expanded its field office there, until it became its largest office worldwide. For Room to Read, implementing more than 1,000 new literacy projects per year, an average of three per day, in countries ranging from Zambia to Nepal posed a "serious logistical challenge" to their team. To help overcome such challenges, ongoing program monitoring was done consistently through a network of hired and trained field employees and trained partner organizations.[34]

Today, improved Internet connections and new communication options across and within countries mean that staff in Nairobi can directly collaborate with colleagues in Singapore, Accra or New York via Zoom, WhatsApp, Skype, and so on. The shutdown of workplaces around the globe due to COVID-19 brought the world's attention to the importance of these technologies, but even prior to that, social entrepreneurs working internationally relied on these communication tools to expand their organizations' reach. Communicating with customers and beneficiaries has been facilitated by the growing prevalence and sophistication of mobile phone technology, especially in emerging markets. Mobile phones continue to proliferate globally, including in rural and low-income regions, and they can act as powerful distribution channels for education, credit, market research, extension services, and much more. Ashoka Globalizer Fellow and founder of ZMQ Software Solutions, Hilmi Quraishi, uses mobile technology to promote health and safety through games, with the aim of changing community behavior.[35] FarmDrive, a Kenyan financial technology company, performs credit scoring using machine learning and alternative information such as agronomic and satellite data in order to lend to smallholder farmers on their feature phones.[36] In many cases, customers and beneficiaries are leapfrogging feature phones altogether and going straight to smartphone devices, through which they can access even more services.[37]

The rise of mobile money payment technology in Sub-Saharan Africa has also supported last-mile business models, revolutionizing sectors like off-grid energy. d.light found that even though its lights cost as little as $8 in the early years, this cost remained a substantial investment for families living on just a few dollars a day. The company therefore became an early pioneer of pay-as-you-go (PAYGo) technology through which individuals can make small installments against the cost of a product via mobile money. d.light developed its own platform which included "payment systems, customer support and inventory management tools" and in 2016 began offering its proprietary system, called d.light Atlas, to its partners.[38] According to the 2020 Off-Grid Solar Market Trends Report, as the availability of mobile money technology grows outside of East Africa, the PAYGo model will increase the affordability of solar products for customers in new markets and help companies achieve profitability and scale.[39]

## #4: Boost Team Performance

The first and most important aspect of technology adoption is not the team's commitment to technology, but the team's commitment to systematic performance measures. As Brian Trelstad, former Chief Investment Officer of Acumen Fund, wrote: "If your organization doesn't care about metrics, don't bother to start building systems to measure performance."[40] Trelstad reinforces that this commitment needs be pervasive throughout the organization, from its board and leadership, to each employee, and in Acumen Fund's case, each investee as well. Similarly, Room to Read leaders emphasize that, "What gets measured, gets done"; as the organization grew, this meant having operational reporting feed into a common dashboard that each country manager up to the C-suite could use to measure organizational performance.[41] Deloitte in its research of top public companies emphasizes the same:

> it's in all actors' interests to help develop the empirical evidence at organization and system level of the way environment and sustainability [E&S] impact contributes to the longer term sustainable success of an organization. This requires the education and immersion of all in this topic up and down the organization and all the way through the value chain.[42]

These measurement systems are critical to accelerate and improve performance and efficiency:

> We [Acumen Fund] started to be more consistent by collecting data quarterly in clearly designed spreadsheets, but as our portfolio team grew from five people in our New York office to 15 people in four offices (including Hyderabad, India, Karachi, Pakistan, and Nairobi, Kenya) we looked for a software solution that would allow us to track performance over time, performance against initial projections, and performance across the portfolio.[43]

According to Hagel III and Brown (2017), the future workplace will be shaped by the concept of "scalable learning," wherein technology is harnessed "to augment the capabilities of people."[44] Technology integrations with scalable learning enable employees to learn faster as the team grows, to upgrade their skills and increase their productivity. "Routine tasks do need to be automated, but for the purpose of freeing up people to explore new approaches to create even more value. In this context, one key dimension of learning is for workers to discover how to more effectively use increasingly powerful digital tools in specific contexts."[45] Furthermore, employees notice whether their leaders are leveraging technology sufficiently. There is research that shows that organizations with "innovative cultures" that embrace technology perform better in the competition for strong talent. Compass, the nonprofit consulting firm, reviewed the nonprofit ecosystem and found a performance gap in outcomes between those nonprofits that invested in necessary technology and those that did not, a gap that widened over time. "Those that ignore technology can fall into a vicious cycle of ignoring change, not innovating, not capturing the value that comes with a flexible, adaptable organizational culture."[46]

Room to Read's founders emphasized that their technical-assistance program allowed the organization to do more for less, a common goal for any scale-up effort.[47] By incorporating some of the startup stack tools widely available today, social entrepreneurs can enhance their team capacity while remaining lean. There are likely some low-effort ways for incorporating technology, such as using Slack to boost team communication, or Smartsheet to manage projects, or file storage tools like Google Drive, Sharepoint or Dropbox to collaborate and share documents. Still, there tend to be great opportunities beyond these solutions and even basic tools often have untapped functionality. To realize the full potential of more comprehensive technology adoptions, organizations typically must build technical talent on the team and foster buy-in throughout the organization.[48]

## #5: Get Organization-wide Buy-in

Of the hundreds of nonprofits Salesforce.org surveyed in 2019, 93 percent considered the lack of skilled technical staff as a challenge to adopting new technologies at their organizations, second only to budgetary constraints.[49] Relying on contractors is common for lean organizations, especially to get the minimum viable product up and running, but while this approach may be wise at the pilot stage in order to make quick pivots, keep overhead costs low, and avoid hiring full-time employees prematurely, it is rarely the right strategy for scaling.[50] In its early days CommonLit, an education technology nonprofit that offers educators digital tools and resources to enhance their literacy programs, contracted junior engineers to develop the first version of their free online platform for teachers and students. But when the early version gained traction and the organization secured a $3.9 million grant from the Department of Education, it built a technical team composed of back-end and front-end engineers with the skill-set and commitment that would enable the organization to meet its growing technical demands, including the requests for additional feature upgrades over time.[51]

For scale, it is important to have a long-term outlook and to have the team capacity to incorporate user feedback and address major technical challenges quickly, especially when the product is reaching thousands, if not millions of customers and beneficiaries.[52] Beyond hiring for technical expertise itself, there are a number of common actions that have made some nonprofits more successful than others at leveraging their technical teams: (1) having technical expertise at the senior management level; (2) making sure digital heads lead, or at a minimum, stay involved in decision-making on new initiatives; and (3) creating a hybrid or intentionally independent digital team structure where digital responsibilities are distributed across multiple teams that actively collaborate. Most critically, successful organizations empower their technical teams by including them in both strategy and decision-making processes.[53]

As we've mentioned, there are numerous simple ways to start using technology – videoconferencing, communication platforms, cloud storage, CRMs, and so on – and in cases where technology is foundational to product or service delivery, having engineers and product managers on the team is a given. Where organizations often struggle is in leveraging technology to radically improve their processes, given that such opportunities require significant upfront investment and the immediate benefits are not always obvious. Consider these example operational workflow challenges: an organization relies on multiple back-and-forth emails to gather basic information from customers; the development team has to constantly compile, clean up and analyze data from various sources just to report to funders or apply for grants; program staff use separate Excel sheets to track expenses that the finance team must then spend hours or days to reconcile. These are common issues that a more significant technology adoption strategy could help resolve.

In studying the GA team's approach, we found that there were several elements that made their technology roll-out a success. Some of these were not surprising: (1) they ran test pilots; (2) they chose industry-appropriate products; (3) they had a qualified technology support team in-house; and (4) they secured the funding to fully implement a measured system adoption organization-wide. The biggest insight that we found, however, was that GA excelled at getting staff at every level and department involved in the process, which ended up being transformational for the organization. For example, Marcus Berkowitz, the VP of Technology and Innovation, led GA's technology upgrade efforts and had the full support of GA's CEO, Andrea Jung. Yet GA didn't take a purely top-down approach, nor did they lean too heavily on only technical staff. Instead, GA's leaders involved the team in various ways and at different points in the process to create inclusion and feedback loops. They did this first by creating a task force, which was made up of leadership members from across departments, to guide key decision-making while preparing and launching the pilot and then organization-wide final product roll-out. They tested the technology product in two very different branches and meaningfully incorporated field staff input on a variety of questions including which features to include, which options should go in the dropdown menu, and how meeting attendance should be recorded. They dedicated significant time to training staff to use the new technology and patiently implemented it throughout the US in a staged approach. Lastly, in order to get each branch excited and comfortable about the adoption, they leveraged nontechnical but highly respected frontline staff in each branch to be "Mambu Champions," who helped their team members adjust and ensured branch issues were resolved in a timely manner.[54]

When it comes to these deeper organization changes, top management cannot rely on the technical team alone to solve all the bugs in a new technology, nor to get full staff buy-in. Technology adoptions that affect the larger team should not leave the team out of the process.

Without cross-organizational, practical insights, candid feedback and enthusiastic support, even platforms that show promise as pilots can fail at organization-wide implementation.

## #6: Keep Supporters Engaged

From the beginning, Kiva realized that building powerful connections between microlenders and small business owners in emerging markets was one of its strengths. While borrowers' stories were first shared in an ad hoc manner and through the self-initiated blogging of a staff member in Uganda, co-founder Matt Flannery found that Kiva's service resonated with donors/lenders because they cared "about the progress of an entrepreneur half-way across the planet. There was, to some degree, a sustained mental and emotional connection. Whether the connection had a positive feel was secondary. These tiny, interpersonal loans were creating a consciousness that didn't exist before."[55] Kiva's platform ultimately became more than just a mechanism to unlock financing; it also became a catalyst for meaningful connections between people with dramatically different life stories.

Social entrepreneurs can utilize numerous technology tools to reach more supporters, improve storytelling and transparency, track funder interest and contributions, and measure impact. Salesforce.org found that nonprofits continue to face higher and higher expectations around engagement, transparency and reporting from donors.

> As individual donors are also consumers enjoying innovation in their personal lives, their expectations as donors regarding their experiences with nonprofits are also rising … Today's donors continue to expect more, as 69% of nonprofits say the demand for transparency regarding funding has increased at least moderately over the past five years.[56]

Room to Read customized a project-specific database, so that timely and specific information on donor funded projects could be generated quickly in order to build a stronger connection between a donor and the work he or she had sponsored. This data also rolled up to more general reports such as their "Global Results and Impact Report" used for a plethora of external audiences.[57]

Increasingly, as mentioned in Chapter 4, social media platforms have become key communication channels through which SEs attract customers, donors, volunteers and advocates. In the US in 2019, 72 percent of American adults were on at least one social media platform (up from 5 percent in 2005) and the number of platforms has grown steadily.[58] According to marketing and communications firm M+R, nonprofits saw their audience size grow by 13 percent on Facebook, 44 percent on Instagram, and 15 percent on Twitter in 2017 over 2016.[59] Making the most of social media as a channel through which to amplify an organization's message requires a well-thought-out strategy and engagement plan. "The power of social media lies in its potential for storytelling," according to TechSoup.[60] Just as SEs hone in on their customer and beneficiary personas to achieve product–market fit, the same detailed understanding should flow into how they share their message with other stakeholders.[61] SEs can drill down into detailed analytics on each platform to evaluate how posts are performing and they can research publicly available statistics on platform use by demographic group.[62]

Social media has also been shown to facilitate "peer-to-peer" fundraising through which supporters share posts, spark excitement and build the supporter network by tapping into their social networks. Peer-to-peer fundraising has the benefit of introducing SEs to new audiences through the trusted avenue of friends and family. Fundraising itself often happens on crowdfunding platforms such as Indiegogo, GoFundMe, and Ketto or via donation-facilitation tools like Facebook's payment platform for nonprofits and Google.org's One Today app. New donor-engagement apps arrive regularly, such as Givelify, which helps donors make donations via the app and offers nonprofit organizations free software to manage incoming contributions so that there is "no need to send [donors] home with a pledge card and hope for the best."[63] Room to Read has heavily invested in social media, running Facebook campaigns to reach financial supporters, growing "double digits every year."[64] Having a social media presence can tie directly to non-donation-based fundraising; Back to the Roots (BTTR) raised $250,000 in startup capital through Kickstarter to launch its aquafarm fish tank product line.[65]

Effective storytelling not only attracts first-time supporters, but also brings the transparency and engagement that donors increasingly expect. While sending out the occasional newsletter still has value, SEs often find greater success by regularly posting content, responding to community comments, and promoting member-led events on their social media accounts.[66] FTUSA, for one, saw online platforms as a means to facilitate connections between consumers and the farmers and factory workers who produce Fair Trade Certified products. According to FTUSA founder, Paul Rice:[67]

> Because almost all of our producer families around the world are online now, a connection via Facebook or some other platform could enable an unprecedented level of transparency into the lives of the people who make the products we buy. Ultimately, we believe this human connection across the world could help build awareness, understanding, and consumer demand for fair trade.

## TECHNOLOGY-RELATED CHALLENGES

Technology clearly has a critical role to play in supporting SEs to go from idea stage, to acceleration, to scale, but it can also introduce challenges of which social entrepreneurs should be aware. We will touch on a few internal and macro-level challenges – maintenance and training costs, IT reliability, data privacy, unintended consequences, and labor market disruptions – and some related mitigation strategies.

The rapid evolution of technology means that SEs must take maintenance costs into account during planning and budgeting and should keep an eye on the obsolescence of their technological infrastructure. When investing in systems, even affordable ones, entrepreneurs should consider what will be needed to stay up to date, both in terms of system costs and in training employees and customers.[68] On the customer side, "Technology education costs might be high: The users of Uber and Alibaba are well versed with technology. But when similar solutions are pushed to everyone, technology know-how and awareness proves to be an unforeseen hurdle."[69] In the prior example of the use of mobile payments in d.light's model, d.light did not introduce mobile money technology, but rather, took advantage of it once the infrastructure had become commonplace. Furthermore, for organizations operating across geographies, or working with different sets of populations (i.e., by age, income, educational levels), their familiarity with technologies can be widely different. For example, mobile money usage is commonplace in Kenya, but less so in Zambia.[70] Organizations need to adapt their models to fit the technologies that their customers and beneficiaries are used to, or otherwise be prepared to take on the additional work of technology acquisition, technical support and customer training.

Within an organization, there are a number of required steps that should be taken to derive the most value from the adoption of new technologies. These activities include the process of choosing which technology product to use, creating working groups, selecting a technology lead, customizing a new system to reflect the optimal process for an organization, migrating data from old to new systems and educating employees to use new systems. GA's technology-driven transformation included many of these steps, and the new platform roll-out took years to complete, including two small-scale pilots, multiple rounds of product iterations and staff training sessions.[71] Vision, patience and strong project management help social entrepreneurs achieve successful roll-outs and long-term success in their technology initiatives.

SEs operating in regions with unreliable networks and more limited technological infrastructure will need fallback plans when faced with the inevitable power cuts, Internet shutdowns, government restrictions and network interferences. The Kearney–Ashoka report found that in India the "lack of quick and effective IT systems, coupled with connectivity constraints in remote locations of India, make it difficult for social enterprises to implement automated processes and ensure quality of operations. As operations scale, the extent of these challenges amplify."[72] While there are still numerous opportunities that technology can offer SEs working in such contexts, some of the principles covered in the chapter will have to be customized to withstand these challenges. This might include proactively developing operating plans for how to continue with service or product delivery without digital channels, purchasing a backup generator for the office, and having clear communication protocols within the team to stay connected and delegate work to staff unaffected by connectivity and power disturbances.

There has been widespread news coverage of companies like Equifax, Under Armour, MyHeritage and Yahoo being hacked, exposing the personal information of millions of people and hurting the reputations of those companies.[73] Such breaches are not only a concern for well-known companies; SEs and nonprofits have experienced such events as well.[74] Hand-in-hand with the opportunities presented by robust data collection come very real data privacy concerns. It is ultimately the responsibility of organizations to follow the necessary steps to protect the personal information they gather about their stakeholders, including employees, volunteers, customers, beneficiaries and donors. Further, if observation is used to track beneficiary use of products, SEs owe it to themselves to ask for those beneficiaries' consent, even if the country in which they are operating does not require it.

We encourage SEs to first assess what data they are collecting and how it might be at risk for privacy breaches. For example, using e-commerce platforms to collect payments, donations and event fees, storing and transferring personally identifiable information like employee records, beneficiary medical information, or collecting preferences of donors and newsletter subscribers, are all examples of actions that gather private data and therefore require enhanced security measures. If an SE (or its vendors) collects personal information, then it should evaluate how and where it is stored and what the legal responsibilities are associated with holding that data. Even when there are no potential legal repercussions, there are likely to be reputational risks should such information be exposed.[75] Ultimately, SEs should follow best practices to ensure they meet legal requirements and avoid negative reputational repercussions. There are now numerous resources available to help SEs determine their risk exposure and analyze the costs and benefits of taking certain actions.

In addition to the business-level challenges associated with technology use, there are macro-level trends associated with the growing presence of technology in our lives that can result in negative and unintended consequences. As way of illustration, consider Facebook and other social media platforms more broadly. Facebook has enabled connections between people across geographies, has helped people receive updates of important life events from friends and family, and in many countries, Facebook acts as an important source of news and locally relevant information. However, there are growing concerns that platforms like Facebook accelerate the spread of misinformation[76] and the invasion of privacy, and its use has been associated with increased symptoms of depression.[77] This issue has become central again in the discussion of privacy in contact tracing of those infected with COVID-19.[78] In another example within the SE field context, researchers at UC Berkeley found that recipients of cook top stoves in Darfur refugee camps overreported their use of the stoves when asked by survey, in comparison to simply observing use patterns by having a sensor attached to the stoves.[79] Ethically, this raises questions around whether the recipients should be notified that they are being observed. But by notifying users, the accuracy of the data collected is then likely to be influenced as users might use the stoves more, as they now know they are being observed. This example illustrates the underlying tension between gaining accurate data to understand product use and effectiveness and the privacy that observed individuals are entitled to have.

Meera Chary of Bridgespan and Christopher Keefe of Omidyar suggest applying design thinking principles in the product development stage and beyond as one way to identify potential negative consequences to product and/or service interventions. They gave the example of Hopelab, which "employed design thinking to develop a video game to encourage children with cancer to stick with their regimes. They were vigilant about testing and monitoring its impact to avoid negative consequences, for example distracting young cancer patients from adhering to their treatments, versus empowering them."[80] A disturbing example of a medical technology having severe unintended negative consequences was the distribution of ultrasound machines in India in the 1970s to improve maternal health during childbirth. Once women discovered the sex of their babies pre-birth, female children were more frequently aborted, leaving a lasting imbalance in the number of males versus females decades later.[81] Clearly, the unintended effects of technology can be complex, and some consequences take years to even become noticeable, leaving the fallout outside of an SE's control. While social entrepreneurs may not be able to anticipate and avoid every potential negative consequence of their intervention, by more actively engaging with beneficiaries throughout the product development and testing process, social entrepreneurs can make important course corrections before beginning large-scale roll-outs in the field.

Another concerning macro trend for many social entrepreneurs is around the role of technology in the "future of work," as many technologies, some highlighted in the chapter, are already disrupting the labor market. Many jobs are being replaced by advanced technologies like artificial intelligence (AI), machine learning and robotics, and researchers suggest that the disruptive force of technology on the labor market will only increase.[82] Individuals who are low-income, lack a four-year degree, or live in specific regions are especially vulnerable to these changes and often do not have the tools to navigate the evolving economy successfully. At the same time, new jobs are emerging and many employers struggle to fill mid-skilled positions, especially in sectors like healthcare, information technology, and advanced manufacturing.[83]

While it is not in scope for this book to dive deeper into the role of technology on job displacement and job creation, it is worth calling attention to this trend. Using technology will have an impact on an organization's workforce, including team composition, size and skill-sets. Many of the insights shared on building a strong team outlined both in this chapter and in Chapter 1 are nevertheless critical, and in some ways even more so with future technological disruptions. Furthermore, there is an increasing number of nonprofits, for-profits and public institutions focused on supporting workers through labor market disruptions. By incorporating best practices for inclusive recruitment and lifelong learning, social entrepreneurs can contribute towards making the labor market work for more people as changing technologies displace old jobs while creating new ones.

# KEY CHAPTER TAKEAWAYS

The COVID-19 pandemic has exposed the inherent vulnerability that comes with being an entrepreneur, where unexpected shocks can change the communication between teams, and the growth trajectory of an organization overnight. Technology has not been a silver bullet during this pandemic, nor will it be in future crises, but it has proven to be a vital component of organizational health and adaptability, allowing many teams to continue to perform in the face of a global health crisis. In this chapter we have discussed ways technology can be a part of building towards a more resilient and scalable model of field reporting, operational excellence, and measurement. As society comes out on the other side of this pandemic, we expect new lessons on technology's role to emerge, and we encourage social entrepreneurs to pay close attention.

## Key Takeaways

- *The development of innovative and affordable technologies has opened up a world of possibilities for resource-constrained SEs to launch and scale.* The startup stack has significantly reduced the costs associated with growing an organization. Digital channels like social media and mobile phone technology have enabled social entrepreneurs to access a broader group of customers, funders and beneficiaries.

- *Ground technology usage in sound principles* for organizational success. Consider creating a framework that evaluates the key factors for success as a way to identify avenues through which technology can measure and increase impact and help the organization achieve scale. In other words, *do not invest in technology just for technology's sake.*
- *Bring on the necessary talent to make the most of technology's potential.* Advanced technologies are becoming increasingly user-friendly and accessible. Still, to reap the full benefits that technology has to offer, invest in skilled technical talent and make sure to include them in relevant decision-making. Further, invest in training and retraining all team members, not just members of the technology team or the chief technologist.
- *Expect deeper technology integrations to take time, effort and resources.* When rolling out new software and tools, be ready to invest more than just money to make them a success. Successful technology adoption is a multistage process of selecting the right technology, discovering how it will change teams' workflows, what data needs to be migrated, what training for staff and other stakeholders might be required, and which team members need to be hired or reassigned to direct the work. Don't shortcut or underestimate how much time it can take to migrate from one platform to another. Maintaining and updating systems to avoid obsolescence are ongoing requirements.
- *Be alert to unintended consequences.* As new technologies arise and old technologies are used in novel ways, there can be unforeseen consequences that emerge over time. There are both macro-level changes taking place, like worker displacement, and negative impacts created at the organization level. At a minimum, SEs should ensure they follow best practices, like protecting personal information, and monitoring how their products and services are being used over time in order to mitigate negative externalities as proactively as possible.

## CASE STUDY
## GRAMEEN AMERICA (GA)

Andrea Jung had just finished another long day at her office in New York and was reflecting on the year ahead. As the newly appointed CEO of GA, a US-based nonprofit that provides small loans for credit- and asset-building to women who live below the poverty line, she knew that her organization was at a critical inflection point.

When Jung first arrived, she was surprised to find that GA still required borrowers to make their loan payments in cash. It was clear to Jung that GA could not continue

**Figure 7.1**     GA logo

37. Menon, Naveen, Varun Arora, Shevika Mishra, Abhishek Malhortra and Abhishek Poddar. "Technology as a Catalyst to Scale." *A.T. Kearney*, www.atkearney.com/communications-media-technology/article?/a/technology-as-a-catalyst-to-scale.

38. "d.light Comprehensive Pay-As-You-Go Solar Financing Platform Now Available to Global Partners." *Omidyar Network*, 29 June 2016, www.omidyar.com/news/dlight-comprehensive-pay-you-go-solar-financing-platform-now-available-global-partners. Accessed 17 June 2020.

39. "Off-Grid Solar Market Trends Report." *International Finance Corporation*, February 2020, p. 46. Lighting Global, www.lightingglobal.org/wp-content/uploads/2020/02/14005VIV_OFF-GRID-SOLAR-REPORT-V13-Exec-Sum-AW4vis.pdf. Accessed 17 June 2020.

40. Trelstad, Brian. "Simple Measures for Social Enterprise." *Innovations: Technology, Governance, Globalization*, vol. 3, no. 3, 2008, p. 112. MIT Press Journals, doi.10.1162/itgg.2008.3.3.105. Accessed 17 June 2020.

41. Ganju, Erin, and Corey Heyman. *Scaling Global Change: A Social Entrepreneur's Guide to Surviving the Start-Up Phase and Driving Impact*. Wiley, 2018, Hoboken, NJ.

42. "Technology Enabled Impact Reporting Practice across the Investment Chain." *Social Impact Investing Implementation Taskforce*, 2018. Impact Investing Institute, www.impactinvest.org.uk/wp-content/uploads/2020/01/Read-the-full-report.pdf. Accessed 17 June 2020.

43. Trelstad, Brian. "Simple Measures for Social Enterprise." *Innovations: Technology, Governance, Globalization*, Summer 2008, p. 112. MIT Press Journals, doi.10.1162/itgg.2008.3.3.105. Accessed 17 June 2020.

44. Hagel, John, III, and John Seely Brown. "Great Businesses Scale Their Learning, Not Just Their Operations." *Harvard Business Review*, 7 June 2017, hbr.org/2017/06/great-businesses-scale-their-learning-not-just-their-operations. Accessed 17 June 2020.

45. Ibid.

46. Laporte, Suzanne, Douglas Kelly, and Tosin Agbabiaka. "Can Technology Transform the Nonprofit Sector?" *Yale Insights*, Yale School of Management, 29 May 2018, insights.som.yale.edu/insights/can-technology-transform-the-nonprofit-sector. Accessed 17 June 2020.

47. Ganju, Erin, and Corey Heyman. *Scaling Global Change: A Social Entrepreneur's Guide to Surviving the Start-Up Phase and Driving Impact*. Wiley, 2018, Hoboken, NJ.

48. Barenblat, Kevin. "How Tech Can Maximize Social Impact." *Stanford Social Innovation Review*, July 6 2017, ssir.org/articles/entry/how_tech_can_maximize_social_impact. Accessed 17 June 2020.

49. Ragones, David. "Nonprofit Trends Report." Report no. 2, *Salesforce*, February 2020, www.salesforce.org/wp-content/uploads/2020/02/2nd-edition-Nonprofit-Trends-Report.pdf. Accessed 17 June 2020.

50. Barenblat, Kevin. "How Tech Can Maximize Social Impact." *Stanford Social Innovation Review*, July 6 2017, ssir.org/articles/entry/how_tech_can_maximize_social_impact. Accessed 17 June 2020.

51. Ibid.

52. Ibid.

53. Mogus, Jason, and Austen Levihn-Coon. "What Makes Nonprofit Digital Teams Successful Today?" *Stanford Social Innovation Review*, 6 February 2018, ssir.org/articles/entry/what_makes_nonprofit_digital_teams_successful_today. Accessed 17 June 2020.

54. Walske, Jennifer M., Elizabeth Foster, and Laura D'Andrea Tyson. "Grameen America: The Pivotal Role of Technology in Scaling." *The Regents of the University of California*, 1 July 2018. Berkeley Haas Case Series B5918, p. 7.

55. Flannery, Matt. "Kiva and the Birth of Person-to-Person Microfinance." *Innovations: Technology, Governance, Globalization*, vol. 2, no. 1–2, 2007, pp. 52–3.

56. Ragones, David. "Nonprofit Trends Report." Report no. 2, *Salesforce*, February 2020, www.salesforce.org/wp-content/uploads/2020/02/2nd-edition-Nonprofit-Trends-Report.pdf. Accessed 17 June 2020.

57. Ganju, Erin, and Corey Heyman. *Scaling Global Change: A Social Entrepreneur's Guide to Surviving the Start-Up Phase and Driving Impact.* Wiley, 2018, Hoboken, NJ.

58. "Demographics of Social Media Users and Adoption in the United States." *Pew Research Center*, 12 June 2019, www.pewresearch.org/internet/fact-sheet/social-media. Accessed 17 June 2020.

59. Peyrot, Amy. "Social Media Director's Guide to 2018 Benchmarks." *M+R*, 31 May 2018, www.mrss.com/about. Accessed 18 June 2020.

60. Harrison, Hanna. "7 Tips for Fundraising on Social Media." *Techsoup*, 8 August 2018, blog.techsoup.org/posts/7-tips-for-fundraising-on-social-media. Accessed 18 June 2020.

61. "How Nonprofits Can Use Social Media to Boost Donations." *Digital Marketing Institute*, digitalmarketinginstitute.com/en-us/blog/how-nonprofits-can-use-social-media-to-boost-donations. Accessed 18 June 2020.

62. Harrison, Hanna. "7 Tips for Fundraising on Social Media." *Techsoup*, 8 August 2018, blog.techsoup.org/posts/7-tips-for-fundraising-on-social-media. Accessed 18 June 2020.

63. "Nonprofit Donation and Church Giving App." *Givelify*, www.givelify.com. Accessed 18 June 2020.

64. Ganju, Erin, and Corey Heyman. *Scaling Global Change: A Social Entrepreneur's Guide to Surviving the Start-Up Phase and Driving Impact.* Wiley, 2018, Hoboken, NJ.

65. "The 25 Most Creative Consumer and Retail Brands – Back to the Roots." *Forbes*, www.forbes.com/pictures/ghmf45lmgk/back-to-the-roots/#1eb8a8e77a84. Accessed 18 June 2020.

66. Rees, Sandy. "Best Practices in Using Social Media for Fundraising." *Get Fully Funded*, 30 July 2019, getfullyfunded.com/social-media-for-fundraising. Accessed 18 June 2020.

67. Walske, Jennifer, and Laura Tyson. "Fair Trade USA: Scaling for Impact." *The Regents of the University of California*, 1 May 2015. Berkeley Haas Case Series B5836, p. 142.

68. Menon, Naveen, Varun Arora, Shevika Mishra, Abhishek Malhortra and Abhishek Poddar. "Technology as a Catalyst to Scale." *A.T. Kearney,* www.atkearney.com/communications-media-technology/article?/a/technology-as-a-catalyst-to-scale.

69. Ibid.

70. Chironga, Mutsa, Hilary de Grandis, and Yassir Zouaoui. "Mobile Financial Services in Africa: Winning the Battle for the Customer." *McKinsey & Company*, 1 September 2017, www.mckinsey.com/industries/financial-services/our-insights/mobile-financial-services-in-africa-winning-the-battle-for-the-customer.    Accessed 18 June 2020.

71. Walske, Jennifer M., Elizabeth Foster, and Laura D'Andrea Tyson. "Grameen America: The Pivotal Role of Technology in Scaling." *The Regents of the University of California*, 1 July 2018. Berkeley Haas Case Series B5918, pp. 11–12.

72. Menon, Naveen, Varun Arora, Shevika Mishra, Abhishek Malhortra and Abhishek Poddar. "Technology as a Catalyst to Scale." *A.T. Kearney,* www.atkearney.com/communications-media-technology/article?/a/technology-as-a-catalyst-to-scale.

73. Mele, Christopher. "Data Breaches Keep Happening. So Why Don't You Do Something?" *The New York Times*, 1 August 2018, www.nytimes.com/2018/08/01/technology/data-breaches.html. Accessed 18 June 2020.

74. Coca, Nithin. "How Data Privacy Regulations Affect Nonprofits – and What They Can Do." *Triple Pundit*, 5 November 2018, www.triplepundit.com/story/2018/how-data-privacy-regulations-affect-nonprofits-and -what-they-can-do/55976. Accessed 18 June 2020.

75. "Cybersecurity for Nonprofits." *National Council of Nonprofits*, www.councilofnonprofits.org/tools -resources/cybersecurity-nonprofits. Accessed 18 June 2020.

76. Frenkel, Sheera, and Katie Benner. "To Stir Discord in 2016, Russians Turned Most Often to Facebook." *The New York Times*, 17 February 2018. Accessed 18 June 2020.

77. Steers, Mai-Ly N., Robert E. Wickham, and Linda K. Acitelli. "Seeing Everyone Else's Highlight Reels: How Facebook Usage Is Linked to Depressive Symptoms." *Journal of Social and Clinical Psychology*, vol. 33, no. 8, 2014, pp. 701–31, doi:10.1521/jscp.2014.33.8.701. Accessed 18 June 2020.

78. O'Brien, Matt, and Christina Lawson. "Here Come COVID-19 Tracing Apps – and Privacy Tradeoffs." *The Denver Post*, 10 May 2020, www.denverpost.com/2020/05/10/coronavirus-tracing-apps-privacy/. Accessed 18 June 2020.

79. Wilson, Daniel Lawrence, Mohammed Adam, Omnia Abbas, Jeremy Coyle, Angeli Kirk, Javier Rosa and Ashok Gadgil. "Comparing Cookstove Usage Measured with Sensors Versus Cell Phone-Based Surveys in Darfur, Sudan." *Technologies for Development: What is Essential?*, edited by Silvia Hostettler, Eileen Hazboun and Jean-Claude Bolay, Springer International Publishing, 2015, Cham, Switzerland, pp. 211–21, doi:10 .1007/978-3-319-16247-8_20. Accessed 18 June 2020.

80. Chary, Meera, and Christopher Keefe. "Technology's Best Bet for Scaling Social Good? Ask the People Who Need the Social Good." *Fast Company*, 9 April 2015, www.fastcompany.com/3044849/technologys-best-bet -for-scaling-social-good-ask-the-people-who-need-the-social-g. Accessed 17 June 2020.

81. Manchanda, Samiksha, Bedangshu Saikia, Neeraj Gupta, Sona Chowdhury, and Jacob M. Puliyel. "Sex Ratio at Birth in India, Its Relation to Birth Order, Sex of Previous Children and Use of Indigenous Medicine." *PLoS ONE*, vol. 6, no. 6, 2011, doi:10.1371/journal.pone.0020097. Accessed 18 June 2020.

82. McKay, Conor, Ethan Pollack and Alastair Fitzpayne. "Automation and the Changing Economy. Part 1: The Case for Action." *The Aspen Institute*, April 2019, assets.aspeninstitute.org/content/uploads/2019/ 04/Automation-and-a-Changing-Economy_The-Case-for-Action_April-2019.pdf?_ga=2.250984582 .1676132748.1589514782-104131720.1586320377. Accessed 18 June 2020.

83. Fitzpayne, Alastair, Conor McKay, and Ethan Pollack. "Automation and the Changing Economy. Part 2: Policies for Shared Prosperity." *The Aspen Institute*, April 2019, assets.aspeninstitute.org/content/uploads/ 2019/04/Automation-and-a-Changing-Economy_The-Case-for-Action_April-2019.pdf?_ga=2.250984582 .1676132748.1589514782.

# 8
# Measuring impact

As we bring this book to a close, we end with the most important differentiator between traditional for-profit entrepreneurial startups and social startups: the social startup's *impact*. In fact, the main purpose of a social startup is to address societal problems (Dees, 1998),[1] which often persist due to government and/or market failures (Austin et al., 2006).[2] But within the field of social entrepreneurship, it's often not enough to solve a social issue on a limited basis – social startups are often seen as catalytic, seeding transformational and systemic change to then be scaled and replicated elsewhere. The challenge for those wanting to be changemakers, then, often surrounds how to evidence that societal change is happening and, secondly, prove that this change is directly attributable to the social startup itself. As scholars assert: "One of the main barriers to capitalizing fully on the activities of social entrepreneurs is that we rarely have good, timely, rigorous, cost-effective measures of social impact."[3] This chapter aims to address this concern by summarizing how best to tie impact to the deep-seated mission of a social startup, including ways in which impact can be measured, both simply and effectively, over time. Through our research on young social enterprises (SEs), we have found that when impact metrics and "business" metrics move in lockstep, an SE is far more likely to collect high-quality and timely data that in turn leads to product, service and business model improvements. In fact, when a startup is young, that is the best time to put good impact evaluation practices in place, so that as the organization scales, so too does its evidenced impact.

Looking across the panel of firms that we interviewed for this book, we asked each of the founders how they defined impact, and how the impact that their organizations delivered met the dual criteria of *intentionality* and *additionality*.[4] Secondly, we looked at each organization's mission statement, asking how the metrics they tracked supported their impact proof statements, and if the impact measurement changed in sync with mission shifts over time, to get as close as possible to proving *causality*: that the programs and/or products delivered by an SE led to intended outcomes. In reality, we found that perfectly matching metrics to mission is one of the most challenging tasks within SEs. The challenge is, as sociologist, William Bruce Canon stated: "Not everything that counts can be counted."[5] Similarly, we would add that not everything counted, counts.

As a result, early-stage social startups and the firms that fund them, are more likely to opt for (in the words of Brian Trelstad, former Chief Investment Officer at Acumen Fund and now Partner at Bridges Fund Management) "frequent, simple measures"[6] that allow founders to change course and diagnose problems early. In the trenches, measuring impact is often intricately tied to core business performance, such as the number of products or services that a social startup delivers to its target constituents. Examples in our sample of firms include: the total number of solar lights sold, the number of loans given to entrepreneurs in developed and

developing countries, the number of low-cost baby incubators given to low-income populations, the number of toilets deployed in Kenyan informal settlements, and the number of meals
served to children in low-income schools.[7] In the field of social impact, there is a counterar-
gument which states that tracking these types of "outputs," related to the number of products
or services deployed, isn't enough. In fact, the principle of *additionality* states: "Don't be
redundant,"[8] meaning that if others are providing similar services to what your social startup is
providing, then there needs to be a proof case of why this product or service is better than other
options currently being delivered. The second key principle is *intentionality*, which means
that an organization's impact shouldn't be accidental; instead, it should be directly tied to the
organization's core mission statement and purpose.

Often, with the delivery of products and/or services, there are secondary ways in which
organizations provide social benefit, such as improved employment, workforce skills building,
and/or greater awareness of social issues, which can lead to wider and deeper funding sources
for the sector. In our sample set of firms, localized product development and delivery led to
an increase in employment opportunities, an unintended impact evidenced in startups located
both in developed countries (i.e., Revolution Foods (RevFoods)) as well as developing countries (i.e., Sanergy). While these are secondary, unintended impacts (positive or negative), the
core activities of the social startup were intentional. In our view, this ancillary and unintended
social impact should still be considered when capturing total organizational impact as many
social problems rarely receive too much attention. The greater problem becomes when "competing" solutions create confusion within beneficiary segments because they are deployed in
an uncoordinated way.

Both professional and academic publications over the last decade evidence that impact
measurement has become an increasingly salient topic for social entrepreneurs when seeking
the funding, support and the validation that they need in order to scale their operations.
Beneficiaries, donors, investors, mentors, partners, distributors, suppliers and just about every
other potential stakeholder can benefit from understanding how an organization derives its
impact, and how it plans to deepen or broaden its impact over time. On a larger scale, when
dealing with widespread program implementation (at the national or global level), the pressure to produce evidence of impact is only amplified. As authors Gertler et al. state:

> Impact evaluations are part of a broader agenda of *evidence-based policy making*. This
> growing global trend is marked by a shift in focus from inputs to outcomes and results,
> and is reshaping public policy. Not only is the focus on results being used to set and track
> national and international targets, but results are increasingly being used by, and required
> of, program managers to enhance accountability, determine budget allocations, and guide
> program design and policy decisions.[9]

However, the process of gathering, organizing and presenting impact data raises a number
of challenges for the leaders of SEs. Throughout this chapter, we will explore the benefits
and costs associated with robust impact measurement, provide a framework for the design of
measurement programs, and discuss relevant tools and methods for communicating impact
performance to key stakeholders.

Before diving into the measurement of an SE's impact, it is important to establish what "impact" means. According to Professors Alnoor Ebrahim and V. Kasturi Rangan of Harvard, the established literature refers to impact as the "significant or lasting changes in people's lives, brought about by a given action or series of actions."[10] Ebrahim and Rangan also highlight a growing emphasis on connecting impact to the "root causes" of a social problem, and then measuring the organization's specific role in the resulting social change, to directly link attribution back to the organization.[11] Regardless of the exact definition of "impact," the trend towards demanding greater accountability and transparency from SEs is clear. This places the onus on SEs, even those that are still early stage, to have a plan for diligently measuring and communicating the results of their organization's work to their stakeholders.

These expectations around "proving" the impact of an SE's work can make impact measurement seem like an onerous reporting process, prompting organizations to approach it from a defensive stance rather than a learning mindset. However, just as tracking finances and keeping detailed books brings value to the business outside of getting a clean opinion from auditors, impact measurement also offers a number of benefits for the SE beyond reporting to funders. Alternatively, validating impact can easily slide into an expensive and time-consuming endeavor, warping organizational priorities. It is our view, therefore, that an SE should align its impact measurement practices with both the stage and resources that are most appropriate for its size and not overinvest in impact measurement when the organization is still nascent. It's further critical that the impact data obtained by the organization is valuable to its leadership team foremost, and not done just to satisfy, for example, a funder's request. Last, impact measurement is least impactful when it is done infrequently – which is why for early-stage organizations, we recommend program monitoring instead of external program evaluation.

## THE BENEFITS OF IMPACT MEASUREMENT

As mentioned previously, collecting data on the social and/or environmental performance of the venture can at times seem burdensome, costly and a distraction from the "core" work of building a financially sustainable SE.[12] Impact measurement is definitely an investment, and sophisticated approaches to measurement can be expensive. However, if done well, impact measurement can also be one of the greatest sources of insight in determining an organization's strategic direction, in aligning team goals and motivation, and serving as a point of external validation for the organization's work. We see four key benefits to impact measurement: *goal-setting, impacting validation, fundraising,* and *ensuring stakeholder engagement.*

As the international nonprofit organization, World Vision, puts it: "Measures can motivate."[13] Many SEs find that setting an overarching impact target can serve as a "north star" in orienting the SE to a shared, consistent and ambitious target against which strategic questions and milestones can be measured. For example, at World Vision, after years of running programs in heterogeneous markets with different definitions of what constituted success, the team set out to define and adopt a common perspective of what *the* problem that they were trying to solve actually was, and how World Vision was uniquely solving it. Rather than keeping an ambiguous goal like "access to clean water," the organization eventually defined "access to clean water" as "having a protected clean water source available 12 months of the year within a 30 minute round-trip walk from a person's household."[14] Converging on this more targeted goal aided World Vision in getting more specific on the problem itself: only 45 percent of the population where World Vision operated in Africa had water access, suggesting that there was another 15 million people in need. Being clear on its goals also gave World Vision a uniform metric to communicate with donors and measure progress against.[15]

Measurement can also serve to validate (or invalidate) an organization's impact. As noted in Chapter 5, validating the SE's *impact* hypothesis is one of the three areas (along with *growth* and *value*) that an SE must consistently employ throughout its life cycle. While isolating the net impact of an SE's work is complex, doing so also ensures that its work is achieving desired results. This validation acts as an accountability mechanism not only for the SE, but also for the other stakeholders involved, such as public funders, who are in some cases deploying tax-payers' dollars to address deep-seated social issues. Further, impact measurement is not merely backward-looking, it is also a way to identify areas for improvement; by analyzing and further disaggregating impact data, social entrepreneurs have the opportunity to identify where their solution's design or implementation might be lacking. Through the process of problem iden-tification, solution delivery and ongoing impact performance measurement, there is never a point in an SE's life cycle when actively seeking out customer and beneficiary feedback is no longer valuable. In this way, collecting and evaluating impact data is not unlike Eric Ries's customer development process as described in Chapter 5.

There are four areas which can be difficult to instrument when it comes to program evalu-ation,[16] which is why we suggest program monitoring instead. The first is difficulty in meas-urement. For example, if the organization's goal is to "empower marginalized populations," how exactly does an organization measure that its services directly helped populations feel less marginalized? The second difficulty can be in the area of data collection. In some cases, there could be privacy laws that prevent organizations from tracking target populations' improve-ments, most particularly over time. Third, often there are many reasons why a population segment might or might not improve – and this probably does not (and probably shouldn't) rest solely on one organization's product or service. This is why proving causality – tightly linking impact performance to one specific solution – can be very difficult to prove in the field. Finally, most solutions require ongoing community engagement and monitoring,[17] as well as an element of "systems thinking" wherein the whole problem and solution are considered a bit more anthropologically and through observation, in order to ensure the social outcome an organization seeks.[18]

For example, let's say that an organization's goal is to provide clean water to a remote village, in keeping with the goals of World Vision as mentioned earlier in this chapter. Even when clean water is provided to a centralized location in a village, water could still become contaminated from the point of collection if beneficiaries use dirty water containers. In the home, water could also become tainted if the same cup is used to dip into the water each time, or if the water container isn't properly covered. Even at the centralized village water pump, if maintenance is not ongoing and the pump stops working, then no clean water is going to the villagers. Further, if a powerful gang overtakes the pump and starts charging villagers for water, then only those with an ability to pay will have access to clean water. By not having ongoing monitoring there could be numerous issues impeding a local village from having access to water, even though the pump itself was installed properly. In fact, one has to look no further than the disastrous implementation of PlayPump[19] to understand how good intentions can go awry without ongoing program engagement and monitoring.

This leads to the final point in this section: that impact measurement should be built not only with the engagement of a larger community of stakeholders but through the eyes of one's beneficiaries as well. Acumen Fund, which built an industry-leading impact management practice that eventually spun off into what is now 60 Decibels, wrote in 2015 that: "Collecting data on social performance opens up a channel to communicate with customers, thus also providing opportunity to gather consumer feedback, data on customer segmentation, and market intelligence."[20] Further, by listening to one's beneficiaries, SEs are demonstrating the continued priority of this stakeholder group, despite the competing and often stronger pulls towards an SE's funders. As impact management expert and co-founder of Social Value International, Jeremy Nicholls, states: "Measuring social impact is about giving power to those affected by the work of an organization. Like financial accounting, it should provide information so that stakeholders—usually, in the case of nonprofits and SEs, the beneficiaries—can hold organizations to account."[21]

## THEORY OF CHANGE

The most important place to start when defining an organization's impact, after clarifying the organization's mission and purpose, is to create the organization's theory of change (ToC), also referred to as a logic model. An organization's ToC is so central to its being, that it has been described as "the explanation and justification for why you are about to embark on this social venture you are planning, why it will work, and why people should join you and invest in your solution."[22] From a historical perspective, the use of a ToC is rooted in the evaluation of USAID development projects during the 1960s.[23] Since then, the ToC has now become the most common framework used in the field of social innovation. As Gertler et al. state: "Theories of change depict a sequence of events leading to outcomes; they explore the conditions and assumptions needed for change to take place, make explicit the causal logic behind the program, and map the program interventions along logical causal pathways."[24] In sum, a ToC aims to represent an organization's approach and how its activities lead, over time, to real change and a positive impact for the social or environmental issue that the SE is tackling.

A ToC is also often designed with one's stakeholders in mind. According to Gertler et al.:

> The best time to develop a theory of change for a program is at the beginning of the design process, when stakeholders can be brought together to develop a common vision for the program, its goals, and the path to achieving those goals. Stakeholders can then start program implementation from a common understanding of the program, how it works, and its objectives.[25]

Given that partnerships are often central to solving social issues, co-creating a ToC with one's partners is therefore key to achieving an organization's mission and desired results. For example, several organizations might be united in addressing hunger, homelessness, disease eradication, lack of affordable healthcare, and so on. The bigger the social issue, the more likely that collaboration is necessary, and that the complexity of an organization's ToC increases:

> One of the key dimensions on which theories of change vary is their degree of complexity, as measured by the number of activities required to create the desired outcomes. For organizations seeking to produce value on a broad array of dimensions, identifying the requisite interventions and ensuring that they are all in place is a complex undertaking. Helping to stabilize troubled families, for example, might entail the provision of counseling, day care, and housing support, as well as economic assistance and job training.[26]

A concrete example of this level of complexity, at scale, can be seen with Aravind Eye Care, located in India. "In 2012 alone, Aravind Eye Hospital (Aravind) performed over 340,000 surgeries, most of them for cataract surgeries in one province in India, and it screened over ten times that number of people. Its outputs are remarkable: providing vision correction to over 3 million individuals since its founding in 1979." [27] However, the organization's outputs (i.e., the number of patients screened or treated) do not fully speak to the organization's impact nor do they fully align with Aravind's mission, which is "to cure needless blindness." To this end, the organization asks how many people who received treatment were satisfactorily cured. Fortunately, receiving surgery or correcting vision is closely aligned with curing blindness (note: some diseases, such as retinitis pigmentosa, cannot be cured as easily through surgery or vision correction, but those diseases are relatively rare). If instead Aravind's mission were to eliminate not only blindness, but poverty as well, addressing that latter mission would be far more complicated. Even though blindness might be associated with poverty, there are clearly other factors associated with poverty as well, such as a lack of access to education, lack of job training, and poor job mobility.

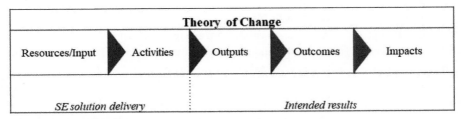

**Figure 8.1**  Theory of change

The key components of a ToC (Figure 8.1) include:

- *Inputs*: the SE's resources, such as funds, staff, technology and expertise.
- *Activities*: the SE's core work as instrumented through its operational activities.

- *Outputs*: the near-term results of the SE's activities, such as "units sold," "students taught," etc.
- *Outcomes*: the *change* in results, such as "reduction in malaria infections," or "increase in college acceptance rates."
- *Impacts*: effect on the root cause of the problem that is attributable to the SE's work that would not have happened were it not for the SE's activities.[28]

The process of measuring defined outputs (with some linkages to outcomes) provides social entrepreneurs with the datasets that can either prove or disprove their underlying hypotheses that, in turn, justify the existence of their organizations. For newly established social startups, forecasting deployment of one's products or services is tracked as "outputs." In contrast, "outcomes" are more closely tied to an organization's mission and/or goals, including goals that are often aspirational. This can be problematic if there is a disconnect between the aspirational goals within an organization's mission statement and the products/services that it actually delivers in the field. For startups, it can be challenging to collect enough meaningful data to evidence product or program effectiveness, with often very few organizational resources, both financial and otherwise. However, instilling an organizational commitment to data collection over time can help ensure that this data remains consistent (critical for year-over-year comparisons) and meaningful, as the organization grows.

At the point of building a ToC, most social entrepreneurs will already have a good sense of the social issues that they are targeting and how their work addresses these issues. However, they might not yet have the empirical evidence to back up that connection, nor a clear idea of the steps needed to map outputs to outcomes. As a result, ToCs can give structure to an otherwise difficult and messy process, enabling organizations more holistically to test their assumptions about their solution's impact. It is also a well-known and widely accepted method for conveying an SE's impact goals. While the highest bar in program evaluation might be through such techniques as randomized control trials (RCTs), which create both a treated and untreated group to test and compare, this method's sophistication means SEs often have to hire third parties to do this work. These evaluations can then cost in the hundreds of thousands of dollars and require extensive data to be statistically significant. As such, most startups lack the data and the funding to conduct RCTs.

We suggest that instead, empirical research from academic institutions can serve as a bridge between data collection (i.e., outputs) and the SE's desired outcomes. For example, RevFoods does track the number of lunches served to lower income children (as that is part of the government reimbursement process), but it does not track how these same children perform scholastically; in other words, the organization cannot prove through its own data collection that its healthy meals result in scholastic achievement. Getting access to this type of data alone is problematic: student identities are considered confidential to school districts. Given the turnover and attrition in school populations, it would be very hard for RevFoods to have continuity in its data over time, even if it had access to student performance information. Instead, RevFoods considers anecdotal feedback from school teachers and administrators on what they are observing in the classroom, and lean into published research that shows that better nutrition leads to better brain function, classroom attention and scholastic performance over time.

In thinking about the current pandemic, we invite you to think of how you'd map out an organization's ToC if it were focused on disease eradication. Clearly, this would be a multifaceted ToC involving public and private partnership, as well as collective action from citizens. What would you add to the ToC in Table 8.1?

**Table 8.1  ToC example**

| COVID-19 Vaccine | | | | |
| --- | --- | --- | --- | --- |
| Resources/Input | Activities | Outputs | Outcomes | Impacts |
| Employees/Scientists | Production of a vaccine | Administering the vaccine | Disease eradication | Reduction of loss of life |
| Financial support | Clinical trial | Efficacy tracking | Minimal negative impact of vaccine | Resumption of economic activity |
| Facilities for drug development | Ongoing reporting & regulatory approvals | Tracking of side effects | Wide drug availability and publication of results | Return to school, colleges, etc. |

*Source:* Authors.

Given the downsides of having an overly ambitious ToC, as the COVID-19 example in Table 8.1 might evidence, why then would an SE take on a large social issue like a pandemic? SEs at times feel pressured to overreach on their ToCs in order to capture donor attention, and to command a large following in the social innovation community. This is especially true when confronted with funders who impose specific versions of the ToC structure and expect complete solutions to be delivered within a short period of time. Sean Stannard-Stockton, the founder and CEO of Tactical Philanthropy Advisors, argues that while the idea of a ToC makes sense in a "static landscape, where you can learn more and more about what works and what doesn't and finally craft the perfect theory," it "fails in a dynamic landscape, such as social change, where what you learned on your last trip might not apply this time."[29] Stannard-Stockton asserts that instead, SEs should focus on building great organizations rather than great ToCs. Acumen Fund takes the following view, which brokers a compromise between these extremes:

> Our principle [*sic.*] objective is not to know with certainty that impact can be attributed to a particular action or intervention. Our objective is to collect data with an appropriate degree of rigor that gives voice to our customers, including a more objective window into their experiences of a given product or service, and helps the businesses we invest in use this data to keep an eye on their social metrics and manage toward ever improving levels of social performance.[30]

As an impact management group, Social Value UK explained: "Your ToC is not a 'magic wand' that can solve all of your planning and evaluation challenges, but it will start your thinking about how you are going to create as much impact as you can."[31] So in building a ToC, we suggest erring on the side of an applied and ongoing method for program management and improvement, and the view that some measurement is better than no measurement. As the famous French writer Voltaire said, "perfect is the enemy of good."[32]

Building a ToC that will scale with the venture adds another layer of complexity. First, an organization has to consider what aspects of its solution are suitable to scaling: "The more complex an organization's theory of change, the more difficult it is to replicate, which is why its leaders' ability to specify the activities that create their program's value is so important."[33] This means, akin to principles around lean product development and creating a minimal viable product (as mentioned in Chapter 5), SEs that want to scale should consider the fewest program elements that are needed to produce the organization's desired impact. As Jeffrey Bradach suggests, before scaling: "an organization has to be able to show that its theory of change is strong, that its initial outcomes are encouraging, and that it has systems in place to track key performance data going forward."[34] Ebrahim and Rangan give the example of City Year, a Boston-based nonprofit which places college-bound students taking a gap year into high schools in less advantaged areas, with the goal of increasing high school graduation rates.[35] While many aspects of the program are worthy of duplication, Ebrahim and Rangan ask if *all* aspects of the program are. For example, is it necessary that all corps members wear red jackets, or that companies sponsor individual teams in order for City Year to reach its desired outcomes?

## BEST PRACTICES IN SOCIAL IMPACT ASSESSMENT

We've discussed the benefits of creating a diligent impact measurement practice early on, but how can an SE actually get started? Matthew Forti, Managing Director of One Acre Fund, advises social entrepreneurs to pursue impact evaluation only when "you are crystal clear about your organization's target population, approach, and outcomes, and have internal data that shows you are consistently reaching that population, delivering intended services, and achieving intended outcomes."[36] A study of 30 leading US nonprofits found that measurement was useful to the organizations for improving outcomes, particularly when they set measurable goals linked to mission, kept measures simple and easy to communicate, and selected measures that created a culture of accountability and common purpose in the organization.[37]

Like many elements of an SE's work, impact measurement is something that can evolve over time as the SE's products and business model are refined, and as the organization attracts the resources and talent it needs in order to implement a more rigorous impact measurement process. But in the beginning, it's most important to start conducting impact measurement simply and consistently to ensure that this practice becomes part of the SE's DNA, rather than a onetime or only occasional event. This means that mission and measurement must align, so that program assessment can be ongoing (and not weakened) when an organization grows its depth and breadth. Regardless of where an SE is in its development, one can apply the straightforward four-step cycle: *Plan, Do, Assess, Review* to organize and implement an impact measurement process, as developed by the G8 Social Investment Taskforce.[38] Each step is described in greater detail in the subsections that follow.

## Plan: Outline Your Impact Model

Diving into implementation without a clear plan often leads to avoidable mistakes, wasted resources, and potentially long-term reputational costs if the organization is measuring the wrong things, or even measuring the right things poorly. Planning for impact measurement is especially important when the SE is in its early stages and developing a clear articulation of its impact story. This story should stem from an analysis of how the SE's activities touch on the root causes of a problem, and how these activities can lead to both near-term outcomes and long-term impact. Through the articulation of the organization's ToC, the SE is able to identify what kind of salient metrics it should measure and then develop the methods for doing so. Over time, this planning stage will hopefully become more iterative and less foundational, although a major pivot and re-evaluation is probably required at different stages of the organization's life cycle.[39]

Planning starts with setting goals for the impact the organization aims to achieve, and this is typically encapsulated in an organization's ToC, discussed in detail earlier in this chapter. The next step is scoping out the most salient metrics to track from the activities, outputs and outcomes that stem from the ToC. The SE is likely to find that there are dozens, if not hundreds, of potential metrics to track, so it is best to consider how the venture will use these metrics. As we've stated before, impact metrics are most powerful when tied to the business model and are tracked as key performance indicators (KPIs). Just as it was critical to differentiate between actionable metrics and vanity metrics during the business model development process, so too is it important to differentiate between those impact metrics that are meaningful and those that are not, by asking three questions: (1) which metrics validate the impact hypothesis? (2) which metrics inform the delivery of the impact? and (3) which metrics are most objectively and clearly linked to the organization's work? As the organization grows and attracts funders, it will likely be encouraged to collect a number of common metrics for the sector, such as "CO2e emissions mitigated" or "beneficiaries reached," and will grow to rely on standardized metrics such as IRIS+.[40] It therefore might be wise to start using sector or industry standard metrics early on, to avoid redoing data collection later, making year-over-year comparisons that much more difficult.[41]

The following sequence of events contains some suggested specific areas to resolve, before measurement (as given from the G8 Social Investment Taskforce, and modified by the authors):[42]

- Define/create a ToC.
- Articulate the expected positive or negative changes that result from the organization's work (outcomes).
- Characterize the most important metrics linked to the organization's mission.
- Be specific as to which goals are driven by the organization, and which goals might be more dependent on the ecosystem, and/or collaborative effort.
- Identify key stakeholders' roles in that ToC and involve them early on.
- Determine a baseline (pre-intervention metrics) if available. If there is no baseline to use for comparison purposes, then consider a counterfactual measure (what would happen

if the SE's solution was not available, for example) by observing a treated or untreated group. If this is not possible, link impact findings to related studies already done that can serve as a bridge in linking an organization's outputs to outcomes.

- Incorporate recognized metrics language that is relevant to the organization's place within its solution domain or region, balancing relevance with generalizability.

## Do: Implement Your Core Mission

At its core, this step is about carrying out the SE's mission through its business model and associated activities. As recommended by the G8 taskforce, this includes: "Efficient and effective data collection and management of performance data, tak[ing] into account the necessary information technology, tools, resources, human capital and methods used to track data."[43] In early 2014, Acumen Fund created the Lean Data initiative, which was inspired by "lean" design principles, such that: "organizations get the best return when they: a) collect a small number of easily verifiable measures linked to their theories of change, b) do this regularly at every level, and c) couple data collection with analysis, learning, and action." This approach involves a shift away from reporting and compliance, moving towards gathering data that drives decisions using low cost-technology, generating high-quality data both quickly and efficiently on beneficiaries.[44]

As an organization scales, it will start collecting data on a broader set of actions and behavior that might seem unrelated to its direct impact, but the organization should continue to keep impact measurement in mind. Trelstad, for example, mentions that at Acumen Fund:

> Defining the outputs is critical. For us, it is not just "bednets," but some dimension of "bednets" properly deployed and used. Moving from narrow definitions of outputs as "products" toward definitions with some dimension of product service and quality acts as an important check on a race to least-cost delivery models.[45]

Most organizations already have feedback loops from customers and other stakeholders embedded throughout their activities. As a result, impact data collection can easily become part of this feedback process by building customer feedback surveys that incorporate questions about the SE's intended outcomes. Further, by disaggregating customer data by beneficiaries' demographics or sociographics (i.e., gender, race, income-level, educational background, geography, etc.), the SE can better understand its reach, and whether or not this falls within its intended beneficiary set.

As we discussed in Chapter 7, outside of surveys and other types of feedback loops (i.e., observation, small group focus groups), feedback from beneficiaries can be built into products in less obtrusive ways, such as installing sensors into products in order to gather real-time data on product use. There are of course ethical issues around data collection that is built into products, which must be navigated, but some argue that these results are far more accurate than relying on surveys or even focus groups, as users are likely to over or understate actual use. Even observation can have issues, as those who are knowingly being observed often behave differently than they might in a more natural context (which is known as the Hawthorne effect).[46]

## Assess: Collect and Measure The Results

This next stage of the process asks: What do the data and stories that have been collected tell you about the type and extent of impact your organization is having? As McCreless et al. put it,

> Each data collection exercise represents an opportunity to create value in multiple ways:
> - By testing assumptions about our impact, and hopefully, demonstrating impact to capital providers;
> - By refining products and services;
> - By channeling feedback from low-income consumers or producers to others engaged in the community (who may in turn be willing to share the cost of the evaluation).[47]

As we have stated in earlier chapters, measurement and data collection are not inherently valuable. More generally, measuring outcomes is possible under two conditions that are uncommon in the social sector: when the causal link between outputs and outcomes is well established, or when the range of the integrated interventions needed to achieve outcomes is within the control of the organization.[48] So what then should an SE consider when evaluating information that has been gathered? The approach should provide salient information and the social entrepreneur must actively assess what the gathered information can tell him about the SE's work and efficacy. This step is about data analysis and distilling what has been measured into valuable organizational insights.[49] The complexity of the impact measurement process, whether through a lean measurement approach or through a more expensive and time-consuming RCT, should align with the resources, requirements and expectations of the venture. More comprehensive studies come at a cost, but these might be required by donors or by industry. For example, Embrace ultimately had to conduct numerous clinical trials to credibly sell its product in India, as the infant warmer was a medical device for use with a very vulnerable population: premature infants. While expensive and time-consuming, the trials also served to prove the product's impact: the trial showed that Embrace's baby warmer had similar efficacy in comparison to a high-end incubator, at a fraction of the cost.

Further, SEs often choose to perform a mix of qualitative and quantitative impact measurements. While quantitative results can demonstrate statistically valid findings, qualitative tests are useful in adding nuance to findings that might otherwise be missed. Qualitative interviews can also be very useful in storytelling – important as we'll discuss later in communicating one's impact to stakeholders. Finally, objectives and measurement tools should be "SMART," which stands for specific, measurable, achievable, realistic and timely. For a diagram that shows the trade-off between time, money and accuracy in the different types of impact reporting that an organization can conduct, see Figure 8.2.

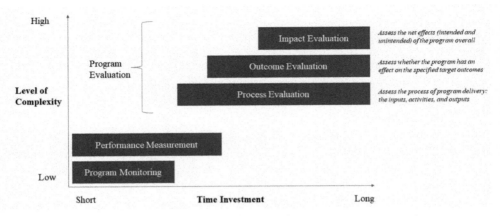

*Source:* Trochim and James Donnelly (2006), modified by authors.[50]

**Figure 8.2**     Methods comparison

The ultimate goal of any impact study is to be sure that it is: (1) *credible*; (2) *actionable*; (3) *responsible*; and (4) *transportable*. First, the data should be *credible*: it should accurately reflect and be representative of the research questions regarding the SE's impact. For a later stage SE, this might entail a rigorous evaluation of impact metrics gathered over time, while for a smaller, earlier stage venture, this might only be achieved by choosing and gathering information on just a few key metrics.[51] Two other characteristics of quality data collection include: (1) data that captures a complete picture of the users' experiences with a product or service; and (2) data that remains consistent over time to enable longitudinal studies or comparisons between activities over time.[52] Next, the data should be *actionable*; the information gathered should be used to adjust the organization's programs and products. As the monitoring and evaluation experts at Innovations in Poverty Action (IPA) stated, "Put simply: If all possible findings lead to the same decision, it is a waste of time and money to collect that information."[53] This underscores the difference between measuring impact to fulfill a reporting burden versus measuring impact to learn and improve organizational impact through data-driven decisions. Third, the data collection process should also be *responsible*, meaning that the resources and systems utilized to perform impact measurement should match the resources the SE has to put towards it. More is not always better, especially if insufficient resources lead to poor processes that undermine the quality of what is being gathered or if the SE does not have the capability (and additional resources) to analyze data once returned. Also, ethical issues do abound in data collection, especially when dealing with marginalized populations; pressing beneficiaries to answer countless surveys or participate in endless focus groups can become not only onerous, but potentially intrude on their privacy as well. Finally, impact data should be *transportable*. For data to be transportable, the SE must be able to take the associated learnings and apply them to other contexts, such as other programs or markets. Transportable also means that one's learnings can be shared and then potentially used by others in the field: "For transportability, you need to know something about why a program works, and be open and transparent about sharing learning with others."[54] Unique to the field of social entrepreneurship is a common commitment to creating shared knowledge, and in collectively solving social problems.

Chapter 7 touched on how technology, such as sensors and mobile phones, can be used in impact measurement. Root Capital, for example, uses tablets to improve the efficacy of its in-person surveying. Acumen Fund's impact measurement group (now 60 Decibels), primarily uses mobile phones for remote surveying.[55] Both organizations have utilized technology to improve their work but have also learned that "asking questions and collecting data via mobile phones takes considerable thought and attention." They therefore advise SEs to give their stakeholders notice before reaching out (such as alerting them that a survey is coming a day or two before). They also ensure that their approach takes into consideration the language and literacy levels of the target group, and limit the survey to fewer than ten questions, if possible, or offer an incentive if a more extensive set of questions is required. Finally, it is important to start any process by informing each respondent about confidentiality.[56]

## Review: Learn To Strengthen Your Impact

As the final step in the cyclical process, "review" is about creating a learning model for the organization and its stakeholders, both by sharing progress and turning the insights derived from the impact assessment into actions. Perhaps an organization's impact measurement reveals areas for improvement that then leads to changes in the product's service delivery model, the product's design, or the organization's marketing and outreach approach. Similarly, proof of success could highlight where the SE can deepen its engagement or find the validation it needs to scale further. Also, assessments could reveal gaps in solution sets, such that additional partnerships might be needed for a total solution delivery.

Finally, the organization might find that its impact is deficient compared to that of other organizations in the same sector. This possibility, in fact, is the reason why some organizations shy away from having robust impact measurements programs, to begin with; it's much easier to rely on storytelling that highlights the transformational change in a few beneficiaries' lives, rather than risk finding that those beneficiaries are simply too few to justify the cost and expense of running a program. If at the end of the day an organization's products and/or services are truly redundant in the sector, there are ways to address this too. We are seeing more nonprofits "merge" with other nonprofits so that beneficiaries are not left stranded and have access to even greater resources and richer solutions. As the Center for Global Development states:

> The value of an individual institution's activities or studies would be multiplied if complemented by collective efforts to identify policy questions of shared importance, to cluster studies around priority issues, to ensure that studies are reliable and valid, to register and disseminate studies, and to build research capacity in developing countries.[57]

The review stage is also about communicating the impact with external stakeholders, which we detail further in the section below.

## COMMUNICATING IMPACT

An example of impact measurement and communication can be seen in the company Sanergy, mentioned in previous chapters. Sanergy has the following mission statement: "Sanergy builds healthy, prosperous communities by making safe sanitation, accessible and affordable for everyone, forever – starting with the urban slums of Nairobi, Kenya."[58] To communicate its impact, the company describes it in the following way:

> Each Sanergy Fresh Life latrine provides sanitation to 77 people and costs only $350 to construct, compared to traditional community toilets that can cost up to $25,000 to build. A single Fresh Life toilet is also expected to generate between $800 and $1,000 per year in profit for the entrepreneur, many of whom operate several latrines or operate them adjacent to existing businesses. The Sanergy model nurtures the growth of a sustainable business ecosystem and offers a pathway to prosperity for local entrepreneurs while addressing sanitary conditions that affect 2.6 billion people.[59]

Note that this paragraph is peppered with facts, demonstrating a social return on investment for its served beneficiaries not only in providing more cost-effective access to sanitation, but in providing income as well. It also links to an ambitious mission statement and contextualizes it within a global scale relating to the importance of sanitation (a United Nations' Sustainable Development Goal).

As we finish this chapter, in addition to measuring impact, as the Sanergy example shows, it's also important to think about how an organization communicates its impact. In a joint report by ACEVO, Social Enterprise UK, SROI Network and others, there are six recommendations for communicating an organization's impact. These include: *Clarity, Accessibility, Transparency, Accountability, Verifiability* and *Proportionality*. *Clarity* is somewhat obvious: impact reporting should show the link between organizational mission, its programming and its effectiveness. Often, an organization might mistakenly be too "into the weeds" in its reporting, preventing those less familiar with a sector from easily comprehending how the organization indeed provides a unique solution to a pressing social problem. Circling back to the chapter's initial concepts, a communication plan should also demonstrate the organization's *additionality* – how it uniquely provides value in addressing social issues above and beyond what others are providing, as well as the organization's *intentionality* – that its efforts match the organization's aims.

An impact communication plan should also be *accessible*, so that relevant information can be found by anyone who looks for it, in a range of formats suitable for different stakeholders. This is followed by *transparency*, such that reporting is open and honest. No solution is perfect, and hiding that imperfection will only build distrust with one's stakeholders. *Accountability* goes hand in hand with timely reporting. It's important to remember that program monitoring is one way an SE can be held accountable to their most important stakeholder, those they serve. Impact metrics should also be independently *verifiable*. Verification can range from informal stakeholder feedback at one end of the spectrum, all the way to an external audit at the other end of a spectrum. We end with the recommendation that impact should reflect *proportionality*: the level and detail of reporting should be commensurate with the size of the organization and the complexity of the social issue that it's trying to address. Impact assessment in scope or expense shouldn't overshadow the actual delivery of the organization's innovative products and services. Similarly, when organizations get larger, spending too little on impact measurement can lead others to believe that impact authenticity isn't that important to the organization after all.[60] In sum, impact measurement helps an organization identify where it isn't meeting targets and needs to improve, where it is successful and should stay the course, and what learnings it can share with the social impact field at large.

## CHAPTER TAKEAWAYS

Given that positive social impact is *the* differentiator between a traditional for-profit and an SE, SEs must therefore diligently measure and validate that they're delivering on their missions. In our research, we found that the most scalable and meaningful approach to measuring impact was by incorporating salient impact monitoring into the SE's "standard" organizational performance tracking practices. Our advice in the complex area of impact assessment can best be summarized in the following takeaways:

- *Impact should be intentional and additional.* The SE's *additionality* validates that its product or service is better than existing options available, and/or that it reaches a previously overlooked population. The point of *intentionality* is that the organization's impact should not be an accident, but rather a well-intended byproduct of the organization's core activities and mission.
- *Impact measurement should primarily be used to increase organizational impact, not to simply meet funders' requirements.* While impact measurement can be a significant part of an SE's reporting requirements, it more importantly serves as an accountability mechanism for all of its stakeholders, including its beneficiaries.
- *SEs can best articulate their impact by framing them within a ToC, which provides the link between the organization's resources and activities and the ultimate outcomes it hopes to achieve.* Constructing a ToC helps SEs test their assumptions between the work they do and the impact they claim, by forcing them to form the logical pathway between their activities (for example: selling solar lamps), the outputs (number of solar lamps purchased or deployed), the outcomes (usage of the solar lamps) and impact (increase household productivity while decreasing exposure to harmful toxins). In sum, a ToC serves as a powerful communication tool for the organization.
- *By following the simple cycle of Plan–Do–Assess–Review, the SE can start small with targeted metrics that tie to their "business" metrics and develop their impact practice over time, as resources allow.* This approach to impact measurement can evolve over time to become more robust, but SEs do not have to wait until they can afford an RCT to incorporate impact measurement into their daily practices.
- *The final step of the cycle, "Review," is also about communicating the results beyond the SE's internal team.* Communicating impact provides an SE the opportunity to demonstrate accountability to its stakeholders and garner the attention and resources it needs to scale. Communicating impact should follow the principles of: *Clarity, Accessibility, Transparency, Accountability, Verifiability* and *Proportionality.*

## CASE STUDY
### BRIDGES FUND MANAGEMENT

In late 2016, in the New York offices of Bridges Fund Management (Bridges), Brian Trelstad, a Partner at Bridges, called his London-based colleague and fellow Partner, Clara Barby, to discuss the firm's impact analysis strategy. Both Trelstad and Barby were early pioneers in impact investing, with years of experience investing in SEs at Acumen Fund and then at Bridges.[61] Over the course of their careers they had wrestled with the challenges of measuring the impact of their investments, challenges they still saw as prescient within impact funds and SEs alike. They further considered how Bridges could grow its impact with its newly launched US-based fund, not only through direct investments but also through field-building work.

By the time of its US launch, Bridges had a long and storied history in impact investing. Bridges had launched in the United Kingdom almost 20 years previously, raising £40 million in its first fund from banks, local authority pension funds, private equity firms, entrepreneurs, and the UK government. At the time, Bridges was one of the few investors asking the question: "How can capitalism better serve society?" and explicitly considering impact alongside financial returns. Michele Giddens, Bridges' co-founder, recalled the hurdles the team faced when raising their first fund:

> What was very different, back in 2002, was that the concept of impact investing didn't really exist. Instead, there was a strong and widespread belief that there was a clear dividing line between trying to do good, which you do via philanthropy, and trying to maximize your risk-adjusted financial returns, which you do by whatever means necessary within the realms of what's legal.[62]

Across the various fund strategies and geographies, Bridges sought to catalyze impact across four themes: Health & Well-Being; Education & Skills; Sustainable Living; and Underserved Markets. In order to evaluate the potential for an investee's impact, the Bridges team would ask three key questions: What is the societal challenge that the investee aims to address? What is the SE's desired outcome? And, what is the strategy to get there? Bridges uses a number of

**Figure 8.3**      Bridges Fund Management logo

tools during its due diligence process prior to investing, including applying a ToC frame-work to determine target outcomes, and creating a materiality analysis to identify the risks and opportunities along Environmental, Social and Governance (ESG) factors. This pre-investment social impact analysis is ultimately summarized into an Impact Scorecard for each venture, known as KPIs. As Bridges put it: "If we get this right, the impact KPIs we track as an investor are simply smart business KPIs for our investees, demonstrating their positive contribution to society and their protection and enhancement of value for investors."[63]

When the Sustainable Development Goals (SDGs) were set by the United Nations in 2016 for attainment by 2030, Bridges incorporated this widely used blueprint by connect-ing its four impact themes to specific SDGs, including: "Good Health and Well Being"; "Quality Education"; "Decent Work and Economic Growth"; "Reduced Inequalities"; and "Sustainable Cities and Communities."[64] Utilizing the SDG terminology was a way for the firm both to hold itself accountable to impact outcomes and to communicate its impact goals more effectively to a global set of stakeholders.

By 2016 the firm had raised more than $1 billion in investment capital across 12 funds. Bridges was also taking on a proactive role in bringing more attention to the nascent im-pact investing ecosystem, not only by leveraging its years of experience and strong track record, but also by forming new teams and entities attached to Bridges. As a comple-ment to its funds, Bridges established a separate charitable arm (now called the Bridges Impact Foundation) to deploy capital towards opportunities within its four themes that were not investable by the company.[65] The Foundation's US office also established the MBA Impact Investing Networking and Training (MIINT) program in 2011, in partnership with the Wharton Social Impact Initiative, to train the next generation of impact investors through experiential learning.[66]

An in-house advisory arm, Bridges Impact+, was also created to build out the team's impact measurement and management practice, and to share best practices and tools with the broader impact community. These services were becoming increasingly important; impact investing was steadily growing in popularity and successfully attracting top talent from the finance world and the social sector. However, the growing interest in and matu-rity of the field were leading to a broad array of approaches to and definitions of impact. Critics began to complain that investment firms were merely "impact-washing" traditional investing in order to attract new clients and to differentiate themselves.

A growing criticism of impact investing was the lack of evidence that these investments were leading to positive societal outcomes. Funds varied in their approaches to impact measurement (if they practiced it at all) and there was no commonly used set of metrics.[67] As Trelstad put it: "even in this relatively small field, many of the players are thinking and talking about impact in very different ways. So finding some common ground – a common language for articulating our goals, and a common framework to measure our success against those goals – remains a huge challenge for the sector."[68]

Bridges' field-building work eventually led to the launch of the Impact Management Project (IMP) in order "to build consensus around the shared fundamentals of impact measurement and management."[69] Barby emphasized the need for advancing impact measurement towards a more standardized approach:

> In financial management, "general acceptance" of norms for how we talk about, measure and manage financial performance enables capital to flow efficiently across value chains and across borders. If we want impact management to become the norm for every enterprise and investor, as the U.N. Sustainable Development Goals demand, we need shared principles, reporting standards and benchmarking methods for impact.[70]

Bridges' co-founder, Philip Newborough, agreed:

> We spent many years developing our own tools and methodologies to help us invest for impact. But what we came to realize was that it doesn't make sense for all the different players in this market to devise their own competing methodologies; it just confuses the market. Far better to come together and agree on some very clear standards and definitions that are accepted across the market – then everyone can compete on maximizing impact and delivering the best possible results within that framework.[71]

As Trelstad and Barby looked to the future, they were heartened by the role Bridges could continue to play in the field of impact investing. As Bridges' funds steered financial capital to high-performing SEs and as platforms like MIINT and IMP drew together thousands of stakeholders, it was hard not to be optimistic about what would be accomplished by SEs and impact investors in the years to come.

## CASE QUESTIONS

1. What role does impact measurement play in the field of social entrepreneurship?
2. What are the challenges in creating a shared language around impact?
3. Do you see any difficulties in aligning an SE's impact measurement practices with what their funders expect? What causes this potential misalignment?

*For more information, see Berkeley Haas Case Series title *Bridges Fund Management: Navigating Changes in the Political Economy* (B5890).

# NOTES

1. Dees, J. Gregory. "The meaning of social entrepreneurship." 1998, available from http://the-ef.org/resources-Dees103198.html.

2. Austin, James, Howard Stevenson, and Jane Wei-Skillern. "Social and Commercial Entrepreneurship: Same, Different or Both?" *Entrepreneurship Theory and Practice*, vol. 30, no. 1, 2006, pp. 1–22.

3. Zeyen, Anica, Marcus Beckmann, and Susan Mueller. "Social Entrepreneurship and Broader Theories: Shedding New Light on the 'Bigger Picture'." *Journal of Social Entrepreneurship*, vol. 4, no. 1, 2012, p. 4.

4. Definition of additionality: defined as the extent to which desirable outcomes would have occurred without a specific intervention, noted in: https://www.pacificcommunityventures.org/2013/09/05/impact-investing-2-0-3-billion-tells-us-next-300-billion.

5. Cameron, William Bruce. *Informal Sociology: A Casual Introduction to Sociological Thinking*. Random House, 1963, New York, NY, p. 13.

6. Trelstad, Brian. "Simple Measure for Social Enterprises." *Innovations: Technology, Governance, Globalization*, Summer 2008, p. 107.

7. Walske, Jennifer, and Laura Tyson. "Built to Scale." *Entrepreneurship and Innovation*, vol. 16, no. 4, 2015, p. 272.

8. Bugg-Levine, Antony, and Jed Emerson. *Impact Investing: Transforming How We Make Money while Making a Difference*. Wiley, 2011, San Francisco, CA, p. 36.

9. Gertler, Paul J., Sebastian Martinez, Patrick Premand, Laura B. Rawlings, and Christel M.J. Vermeersch. *Impact Evaluation in Practice*. The World Bank, 2016, Washington, DC, p. 3.

10. Ebrahim, Alnoor, and V. Kasturi Rangan. "What Impact? A Framework for Measuring the Scale & Scope of Social Performance." *California Management Review*, Spring 2014, vol. 56, no. 3, pp. 118–41.

11. Ibid.

12. Adams, Tom, Rohit Gawande, and Scott Overdyke. "Innovations in Impact Measurement." *Acumen.org*, November 2015, acumen.org/wp-content/uploads/2015/11/Innovations-in-Impact-Measurement-Report.pdf.

13. Probus, Larry. "Measuring Impact: Keep It Clear and Simple." *SSIR*, 15 March 2013, ssir.org/articles/entry/measuring_impact_keep_it_clear_and_simple.

14. Ibid.

15. Ibid.

16. Brest, Paul, and Kelly Born. "Unpacking the Impact in Impact Investing." *SSIR*, 14 August 2013, ssir.org/articles/entry/unpacking_the_impact_in_impact_investing.

17. Walske, Jennifer, and Sophi Martin. "Applying Lean Startup Methodology in Developing Countries." *VentureWell*, 18 January 2017, www.venturewell.org/applying-lean-startup-methodology-developing-countries.

18. Brown, Tim. "Designers – Think Big!" *TED*, July 2009, www.ted.com/talks/tim_brown_urges_designers_to_think_big.

19. Murphy, Tom. "How PlayPumps are an Example of Learning from Failure." *Humanosphere*, 3 July 2013, www.humanosphere.org/basics/2013/07/how-playpumps-are-an-example-of-learning-from-failure.

20. Adams, Tom, Rohit Gawande, and Scott Overdyke. "Innovations in Impact Measurement." *Acumen.org*, November 2015, acumen.org/wp-content/uploads/2015/11/Innovations-in-Impact-Measurement-Report.pdf.

21. Nicholls, Jeremy. "People, Power, and Accountability." *SSIR*, 23 June 2014, www.ssir.org/articles/entry/people_power_and_accountability.

22. Chahine, Teresa. *Introduction to Social Entrepreneurship*. CRC Press, Taylor & Francis Group, 2016, Boca Raton, FL, p. 78.

23. Ebrahim, Alnoor, and V. Kasturi Rangan. "What Impact? A Framework for Measuring the Scale & Scope of Social Performance.", *California Management Review*, vol. 56, no. 3, 2014, pp. 118–41.

24. Gertler, Paul J., Sebastian Martinez, Patrick Premand, Laura B. Rawlings, and Christel M.J. Vermeersch. *Impact Evaluation in Practice*. The World Bank, 2016, Washington, DC, p. 3.

25. Ibid., p. 22.

26. Bradach, Jeffrey L. "Going to Scale." *SSIR*, Spring 2003, ssir.org/articles/entry/going_to_scale.

27. Ebrahim, Alnoor, and V. Kasturi Rangan. "What Impact? A Framework for Measuring the Scale & Scope of Social Performance." *California Management Review*, vol. 56, no. 3, 2014, pp. 118–41.

28. Trelstad, Brian. "Simple Measures for Social Enterprise." *Innovations*, Summer 2008, https://www.mitpressjournals.org/doi/pdf/10.1162/itgg.2008.3.3.105.

29. Brest, Paul. "The Power of Theories of Change." *SSIR*, Spring 2010, www.sc4ccm.jsi.com/wp-content/uploads/2016/07/The-Power-Of-Theories-Of-Change.pdf.

30. Adams, Tom, Rohit Gawande, and Scott Overdyke. "Innovations in Impact Measurement." *Acumen.org*, November 2015, acumen.org/wp-content/uploads/2015/11/Innovations-in-Impact-Measurement-Report.pdf.

31. Aps, Jaan, Ben Carpenter, Agata Fortuna, Jeremy Nicholls, Gonca Ongan, Serra Titiz, Elif Urgan et al. "Maximize Your Impact: A Guide for Social Entrepreneurs." *Social Value UK*, 24 October 2017, http://www.socialvalueuk.org/app/uploads/2017/10/MaximiseYourImpact.24.10.17.pdf.

32. "A Quote from Philosophical Dictionary." *Goodreads*, www.goodreads.com/quotes/215866-le-mieux-est-l-ennemi-du-bien-the-perfect-is-the.

33. Bradach, Jeffrey L. "Going to Scale." *SSIR*, Spring 2003, ssir.org/articles/entry/going_to_scale.

34. Ibid, p. 20.

35. *City Year*. www.cityyear.org.

36. Forti, Matthew. "Seven Deadly Sins of Impact Evaluation." *SSIR*, 22 February 2012, ssir.org/articles/entry/seven_deadly_sins_of_impact_evaluation.

37. Ebrahim, Alnoor, and V. Kasturi Rangan. "What Impact? A Framework for Measuring the Scale & Scope of Social Performance." *California Management Review*, vol. 56, no. 3, 2014, pp. 118–41.

38. "Measuring Impact." *Social Impact Investment Taskforce*, September 2014, s3.amazonaws.com/giin-web-assets/iris/assets/files/metric-details/GSG-IRIS-Measuring-Impact-WG-paper.pdf.

39. Ibid.

40. Iris+. *The GIIN*, www, iris.thegiin.org.

41. Brest, Paul. "The Power of Theories of Change." *SSIR*, Spring 2010, www.sc4ccm.jsi.com/wp-content/uploads/2016/07/The-Power-Of-Theories-Of-Change.pdf.

42. "Measuring Impact." *Social Impact Investment Taskforce*, September 2014, s3.amazonaws.com/giin-web-assets/iris/assets/files/metric-details/GSG-IRIS-Measuring-Impact-WG-paper.pdf.

43. Ibid.

44. Forti, Matthew. "Measuring to Improve vs. Improving Measurement." *SSIR*, 7 May 2013, ssir.org/articles/entry/measuring_to_improve_vs._improving_measurement.

45. Trelstad, Brian. "Simple Measures for Social Enterprise." *Innovations*, vol. 3, no. 3, 2008, https://www.mitpressjournals.org/doi/pdf/10.1162/itgg.2008.3.3.105.

46. Spencer, Elizabeth A., and Kamal Mahtani. "Hawthorne Effect." *Catalog of Bias*, 12 January 2018, catalogofbias.org/biases/hawthorne-effect/.

47. McCreless, Mike, C.J. Fonzi, Genevieve Edens, and Saurabh Lall. "Metrics 3.0: A New Vision for Shared Metrics." *SSIR*, 4 June 2014, ssir.org/articles/entry/metrics_3.0_a_new_vision_for_shared_metrics.

48. Ebrahim, Alnoor, and V. Kasturi Rangan. "What Impact? A Framework for Measuring the Scale & Scope of Social Performance." *California Management Review*, vol. 56, no. 3, 2014, pp. 118–41.

49. "Measuring Impact." *SSIR*, September 2014, s3.amazonaws.com/giin-web-assets/iris/assets/files/metric-details/GSG-IRIS-Measuring-Impact-WG-paper.pdf.

50. Modified from Trochim, William M., and James Donnelly. *The Research Methods Knowledge Base*, Atomic Dog Publishing, Inc., 2006, Cincinnati, OH, in "Introduction to Impact Measurement." *REDFworkshop*, 26 April 2019, redfworkshop.org/learn/impact-measurement.

51. "Goldilocks: Finding the Right Fit in Monitoring & Evaluation." *Innovations for Poverty Action*, February 2016, www.poverty-action.org/sites/default/files/publications/Goldilocks-Finding-the-Right-Fit-in-Monitoring-and-Evaluation.pdf.

52. Aps, Jaan, Ben Carpenter, Agata Fortuna, Jeremy Nicholls, Gonca Ongan, Serra Titiz. Elif Urgan et al. "Maximize Your Impact: A Guide for Social Entrepreneurs." *Social Value UK*, Autumn 2017, http://www.socialvalueuk.org/app/uploads/2017/10/MaximiseYourImpact.24.10.17.pdf.

53. Ibid.

54. Ibid.

55. Adams, Tom, Rohit Gawande, and Scott Overdyke. "Innovations in Impact Measurement." *Acumen.org*, November 2015, acumen.org/wp-content/uploads/2015/11/Innovations-in-Impact-Measurement-Report.pdf.

56. Ibid.

57. Savedoff, William D. "When Will We Ever Learn? Improving Lives through Impact Evaluation." *Center for Global Development*, May 2006, Washington, DC.

58. *Guidestar.org*. www.guidestar.org/profile/36-4688468.

59. "From Public Health Hazard to Organic Fertilizer: Franchising Human Waste in Kenya's Slums: Development Innovation Ventures (DIV) Portfolio." *U.S. Agency for International Development*, 26 May 2016, www.usaid.gov/div/portfolio/s2sanergy.

60. "Principles of Good Impact Reporting." *New Philanthropy Capital*, March 2012, www.thinknpc.org/wp-content/uploads/2018/07/Principles-of-good-impact-reporting-final.pdf.

61. "Our Team." *Bridges Fund Management*, www.bridgesfundmanagement.com/us/our-team/.

62. Walske, Jennifer, and Laura D. Tyson. "Bridges Fund Management: Navigating Changes in the Political Economy." *The Regents of the University of California*, 30 June 2017. Berkeley Haas Case Series B5890, p. 6.

63. "2013 Impact Report." *Bridges Ventures*, February 2014, www.bridgesfundmanagement.com/wp-content/uploads/2017/08/Bridges-2013-Impact-Report-screen.pdf.

64. Walske, Jennifer, and Laura D. Tyson. "Bridges Fund Management: Navigating Changes in the Political Economy." *The Regents of the University of California*, 30 June 2017. Berkeley Haas Case Series B5890, pp. 7–8.

65. Ibid.

66. Gan, Joanne. "Global MIINT Competition Brings Together Ten Business Schools to Compete for $50,000 Impact Investment Opportunity." *MIINT*, 17 April 2015, www.themiint.org/news/2015/4/17/global-miint -competition-brings-together-ten-business-schools-to-compete-for-50000-impact-investment-opportunity.

67. "Bridges Impact Ltd. Trustees Annual Report and Accounts." *Bridges Impact Foundation*, 31 March 2019, www.bridgesfundmanagement.com/wp-content/uploads/2019/10/Bridges-Impact-Foundation-Annual -Report-2019.pdf.

68. "The Challenge for Impact Investing Is Management, Not Measurement." *LSE Business Review*, 24 September 2017, blogs.lse.ac.uk/businessreview/2017/03/02/the-challenge-for-impact-investing-is-management-not -measurement/.

69. "Bridges Impact Ltd. Trustees Annual Report and Accounts." *Bridges Impact Foundation*, 31 March 2019, www.bridgesfundmanagement.com/wp-content/uploads/2019/10/Bridges-Impact-Foundation-Annual -Report-2019.pdf.

70. "A New Global Standard for Impact Management." *Bridges Fund Management*, 11 July 2019, www.b ridgesfundmanagement.com/us/a-new-global-standard-for-impact-management-and-measurement/.

71. Ibid.

# Conclusion to *Scaling the Social Enterprise*

The field of social entrepreneurship has evolved from a novelty to the mainstream. While a myriad of terms are used to describe businesses that want to do well and do good, such as "social innovation," "conscious capitalism" and "double- (or triple-) bottom lines," the trend is clear: nonprofits are being asked to be more innovative and for-profit firms are expected to be more socially conscious. Indeed nonprofits are increasingly embracing entrepreneurial approaches and innovations to deepen their impact and achieve financial sustainability,[1] and traditional businesses are beginning to recognize that issues like climate change and social justice are closely intertwined with their strategic priorities and financial performance.[2] Impact investing, a vital source of funding for many social entrepreneurs, has grown from a market size of $25 billion in 2013[3] to $715 billion in 2019.[4] Yet, while new social enterprises (SEs) are founded on a daily basis, there remain few examples of SEs that have been able to scale effectively. Further, research on entrepreneurship and business strategy is extensive but their application to SEs remains scant, even though SEs are tackling some of the most complex challenges.

To that end, our research explores how early-stage SEs can be built to scale through an in-depth comparative case analysis of eight SEs: Sanergy, Kiva, World of Good, Revolution Foods (RevFoods), Back to the Roots (BTTR), Fair Trade USA (FTUSA), d.light and Embrace, and then complementing this work with findings from published academic and practitioner research. These SEs' founders have each been confronted with barriers to scaling and have garnered hard-won lessons from which we can all learn. We specifically focused on the decisions they made during the first few years, when their organizations were most vulnerable. Key insights emerged that can be summarized as:

- Securing the organization's key human, social and financial capital;
- Building a brand and garnering early media attention;
- Developing the right business model and value chain to deliver impact;
- Incorporating the technology and impact measurement infrastructure needed to achieve the greatest level of impact using the resources available.

Throughout this book, we have also sought to elucidate theory by pulling in the practical experience of social entrepreneurs and impact investors. Finally, given the timing of this book's completion, we saw an opportunity to incorporate some of the emerging lessons from SEs currently navigating the economic, social and political tolls of the COVID-19 public health crisis.

We structured the book to focus around the building blocks for organizational efficacy and growth. In the social sector and startup world, access to financial resources gets much of the attention but, as we articulated in Chapter 1, human capital is even more critical at an organization's launch. The eight founding teams that we interviewed underscored that early-stage SEs should hire slowly and intentionally given the significant impact each new addition makes to not only the team's productivity but also its culture and mission. Research also emphasizes the importance of establishing a founding team with complementary skill-sets, diverse perspectives, role clarity and high levels of trust amongst members. Further, the SE's talent resources should go beyond the team to include partners, experts and advisors to ensure a vibrant stakeholder network. We explored the role of such stakeholders in Chapter 2, demonstrating that proactively building and managing a network of relevant stakeholders should always be an organizational priority. From industry experts to sector alliances, network connections offer some of the most precious resources for social entrepreneurs by providing guidance, introductions and credibility. The complexity and structural nature of most social issues means that an SE can rarely be successful in solving a complicated social problem alone; these issues persist at scale and must be solved at scale.

While having the right team and social capital are foundational, they are not sufficient for scaling; financial resources are absolutely necessary to fuel the growth of an SE. Further, the type of capital an SE can access will largely be determined by its corporate form, the focus of Chapter 3. Choice of corporate form has other implications beyond financing; for SEs like Kiva and FTUSA, the nonprofit structure was important for gaining the trust of both large corporations and beneficiaries and became a reflection of each organization's mission. For some organizations, such as BTTR and RevFoods, their for-profit structure enabled them to secure both large amounts of venture capital and distribution contracts with well-known retailers. SEs today have more options than ever before and are not limited to the traditional 501c3 or C Corporation structure. In fact, a growing number of SEs are attaining B Corp certification, incorporating as Benefit Corporations, or establishing hybrid nonprofit–for-profit structures (as several organizations in our study did) to advance their double-bottom line goals.

Chapter 4 centers on brand building and the significant role that media attention has played in enabling SEs to amass the resources and attention needed to propel them from obscurity into known entities. Studying current trends alongside the practical experiences of the eight SEs in our research, we found that organizations that received early media attention, which we term as becoming "media darlings," benefited from enhanced credibility that in turn led to new customers, increased access to suppliers, distribution channels and funders, and spurred organizational growth. Together, Chapters 1 to 4 focused on how early-stage SEs can amass the financial, social and human capital needed to enable mission delivery.

In Chapters 5 and 6, we dove into mission implementation. One major element of social entrepreneurship is that entrepreneurs marry startup concepts like lean innovation principles and customer development with a deep commitment to positive impact. The greatest contribution these business concepts make to social innovation is the focus on delivering a product or service that users not only need, but also want. Further, delivering a social innovation in an economically efficient manner sets the organization up to deliver impact at scale more easily. We found that testing hypotheses and remaining focused on validating product–market fit and replicability greatly accelerated the pathway to scale for most organizations. Chapter 6 further demonstrated the importance of developing a robust business model early on, including the careful consideration of how the SE's value chain can be a differentiator or risk for the organization. We specifically looked at strategic management theory including the wide body of value chain research on established firms and determined its applicability to early-stage social startups. Alongside the standard considerations of setting up high-quality manufacturing and distribution partnerships, SEs must also consider the mission alignment of their value chains. Specifically, they often must handle greater complexity and costs to get their products to overlooked consumers, while at the same time diligently monitoring the associated social and environmental costs of their supply chain, such as labor conditions and carbon emissions.

Lastly, we looked at the practices that SEs implement to foster ongoing learning and growth, namely technology integration and impact measurement. In Chapter 7, we studied the various use cases for technology within the SE context. Investing in technology infrastructure requires the outlay of time and resources and must be a well-designed process, but SEs that adopt such technology are then better able to deliver their services to hard-to-reach populations, increase the productivity of their staff, and communicate their impact with key stakeholders in a faster and more vibrant way. Similarly, in Chapter 8 we went into depth on a thread that ran throughout the earlier chapters: the importance of robust impact measurement and management practices. The process of establishing impact targets and a theory of change is foundational to strong stakeholder communication and business model development. It is our view that measuring impact should be both ongoing and "baked into" business operations, allowing the organization to then track it alongside other business performance indicators. Further, by implementing ongoing impact measures, SEs are not only in a position to validate their impact and attract more supporters: doing so also builds team motivation and ensures organizational goal alignment.

As we began the book we noted that there are millions of nonprofits and startups delivering positive impact in the world at a modest scale today, and this number is growing. The number of nonprofits in the US alone grew by 75 percent from 2000 to 2016. Yet, of the 1.3 million nonprofits in the US, 92 percent have budgets of less than $1 million.[5] While it is not always the intention of "grassroots" SEs to scale beyond this level, research highlights that SEs that lack scale are likely to struggle in raising funds,[6] achieving financial sustainability, and meeting the demand for their services.[7] In fact, the 2018 State of the Nonprofit Sector Survey found that the majority (57 percent) of nonprofits could not meet the demand for their services, especially those organizations serving low-income populations.[8] This phenomenon has likely only been heightened during COVID-19.

Our goal in writing this book was to give social entrepreneurs, and prospective ones, the insights and tools they need to achieve impact along what is an immensely challenging career path. Being a social entrepreneur can sound romantic; it captures the positive connotations of entrepreneurship, suggesting creativity, intelligence and grit, along with the halo effect of doing good in the world. As a society, we celebrate the success stories of entrepreneurs and admire those who also lead organizations in a visionary way, like Muhammad Yunus, who earned the Nobel Peace Prize for his work in founding Grameen Bank. Hearing about these success stories and leaders is important as it draws needed attention and talent to the most pressing challenges the world is facing. Yet, it often glosses over the hard work, moments of doubt, and mistakes that these SE leaders went through during the early years. These haloed accounts also fail to capture the practical steps that each founder took early on in order to successfully navigate the inevitable challenges that they each faced.

Today, we face momentous social and environmental challenges. As of the writing of this book, the COVID-19 pandemic has ravaged our global population, rapidly upending routines and demonstrating the razor-thin edge at which so much of the world lives. The impacts of climate change on our way of life are no longer far-off threats; they are at our doorsteps, resulting in record-breaking wildfires in Australia and California,[9] droughts in India[10] and Afghanistan,[11] and cyclones and pest outbreaks in southern Africa,[12] to name a few. In the US, the senseless murders of George Floyd, Breonna Taylor and Ahmaud Arbery, amongst so many other Black Americans, have spurred a reckoning with structural racism that has compelled the country to confront the deep inequities baked into social and economic structures around the globe.[13]

The current crises have also shown the resilience of social entrepreneurs, as well as their proximity to the communities that often feel the brunt of social injustice, climate change and disease. In our set of eight SEs alone, we saw numerous examples of SEs stepping up in new ways to make sure that they continue to deliver on their missions, and in many cases, expand them. Sanergy began distributing hygiene products in Nairobi's informal settlements as part of a COVID-19 response coalition because it had the most developed distribution network within these low-resource areas.[14] RevFoods quickly adapted to ensure its healthy meals and snacks reached children no longer in school, ultimately distributing more than 30 million meals through school and community partners.[15] The pandemic's economic toll has hurt small businesses in the US and abroad, especially those in communities of color. Instead of pulling back its lending amidst the uncertainty, Kiva increased its support and directed much-needed resources to these businesses.[16]

The world needs more SEs proving out and bringing to market new innovations. But just as much, the world needs these proven solutions to reach further. Through this book's snapshot of eight successful SEs and the findings that are reinforced by broadly published theory, we hope to have provided insights that will not only teach a man to fish, as Bill Drayton would say, but also to revolutionize the fishing industry.[17]

# NOTES

1. Martin, Roger L., and Sally Osberg. "Social Entrepreneurship: The Case for Definition." *SSIR*, Spring 2007, ssir.org/articles/entry/social_entrepreneurship_the_case_for_definition.

2. "Business Roundtable Redefines the Purpose of a Corporation to Promote 'An Economy That Serves All Americans.'" *Business Roundtable*, 19 August 2019, www.businessroundtable.org/business-roundtable -redefines-the-purpose-of-a-corporation-to-promote-an-economy-that-serves-all-americans.

3. Mudaliar, Abhilash, Aliana Pineiro, and Rachel Bass. "Impact Investing Trends: Evidence of a Growing Industry." *The Global Impact Investing Network*, December 2016, thegiin.org/assets/GIIN_Impact %20InvestingTrends%20Report.pdf.

4. Hand, Dean, Hannah Dithrich, Sophia Sunderji, and Nashin Nova. "Annual Impact Investor Survey 2020." 10th edn, *Global Impact Investing Network*, June 2020, thegiin.org/assets/GIIN%20Annual%20Impact %20Investor%20Survey%202020.pdf.

5. *Nonprofit Impact Matters*, 2020, www.nonprofitimpactmatters.org.

6. Phillips, Mary. "Growing Pains: The Sustainability of Social Enterprises." *The International Journal of Entrepreneurship and Innovation*, vol. 7, no. 4, 2006, pp. 221–30, doi:10.5367/000000006779111648.

7. *Nonprofit Impact Matters*, 2020, www.nonprofitimpactmatters.org.

8. Ibid.

9. Di Liberto, Tom. "Over a Million Acres Burned in California in Second Half of August 2020: NOAA Climate. gov." *NOAA Climate.gov*, 26 August 2020, www.climate.gov/news-features/event-tracker/over-million-acres -burned-california-second-half-august-2020.

10. Roy, Edmond. "India's Latest Crisis: 600 Million People Struggle with Drought." *The Interpreter*, 17 July 2019, www.lowyinstitute.org/the-interpreter/india-s-latest-crisis-600-million-people-struggle-drought.

11. Lai, David. "Bracing for the Harsh Winter: Lives of Drought-Hit Afghans in Herat Province." *World Health Organization Afghanistan*, 29 December 2018, whoafghanistan.exposure.co/bracing-for-the-harsh-winter.

12. Hillard, Laura. "Cyclone Idai Reveals Africa's Vulnerabilities." *Council on Foreign Relations*, 4 April 2019, www.cfr.org/in-brief/cyclone-idai-reveals-africas-vulnerabilities.

13. "Explained: The Protests for Racial Justice." *DoSomething.org*, 2 June 2020, www.dosomething.org/us/ articles/explained-the-protests-for-racial-justice.

14. *Safe Hands Kenya*. 2020, www.safehandskenya.com.

15. "White Paper: Reinventing School Meal Program for Health and Flexibility during COVID-19." *Revolution Foods*, 27 July 2020, www.revolutionfoods.com/blog/whitepaper-reinventing-school-meal-program-during -covid.

16. "Kiva's Response to COVID-19." *Kiva*, 2020, www.kiva.org/blog/covid.

17. Janus, Kathleen Kelly. "Planting the Seeds for Social Startup Success: 10 Things to Remember When Starting a Social Enterprise." *Porchlight Books*, Porchlight Book Company, 7 February 2018, www.porchlightbooks .com/blog/changethis/2018/planting-the-seeds-for-social-startup-success-10-things-to-remember-when -starting-a-social-enterprise.

# INDEX